EMOTIONAL
LABOR

EMOTIONAL
LABOR

PUTTING THE **SERVICE** IN PUBLIC SERVICE

MARY E. GUY

MEREDITH A. NEWMAN

SHARON H. MASTRACCI

M.E.Sharpe
Armonk, New York
London, England

Library of Congress Cataloging-in-Publication Data

Guy, Mary E. (Mary Ellen)
  Emotional labor : putting the service in public service / by Mary E. Guy,
Meredith A. Newman, and Sharon H. Mastracci.
    p. cm.
  Includes bibliographical references and index.
  ISBN 978-0-7656-2116-0 (cloth : alk. paper) — ISBN 978-0-7656-2117-7 (pbk. alk. paper)
  1. Public service employment—United States—Psychological aspects. 2. Social workers—
United States—Attitudes. I. Newman, Meredith A., 1949– II. Mastracci, Sharon H.,
1968– III. Title.

HD5713.6.U54G89 2008
331.12'042—dc22   2007032403

Printed in the United States of America

The paper used in this publication meets the minimum requirements of
American National Standard for Information Sciences
Permanence of Paper for Printed Library Materials,
ANSI Z 39.48-1984.

∞

BM (c)   10   9   8   7   6   5   4   3   2   1
BM (p)   10   9   8   7   6   5   4   3   2   1

We dedicate this book to public servants everywhere,
who know all too well what emotional labor is about.

Contents

CONTENTS

List of Tables and Figures

Tables

Figures

Foreword

Steven Maynard-Moody

Every once in a while, scholars show us clearly what was unseen and unrecognized but there, right before our eyes, for all to see. Our first reaction to such insight is, "Well, of course," and that is quickly followed by "Why didn't I recognize this before?" Obvious but unseen topics or problems exist—and have existed—in the social world but have received scant attention in our theories and research. Our journals, books, and discourse can become blinders that narrow attention to what has been studied, overlooking what calls out for study. *Emotional Labor* is the rare book that broadens our field of vision by examining with insight and care a topic that has been mostly overlooked yet is obvious and essential.

We all know that work organizations are not cold, dispassionate places. Often emotions run high, but even without *Sturm und Drang,* work remains emotional: we care about our work, work depends on relationships (some colleagues we like, others we cannot abide), and our personal lives intrude into our workplaces. As long as work requires humans, emotions will never be far from the surface. At work we experience joy, fear, belonging, isolation, compassion, disgust, anguish, friendship, boredom, love, hate—in short, the full spectrum of emotions.

All work, therefore, is emotional labor, but some forms of work demand emotional connections with others: teachers, therapists, and social workers, for example, must make emotional connections with kids and clients to get their jobs done. In the cold language of organization theory, emotional connection is the "job technology." Other forms of work require holding emotions at bay—stuffing them—so they do not cloud judgment or prevent needed but painful choices: for example, first responders to accidents cannot allow gut-wrenching horror to cloud medical decisions, and 911 operators cannot freeze when the caller cries, "What do I do! My child stopped breathing?" Other jobs, such as policing, repeatedly involve uncomfortable and unsettling encounters. Even routine traffic stops elicit frustration with argumentative citizens and fear of the unpredictable: is he rooting in the glove box for his registration or for a gun? Whether the work involves making emotional connections or stuffing emotional responses or both, all forms of emotional labor require subtlety and skill and take their toll in disengagement and burnout. These are demanding jobs.

The centrality of emotions to understanding organizations and management has been overlooked for several reasons. One is that the subject is elusive. *Emotional Labor* is a book of intellectual courage. The authors examine the sparse literature and empirical evidence on the subject. They carefully define their subject: "Emotional labor is that work which requires the engagement, suppression, and/or evocation of the worker's emotions in order to get the job done. . . . Simply put, emotional labor requires affective sensitivity and flexibility with one's own emotions as well as those of others." The authors then proceed to examine three prototypical settings for emotional labor: the Tallahassee Police Department 911 Call Takers, the Illinois Department of Corrections, and the Cook County Office of the Public Guardian. These three sites present a range of jobs and skill levels and a mix of male-dominated, female-dominated, and gender-mixed workplaces. The research upon which this book rests is based on careful, up-close fieldwork and a standardized survey.

Another reason why emotional labor has received so little scholarly attention is gender bias in our theorizing, suggest the authors. Emerging feminist organization and public administration theory gives greater emphasis and value to emotions, while traditional male theory is preoccupied with leadership and command. Given this gender bias in our research and theory, one of the surprising—and reassuring—findings of this research is that there are no meaningful differences in the centrality and experience of emotional labor between men and women who perform the same job. Emotional labor is not a "woman's issue" in the sense that men do not experience the same feelings, pressures, and concerns.

Emotional labor is a "woman's issue," however, in the sense that many emotionally demanding jobs are in women-dominated professions. This, the authors claim, may be an overlooked aspect of cross-job-pay differences that account in part for persistent gender pay inequality. Based on a content analysis of job descriptions, the authors suggest that skills associated with emotional labor are not identified as "bona fide occupational skills" and appropriately compensated. Emotional labor is taken for granted, not paid for.

And so, as you finish reading this foreword and begin reading this book, be prepared for new ideas and insights; you are exploring mostly uncharted terrain. We have known for some time the rough outlines of this territory and suspected all along that emotional labor was "out there" in our organizational world. But it took three courageous explorers—Mary Guy, Meredith Newman, and Sharon Mastracci—to take us into the hinterlands of this essential topic.

Acknowledgments

There are many people who helped bring this work to fruition. Foremost are the workers who talked with us so that we could understand the work they perform. We are grateful to the staffs of the Cook County Office of the Public Guardian, the Illinois Department of Corrections, and the Tallahassee Police Department for giving their time to participate in the interviews and focus groups, and to complete the surveys. Without their firsthand experience, this book would not have been possible. We quote from them throughout these chapters because their words illuminate and amplify our thesis. To protect their anonymity, we note without citation where we have drawn quoted material from our interviews.

We are grateful to Warren Barclay and Jannah Bensch for providing personnel data from the state of New Jersey; to Arthur H. McCurdy, Denise L. Hall, and Donna L. Lantz for providing data from the state of Oregon; and to Steve Karr for providing data from the state of Illinois.

We wish to thank Seung-Bum Yang for his assistance in designing and testing the questionnaire and performing analyses; to Wenjue Lu for assisting with the data analysis and presentation; to Bess Newman for transcribing interview tapes; to Melanie Hicks Tozzi for her work in arranging and conducting the focus groups for the 911 call takers; and to Karen Kunz for her assistance in compiling the Illinois Department of Corrections employment data.

We wish to acknowledge Sage Publications, Inc. for granting permission to use material in Chapter 6 that is drawn from Sharon H. Mastracci, Meredith A. Newman, and Mary E. Guy, 2006, "Appraising Emotion Work: Determining Whether Emotional Labor is Valued in Government Jobs," 2006, *American Review of Public Administration,* 36 (2): 123–138 and Wiley-Blackwell Publishers for granting permission to use material in Chapter 7 that is drawn from Mary E. Guy and Meredith A. Newman, 2004, "Women's Jobs, Men's Jobs: Sex Segregation and Emotional Labor." *Public Administration Review,* 64 (3): 289–298.

Our interpretation of emotional labor and its many facets was enriched by the insights of our colleagues as they reflected on our chapters and provided feedback. Foremost among these is DeLysa Burnier, who thoughtfully critiqued this work on multiple occasions.

Collaboration on this book was a team effort, with the three of us sharing the workload. Our understanding of emotional labor was enabled and enriched by the perspectives each of us brought and shared. Too many hours to count were spent in conference calls, meetings, and messaging. We are grateful to one another for the collective outcome of our work.

Mary Guy wishes to thank all her mid-career students. Over the years, they have become her teachers, opening windows so she could see the nature of their public service. May this book help to advance everyone else's understanding of their labors.

Meredith Newman wishes to dedicate this book to her mother and father (in memoriam), her husband Herb, and Bess and William—who have supported, loved, and inspired her, and continue to do so. She wishes to personally thank Rita Kelly (in memoriam) and Nicholas Lovrich for their friendship, kindness, and mentorship over the years.

Sharon Mastracci wishes to dedicate this book to her mother, Janice Hogan, and her husband, Tony. Personal thanks also to Victoria Rodriguez for her continued support and inspiration, and to Mary Guy and Meredith Newman for being the best collaborators and colleagues anyone could ask for.

EMOTIONAL
LABOR

— 1 —

Emotional Labor and Public Service

This book is about public service and what it takes to perform it. Many, if not most, public service jobs require interpersonal contact that is either face-to-face or voice-to-voice. Those who staff the counter at the driver's license examining station are expected to greet the 100th applicant of the day with the same sincerity as they greeted the first. Those who staff the phone lines for the Social Security Administration are expected to be "nicer than nice." Caseworkers must care about strangers, and inspectors who work for planning and zoning departments are required to treat each aggravated homeowner with fairness and courtesy. In the aftermath of a hurricane, Federal Emergency Management Agency (FEMA) officials must address not only physical disaster but emotionally traumatized citizens. This work is relational in nature and is called *emotional labor.* Such work "greases the wheels" so that people cooperate, stay on task, and work well together. It is essential for job completion and is a prerequisite for quality public service.

A generation ago, Peter Drucker called attention to the fact that the future workplace would be staffed not by manual laborers but by knowledge workers. Long before other sectors of the economy came to appreciate the centrality of knowledge work, public service organizations routinely relied on this new type of worker. There is no quarrel that the preponderance of the public work force consists of knowledge workers. The dimension that is missing from discussions of government's human capital is the importance of emotion work, or emotional labor.

For too long, the emphasis on tangible, testable skills has "disappeared" emotional labor—that work which goes beyond cognitive, physical, or

3

mechanical skills but is required for job completion. The result is that agencies adopt the rhetoric of *service* but end up disappearing the very action that is essential between citizen and worker. Trapped in the canon of scientific management, notions of organizational effectiveness fail to account for the centrality of emotion work even when it is directly related to organizational goals. The following excerpts from interviews provide examples:

Police dispatchers answer calls from citizens who are in dire straits. They must manage their own emotions as well as those of the person at the other end of the telephone line. A 911 call taker explains:

> We don't get people who call up and say, "Oh, I'm happy. You're doing a wonderful job." We talk to people at their absolute worst, on probably the worst day of their life. They can cuss and swear, and we're not allowed to cuss and swear back. There are days that you'd like to, but you can't. Our job is to get the information and get an officer to the scene of an accident or crime or fire. So, it is difficult.

Most human service professionals work in public service rather than in for-profit businesses. Their work is different from that required in market-based occupations. In the words of another 911 call taker:,

> I mean everybody talks a lot about closure. I think if your job is other people's grief or other people's pain, you don't necessarily get to have closure with that. You don't have some resolution of the issue. You just carry it around with you everywhere.

Although emotion work is intense, it is also energizing. A social worker at the Office of the Public Guardian tells us,

> People tease me and they say, "You look exhausted," but I smile. It's because I really believe I am making a huge difference in these children's lives. I'm almost reenergized. I mean, it's like there's a re-energy that comes from this positive feedback that I get.

We want to open a dialogue about emotional labor in public service and to clarify and illuminate its characteristics, subtleties, and centrality. To this end, the book presents the substance of emotion work through the words of practitioners who exercise these skills daily. Survey data are used to show the larger picture of how it affects job satisfaction on the upside and burnout on the downside. We close with a discussion of how this subject informs the practice of public service and how it affects human capital.

What Is Emotional Labor?

First, to the point: What is emotional labor? It is a component of the dynamic relationship between two people: worker and citizen or worker and worker. Emotional labor shares similarities as well as differences with physical labor—both require skill and experience and are subject to external controls and divisions of labor. The English language comes up short when we try to describe it. A number of terms capture one aspect or more, but none captures its entirety. For example, the list below names some of the dimensions to emotional labor. Some jobs require workers to exercise several of these; others require the performance of none, one, or only a few:

- Verbal judo: used in law enforcement to describe "tough talk" banter
- *Caritas:* captures the caring function in human services
- Game face: used in law enforcement to signify displays of toughness
- Compassion fatigue: used in social work to describe burnout resulting from too much *caritas*
- Emotion management: focuses on the worker's job of eliciting the desired emotional response from the citizen
- Professional face: used to describe the status shield that workers don to distance themselves emotionally from the interaction; it is a role-playing function.
- Show time: similar to game face
- Deep acting: refers to convincingly pretending to feel a given emotion
- Emotional chameleon: the ability to switch expressions of emotions on and off
- Good cop, bad cop: role playing in which one worker pretends to be sympathetic while the other pretends to be tougher than tough
- Spider sense: the ability to intuit the other's emotional state
- Rapport: the ability to establish a deep understanding and communication with the other
- Stage left: refers to playacting in expressing an emotion, as if on stage
- Emotional suppression: that which is required to disregard one's own feelings
- Emotional mirror: the ability to reflect and adopt the emotions of the other
- Emotional armor: the ability to gird oneself against one's own emotional response
- Emotional equilibrium: refers to maintaining a balance between extremes of emotion

- Emotional teflon: the ability to protect oneself from an emotional reaction
- Emotional anesthesia: the lack of any emotional response; may occur after prolonged exposure to extreme emotional stimuli
- Emotional engagement: the ability to connect with the other and empathize
- Emotional mask: that which results when workers convincingly suppress their own emotions in order to act as if they feel a contradictory emotion, or no emotion
- Emotional façade: the ability to express an emotion one does not actually feel

As the list shows, there are a variety of dimensions that attach to emotional labor. Although some workers can don emotional armor and endure emotionally draining experiences, others cannot. Although some are energized by emotional encounters, others find them exhausting. Whereas some are skilled at emotional suppression, others excel at developing rapport and emotional engagement. This is our point: Emotion work is as individual as cognitive work. It is a skill and is subject to individual differences.

Definition

Any definition of emotional labor begins with the seminal work of sociologist Arlie Hochschild (1983). Hochschild uses the term to mean "the management of feeling to create a publicly observable facial and bodily display" intended to produce a particular state of mind in others; "emotional labor is sold for a wage and therefore has *exchange value*" (1983, p. 7). Emotional labor is a "gesture in a social exchange; it has a function there and is not to be understood merely as a facet of personality" (Hochschild 1979, p. 568). In other words, the worker must perform the work in order to complete the job; it is a type of labor.

Related Terms

Two related terms are germane to this definition. First is the term *emotion work*. Hochschild differentiates between emotional labor and emotion work, treating *labor* as that action that is required by an employer and *work* as the nature of the action itself. To put it differently, to perform emotion work, one must expend emotional labor. This differentiation is slim and nuanced. You will see the terms used in this manner through the chapters.

Emotion work becomes a public act, "bought on the one hand and sold on the other" (Hochschild 1983, p. 118). It requires that workers suppress their private feelings in order to show the "desirable" work-related emotion. In other words, the focus is on an emotional performance that is bought and sold as a commodity. Another way to look at the subject is to think of emotional labor as that work that is performed under the direction of someone else. Emotion work, on the other hand, is the performance of emotional labor at one's own discretion (Tolich 1993). The distinction here is who controls the performance. If it is regulated by the employer, it is defined as emotional labor, and if it results from the autonomous choice of the employee, then it is emotion work. We will examine feedback from employees in Chapter 8 indicating that emotion work is energizing and gives meaning to one's work. These findings point to emotional labor and emotion work as multidimensional phenomena.

The second term is *emotional intelligence*, the ability to manage one's own emotions and to sense those of others. Knowledge born of this intelligence is used to govern one's actions. Just as with cognitive intelligence, there are gradations in skill. Suppressing or managing one's own feelings requires sophisticated skill levels, for example. Related competencies include self-awareness, self-control, empathy, active listening, and the skill to resolve conflicts and cooperate with others.

Emotional Labor Versus Cognitive Work

Cognitive skills and emotion work skills are separate but related dimensions for successful job performance. The former includes the application of factual knowledge to the intellectual analysis of problems and rational decision making. The latter includes analysis and decision making in terms of the expression of emotion, whether actually felt or not, as well as its opposite: the suppression of emotions that are felt but not expressed. More specifically, emotional labor comes into play during communication between worker and citizen, and it requires the rapid-fire execution of

1. *Emotive sensing*, which means detecting the affective state of the other and using that information to array one's own alternatives in terms of how to respond
2. *Analyzing* one's own affective state and comparing it to that of the other
3. *Judging* how alternative responses will affect the other, then selecting the best alternative
4. *Behaving*, such that the worker suppresses or expresses an emotion—in order to elicit a desired response from the other.

In sum, service exchanges between worker and citizen require the worker to sense the right tone and medium for expressing a point and/or feeling and then to determine whether, when, and how to act on that analysis. To

7

ignore this combination of analysis, affect, judgment, and communication is to ignore the "social lube" that enables rapport, elicits desired responses, and ensures that interpersonal transactions are constructive.

Too often dismissed as "nurturant" or "supportive," emotion work has traditionally been thought to be something that women do naturally. With this in mind, emotion work is not delineated in job descriptions, nor is it compensated. It is, instead, treated as a "comes with" for many—if not most—jobs that disproportionately employ women. This view is too narrow. Police officers and prison guards will tell you that they engage in emotion work every day, but at the other extreme. Rather than being nurturing and gentle, their jobs require them to wear a gameface, to act tougher than they actually feel, to engage in verbal judo with law breakers. Neither extreme of emotional labor will be found in job descriptions. Only the cognitive skills will be listed. Why?

Emotional Labor as Work

The commonly accepted notion of *work* is rarely examined. Such neglect has become its own straitjacket as it led to disregard for any labor other than that which is physical or cognitive. This ideology of work is buttressed by four institutional forces, each of which conceals, rather than reveals, emotion work. First, the civil service is built on a foundation of formal descriptions that specify tangible elements of each job. Though reforms have been introduced over the years, the basic understanding of what does, and does not, constitute "skill" remains mired in the empirical tradition—that if it is tangible and measurable, it exists, and if it is not, then it is dismissed.

The discounting of emotion work and the elevation of observable work results in the disappearance of emotional labor skills from job descriptions, performance appraisal, and reward systems. By way of contrast, our lack of attention to emotional labor parallels the lack of attention across the social sciences to that which defies measurement. The fields of sociology, political science, and psychology through the latter half of the twentieth century benefited immeasurably from computerization. The growing convenience of data collection and statistical analysis led social scientists to focus almost solely on variables that lent themselves to empirical observation and quantification. Trapped in this cascade, researchers found themselves swept downstream, measuring that which could be counted and observing that which could be seen. In human resources (HR) circles, the trend resulted in "objectively" defining skills, knowledge, and abilities; constructing tests and measurements to assess these; and writing performance appraisal instruments that would allow supervisors to "fairly and objectively" assess each

Figure 1.1 **What If a Job Announcement Said This?**

Department of Motor Vehicles
Position Available: Service Representative

Customer service representative sought. Ability to smile and interact cheerily all day, everyday, is a must. Ability to mollify frustrated citizens and repeatedly provide the same explanation of driver's license rules is highly desirable. Additional job requirements include operating office equipment, accessing electronic databases, and performing data entry.

---

worker's performance on a Likert scale. Such a scale is itself an attempt to "objectify" qualitative assessment.

Second, the structural elements of organizing, articulated by scientific management and reinforced by top-down command-and-control structures, taught us to treat workers as interchangeable parts whose contributions reside in the performance of clearly enumerated duties. A rational division of labor, hierarchical control, performance standards, selection and advancement based on technical competence, formal record keeping, and communication are ingrained in the way we think about job classification. Relational work is absent from the list of knowledge, skills, and abilities (KSAs) except in the obligatory requirement to "establish and maintain good working relationships."

The process of job construction—where tasks are lumped together to form clearly defined jobs—emerged from the engineering approach of scientific management. Job descriptions are designed to depersonalize work and separate it from the person. By doing so, workers can be treated as interchangeable parts, where any employee with X skill can perform any job with Y requirements. A corollary to this is that only those tasks that are observable are delineated. This assures an impersonal, objective evaluation that protects against favoritism due to race, age, gender, or any other characteristic that differentiates one worker from another. It also assures that all those labors that are *relational* in nature will be unrecognized and uncompensated. This "objective" approach to task elements and performance evaluation rests on an ideology of work that is buttressed by norms suited to industrial but not service jobs. Missing from this modus operandi is any mention of relational work that involves caring and nurturing, and the emotion work that is required to perform such tasks well. For example, consider the hypothetical job ad in Figure 1.1. It seems ludicrous compared to our usual expectations for a job ad because it highlights the emotional demands of the job.

The third institutional force is that of so-called "market value." This is shorthand for cultural understandings of worth. Market value blinds us to a panoply of culturally based assumptions. For example, prior to the mid-1800s, it was unthinkable that a woman would hold a government post (Van Riper 1976). Over time, it became grudgingly accepted for women to work as clerks as long as they did not take income away from men. Over time, women stenographers were welcomed because of their ability to radiate sympathetic interest, agreeableness, and courtesy in the office (Kanter 1977), all a precursor to what agencies and citizens now take for granted in any exchange between government and citizen. But because these attributes were introduced to the workplace as lagniappe, they have been viewed as "icing on the cake," unnecessary for the bare-bones performance of the job and undeserving of compensation.

Fourth, urbanization and industrialization meant that a dichotomy emerged between home and work, with each domain evoking different behaviors. Home became a refuge from the dehumanization of the workplace. The concept of nurturing and sustaining while simultaneously performing manual labor, as had occurred on the family farm, disappeared from the definition of work. In its place came a paradigm of "formal" job duties. Relational work was defined away, not germane to the task at hand. Work and accompanying job descriptions focused on the tangible production of marketable goods and services. Behavior that mediated the process and produced positive relationships, a sense of community, and resolution of conflict did not fit easily into quantifiable elements, so it was treated as extraneous, despite the suasion of Mary Parker Follett (Newman and Guy 1998).

The confluence of these institutional factors cemented notions about what is, and what is not, *real work*, resulting in emotional labor being "disappeared." When performed at its best, like fine background music, emotional labor goes unnoticed. Unbeknownst to the citizen, it facilitates interaction and elicits a desired response, contributing to productivity from the agency's point of view and achieving the goal of the exchange from the citizen's point of view. This is most notable in jobs that require positive interactions, such as caseworker, receptionist, public health nurse, counter clerk, and public schoolteacher. But emotional labor is just as necessary for jobs that require "negative" interactions; for example, police officers need to exert authority and control in hostile situations. To do their jobs well, all must employ skills similar to those of the method actor: they invoke and display emotions, just as actors do when playing roles.

Workers whose jobs require emotional skills must perform each day as if on stage, gauging the emotional response of citizens and shaping their own behavior so as to elicit the desired response. Although lunch breaks and the end of the workday allow the worker to exit the stage and leave the acting behind, the rest of the workday requires theater. Cognitive skills are also required in the job but cannot be exercised effectively unless paired with emotion skills. Primary among these emotion skills is the ability to care about the other person and to empathize.

Caring

Borrowing from nursing, where caring is a subject of much concern, we can find literature that helps to make the connection between public service and face-to-face exchanges. The work of renowned nursing theorist Martha Rogers is replete with the value of caring as an essential component in the nurse-patient relationship. A similar argument, though on an aggregate scale, can be made for the administrator-citizen exchange. Rogers (1994 [1990]) believed that "attitudes of hope, humor, and upbeat moods" are often more effective curatives than drugs (p. 248). Going further, she made the distinction between technology and human-to-human interaction: "Machines do *not* provide human services. . . . Nonetheless, when used wisely and with judgment machines can be useful adjuncts as tools of practice." She explained that the use of machines requires practitioners "who are committed to people and their world as the focus of their concern, and who are socially responsible" (Rogers 1994 [1985], p. 289).

The history of public service moves in the opposite direction. With an emphasis on purely administrative functions (planning, organizing, staffing, directing, coordinating, reporting, and budgeting), the elements of administrative work have historically focused on doing "things." Yet, recent examples demonstrate that "things" without believable expressions of care undermine public confidence. For example, Mayor Rudy Giuliani emerged as a folk hero to the citizens of New York City for his expressions of compassion coupled with leadership in the days following the attack on the World Trade Center in 2001. Conversely, the George W. Bush administration became mired in charges of incompetence in 2005 after Hurricane Katrina displaced thousands and federal officials failed to couple rescue efforts with expressions of empathy for the displaced.

Physical labor and emotional labor go hand in hand, creating a synergy. Neither replaces the other, but either by itself fails to accomplish the mission. As a noun, *care* refers to both abstract and concrete phenomena that relate to assisting, supporting, or enabling activities that focus on the needs of others, the goal of which is to ameliorate a human condition. As a verb, *care* refers to the performance of those actions. Effective caring requires a congruency between the situation, citizen's needs, and the state's response.

What effect does emotion work have on workers? What motivates individuals to seek those jobs despite the emotional consequences? To what extent does emotional labor enhance employees' work lives and contribute to job satisfaction? Research has found that emotional labor's effect on well-being depends on job autonomy, with those holding jobs higher in autonomy reporting lower negative effects of emotional labor than those with low autonomy (Erickson 1991). Other research has identified a positive correlation between emotional labor and job satisfaction (Ashforth and Humphrey 1993; Wharton 1993). This suggests that there are benefits to emotion work, such as stress reduction in interpersonal transactions. These chapters address these questions in the public service context while allowing you to see "around the corner" and learn more about the nuances of emotion work.

Inquiring About Emotion Work

Emotional labor has been defined in a variety of ways, including the "management of feeling to create a publicly observable facial and bodily display" (Hochschild 1983, p. 7), as well as the "effort, planning and control needed to express organizationally desired emotion during interpersonal transactions" (Morris and Feldman 1996, p. 987). Whatever the definition, it is inherent to public service; it is the invisible but necessary element in person-to-person transactions. People's perceptions of the quality of the public services they receive rest on this dynamic exchange between citizen and state. Service management literature also provides greater understanding of emotional labor's importance in the service sector (Bowen, Chase, Cummins, and Associates 1990; Bowen and Schneider 1988; Brown, Gummesson, Edvardsson, and Gustavsson 1991).

Substantial expansion of the work paradigm is required if we are to comprehend and appreciate the dynamics of the exchange in service transactions. To correct this shortcoming in our understanding of public service, we reveal the centrality of emotion work in the service exchange. We do this by presenting the results of extensive research into the workdays of civil servants. Based on interviews and focus groups, you will read in their own words how social workers, 911 operators, corrections officials, detectives, and guardians ad litem experience their work. Passages from these interviews are interspersed throughout the book because they "flavor" the empirical data acquired from surveys administered in three agencies: an urban county office, the Cook County Office of the Public Guardian; a state agency, the Illinois Department of Corrections; and a city police department, the Tallahassee Police Department Dispatch Unit.

Interviews and focus groups were conducted for the purpose of understanding emotion work and to learn what themes emerged as workers related their experiences. The interview questions listed in Table 1.1 were used for

Table 1.1

Interview Questions

1. Tell me about a typical day at your job.
2. What is the work environment like?
3. Do you need to engage in relationship-building in your job?
   a. Describe the kinds of things that you do to build relationships.
   b. Is this with supervisor? Co-workers? Clients?
4. Do you need to establish rapport on your job?
   a. Describe the kinds of things that you do to build relationships.
   b. Is this with supervisor? Co-workers? Clients?
5. Do you need to engage in emotion management—which means managing your own emotions as well as "taming" the emotions of others?
6. What kinds of stresses occur during the normal course of the day?
7. What kinds of emotions are required to adequately address or handle those stresses?
8. How do you deal with the emotional aspect of the job?
9. Do you feel your job has more, less, or about the same level of stress and emotional requirements as other positions in your agency? Why or why not?
10. Is there a particular term or word for how you deal with callers' emotions?
11. How do you prepare for the stresses of your job?
12. Do you often feel "wiped out" at the end of the day?
13. How do you unwind from a tough day?
14. What is the hardest thing about your job?
15. What is the most rewarding thing about your job?
16. Do job stresses affect your personal life?
17. Do you have a term for dealing with the emotional distress that you observe in your work?
18. Every occupation has its own humor—in the form of "sick jokes"—and this serves as a release for tensions. Is this a means for you to release tension?

one-on-one interviews as well as for focus groups. These questions initiated a lively give-and-take as workers discussed their work experiences in their own words. Emotion work is not a term workers are familiar with, and as we embarked on the interviews, it became clear that workers had their own language for it.

These interviews were recorded and transcribed and provide the quotes that are used throughout these chapters to explain and embellish key points. It is the lived experience of workers that reveals the nature of emotion work and what it takes to do it well. This information can be understood only through their words. Interviews and focus groups allowed us to discern patterns and make fine distinctions between meanings—distinctions that are not possible with the blunter instrument of survey data. They also enabled us to make inferences that we then explored using statistical analyses. Following the interviews and focus groups, the survey was distributed to all workers at the Office of the Public Guardian and Department of Corrections, as well as to 911 call takers (see Appendix A).

The section that follows describes each of the research sites, explains the nature of the work performed, and the employees who were interviewed and surveyed. Interviews and focus groups were plentiful enough to achieve data saturation. That is, at each facility, there was enough repetition to lead us to believe that we had heard all dimensions to the emotion work that was performed there.

"A Million Crises Every Day": The Cook County, Illinois, Office of the Public Guardian

Our first research site was the Cook County Office of the Public Guardian, which is in Chicago, Illinois. The purpose of the office is to provide legal guardianship for children and vulnerable adults who have no one to care for them. The mission of the Office of the Public Guardian is "To supply our clients with competency, diligence, integrity, professionalism, and understanding during our relentless quest to help improve the quality and dignity of their lives. To supply our judiciary and adversaries with genuine respect, dignity, credibility, and civility."[1]

How often do the mission statements of government agencies include terms like "relentless quest," much less identify "adversaries" and underscore the need to grant them "genuine respect, dignity, credibility, and civility"? Rarely do institutional staples like mission statements capture the work and spirit of an organization, but then again, rarely are such statements understood by members of the organization as their driving force, their passion, their raison d'être.

Employees of the Cook County Office of the Public Guardian (OPG) are bureaucrats and technocrats as those concepts are commonly understood. Most are also crusaders who perceive their role in fulfilling this mission as more avocation than way to a paycheck. Most of them could make more money just by stepping out the door to work in private sector firms. In recent years, one high-profile tragedy, as well as the dramatic organizational change that followed, only solidified the dedication of OPG employees to the office, their mission, and their clients. Following is a description of this unique government agency; its leadership, work, and work force; the aforementioned tragedy and some of its consequences; and this project's interaction with OPG for the purpose of examining the emotion management demands related to its work.

Government must intercede when its most vulnerable citizens are unable to make decisions on their own, when family members are unable or unwilling to do so, or when no family members can be found. Children can be removed from their homes when their parents have been deemed incapable of caring for them, whether because they are abusive, endangering, or neglectful, or because they are incarcerated or embroiled in a protracted and hostile custody battle. Children in heated custody disputes may not have anyone who can make unselfish decisions that are in their best interests. Children in foster care cannot operate as primary decision makers within the system, and due to the nature of their circumstances, no parent or legal guardian is there to determine their housing, education, and health care needs. And, children are not the only citizens susceptible to such precarious conditions; adults can become similarly powerless and vulnerable. Alzheimer's disease can incapacitate the elderly; and chronic, severe mental illness can prevent adults of any age from making informed decisions and acting in their own best interests.

Through the judicial system, government intervenes to protect hapless citizens and manage their affairs when private options are unacceptable. Attorneys are appointed by judges to serve as guardians ad litem (GALs) to make decisions on vulnerable people's behalf in order to help them live lives that are as normal as possible. In Cook County, GALs are government employees. This represents a deliberate commitment on the part of Cook County that is unlike any other public guardianship in the United States. Elsewhere, courts assign clients to private sector legal guardianships and volunteer court-appointed special advocates (CASAs). In fact, OPG is the only office of its type (P. T. Murphy, personal communication, August 13, 2004).

Cook County, Illinois, comprises nearly sixty departments and commissions covering a broad array of diverse government activities and services, including the sheriff's office, the Brookfield Zoo, the Cook County hospital (home of the long-running NBC series *ER*), and the Chicago Botanical Garden. Its 1,000 square miles and 5.3 million residents make it the largest county in the United States and the second most populous one. Cook County not only covers about as much land area as does the state of Rhode Island, but it has more residents than roughly 125 other countries. Its population is among the most ethnically and economically diverse of all places in America. With respect to governance, Cook County is larger than many states: It is among the twenty largest governments in the nation, with the largest criminal justice system and the third-largest public health system. Moreover, the city of Chicago, the third-largest city in the United States, is only one of 133 municipalities within Cook County.[2]

Suffice it to say, Cook County, Illinois, is a relevant and fascinating government to study. Moreover, the county's interpretation of its role in serving and protecting its most vulnerable citizens differs from any other public sector administrative entity in the country and from any other guardianship agency. The origin, growth, and vision of this unique agency emanate from its initial and longtime leader, Patrick Murphy.

In 1978, amid a corruption scandal in a small, newly formed Cook County department, then governor Jim Thompson appointed a charismatic and idealistic young attorney to the public guardianship agency to demonstrate his administration's commitment to good governance. This attorney, Patrick Murphy, was meant to serve as window dressing for three months, after which the scandal-of-the-moment was predicted to blow over. However, Murphy's tenure would end up being a lengthy one. During more than twenty-six years, Mr. Murphy single-handedly built the OPG from a handful of attorneys, social workers, and assistants—six employees in all—to its current status: nearly 300 employees, half of whom are attorneys, serving over 15,000 clients. If he was grateful to the governor for his position, one might not be able to tell: not only did Murphy investigate his own agency's fund allocations, but he also pursued charges against Governor Thompson. Unlike the typical political appointee, Murphy also states flatly and without any hint of hubris that "the politicians can't touch us" (P. T. Murphy, personal communication, August 13, 2004). He has built an office with a strong reputation for citizen advocacy, and years of diligent service delivery have allowed everyone at OPG to proceed boldly, with little fear of the vagaries of favoritism or the calculus of horse trading by county- or state-level power brokers.

The Office of the Public Guardian had been shaped by Patrick Murphy's leadership and vision so much so that we heard "OPG" and "Patrick" used synonymously on more than one occasion, as in "I came to work for Patrick" rather than "I work for OPG." Such organizations can suffer institutional crises when longtime leaders leave. After his long run at OPG, Patrick Murphy ran for a judgeship on the Cook County Circuit Court in reaction to the county's mismanagement of a tragedy that struck the agency, which is described below. It proved to be a testament to the staff's dedication to mission, to Murphy's stewardship of a resilient organization, and to the strength of its new leadership that the new director, Robert Harris, could seamlessly assume the mantle as director of the agency on January 1, 2005.

Types of Work Performed at OPG and Types of Employees

Half of all OPG staff members are attorneys, and they serve as legal counsel and GALs for foster children and for children embroiled in custody proceedings. In addition to the attorneys, OPG's work force is composed of approximately two dozen paralegals and clerks; several caseworkers or public guardian advocates (PGAs) and investigators; and several support staff, computer technicians, administrators, and managers. One health consultant and one psychiatrist are also on staff for courtroom and client support. Paralegals are assigned to attorneys to support their caseload. Investigators and PGAs conduct site visits at foster homes, follow up on problem placements, and maintain contact with other people and institutions that their clients rely on for services, including mental health professionals, health clinics, nursing homes, schools, probation officers, and substance abuse treatment facilities. Support staff, administrators, and managers range from the receptionists working at the front desk, either downtown or in the Roosevelt Road building, to attorneys who supervise teams of GALs and may no longer maintain a caseload of their own, to social workers who supervise teams of PGAs.

The educational attainment of OPG employees is high. About half of its work force has earned law degrees and the office's reputation has attracted candidates from the nation's top law schools, including the University of Chicago, Georgetown, UC-Berkeley, Harvard, and Stanford. According to results from questionnaires administered as part of this research, 55.4 percent of respondents hold the Juris Doctor (JD) degree. Investigators and caseworkers (PGAs) are required to have earned at least the baccalaureate degree. According to survey results, 12.2 percent of OPG respondents graduated from college, 5.8 percent had some postgraduate education, and 10.1 percent had earned master's degrees. Only 1.4 percent of the OPG respondent population ceased their education upon earning the high school diploma, making educational attainment at OPG higher than the public sector and higher than the general work force overall.

The Cook County Office of the Public Guardian is also a female-dominated organization: fully three-fourths of its work force are women. Just over half of OPG's employees are white, with significant proportions of African American employees (31.9 percent) and Hispanics (10.1 percent). Most are either early in their careers or OPG is their first employer: over two-thirds are between 25 and 39 years old, and over half of all workers have not had employment prior to OPG. Because one-quarter of respondents have been with OPG for ten years or more, it is clear that many attorneys started working there as soon as they finished law school. The age distribution of OPG employees has its greatest concentration in the 30–35 age range.

Main job types include attorneys or GALs, paralegals, caseworkers and investigators, and support staff. Serving as both legal counsel and GALs, OPG attorneys both represent their clients' wishes to the court and generally determine them, as well. Among their many duties, OPG attorneys are required to maintain regular communication with teen clients to advise them of the status of their cases, visit at least fifteen foster children each month, and work closely with others involved in their clients' lives, including foster parents, therapists, and social workers. Paralegals, too, must visit at least fifteen placements each month, and in addition to carefully documenting all aspects of cases, they must prepare materials for hearings and run interference for several attorneys, whose clients sometimes just need to talk. Investigators and caseworkers have fewer ongoing interactions with clients, but rather are called in as part of the Incident Review Team (IRT) when crises occur. Investigators are required to serve subpoenas, look into incidents, develop investigative plans, conduct surveillance, interview witnesses, document incidents through written descriptions and photographs, and testify in court. Caseworkers must conduct home visits, interview clients and caregivers, and report on the health and well-being of clients.

Everyone must document every aspect of work on each and every case, making highly detailed notes. All client communication and documentation must be held to the strictest privacy standards, as it is all confidential and subject to attorney-client privilege. Failing to maintain confidentiality or failing to take detailed notes can jeopardize a client's case and delay removal from an abusive home, placement, or adoption into a good home. The margin for error is slim.

Cultural Climate and Morale

Work at the Office of the Public Guardian is not for the impatient, those easily discouraged or upset, or anyone who demands a set schedule. OPG does not intercede when a family is functional. Like 911 operators, OPG is involved only when something has gone wrong—very wrong. The consequences can be life threatening. OPG staff are aware of the importance of their work: Over 93 percent of survey respondents indicated that they "are doing something worthwhile in their jobs" either often, usually, or always. Only 10 percent indicated that their job is commonly (either often, usually, or always) "a waste of time and energy." Most (51.8 percent) gain "a sense of personal accomplishment" either usually or always from their jobs, and 54.0 percent of survey respondents "feel like their work makes a difference." They are not unaware of the stresses of their jobs. Whereas one-quarter of the OPG respondents indicated that they rarely or never "think about getting a different job," 13.9 percent said that they always do, and 25.5 percent indicated that they think about getting a different job at least sometimes.

Mission trumps structure at OPG. Senior attorneys mentor and advise attorneys with less experience, and Incident Review Teams have point persons, but evidence of institutional hierarchy is almost nonexistent. Organizational form follows agency function.

The Nature of Emotional Labor at OPG

Working with children, teenagers, and elderly clients brings about "a million crises every day."[3] These range from breakdowns with living situations, whether in long-term foster care, group homes, or adoptive homes, to discipline problems at school or trouble with the law, to problems with caretakers involving abuse of the client, substance abuse, or other endangering situations, to sickness or injury, to problems with family visits. The Incident Review Team is brought in on cases only when such a crisis has occurred, so whereas attorneys are able to see their clients when things are going well, caseworkers and investigators witness crisis after crisis. Beyond working in stressful situations, some of the emotion management demands on investigators and PGAs are readable "between the lines" in their job descriptions. Investigators are required to, among other tasks, "[u]se creative efforts in obtaining information; [l]ocate witnesses and clients; [c]onduct extensive interviews of witnesses and clients; and be able to handle a heavy caseload, multiple tasks, and meet constant deadlines" (Job Description for Investigators, Office of the Public Guardian). Both caseworkers and investigators are advised, "Clients should be interviewed alone and individually. . . . Vocabulary and manner must be adapted to the age and comprehension level of each client, while avoiding leading questions" (Cook County Public Guardian Interview Form [revised 2/02]).

Although GALs are not only called on to work with clients when crises occur, their regular and ongoing interactions with large numbers of clients create a stressful work environment that requires them to play many roles. "As the minor's attorney, the GAL is to present the minor's wishes to the court. As the minor's guardian ad litem, the GAL is to present to the court what s/he believes to be in the minor's best interest" (Job Description for Attorney and Guardian *ad litem* II [GAL II], Office of the Public Guardian [revised 11/2/99]). GALs must not only manage over 300 cases but also regularly make decisions that directly shape the well-being of their clients. GALs must also "effectively and professionally advocate before judges, hearing officers, and administrative law judges; conduct negotiations and promote discussion . . . to resolve matters; [and] provide information and communicate in person, by phone, and by correspondence, with ordinary courtesy and tact, with a diverse group of clients, staff, attorneys, and other professionals" (Job Description for Attorney and Guardian *ad litem* II [GAL II], Office of the Public Guardian [revised 11/2/99]).

Emotion management demands are high on caseworkers, attorneys, and investigators, who must manage heavy caseloads while communicating effectively with young clients, their biological parents, and their current caregivers; and other therapists, social workers, schoolteachers, judges, and health care workers, each of whose backgrounds differ greatly from one another and probably from the attorney's own. Neither attorneys nor caseworkers nor investigators can display shock or distress when a client reports abuse, neglect, or endangerment; and each must engender the sort of trust necessary to elicit that kind of information. Multiply each home visit, incident review, or hearing by the number of cases in the heavy caseloads carried by each attorney, and one gets a glimpse of the nature of emotion management demands by county workers at OPG.

OPG employees experienced a crisis of their own in October 2003 that exacerbated workplace stress as well as galvanized their commitment to the office and to each other. At around 5:00 p.m. on Friday, October 17, 2003, a fire broke out at the Cook County Administration Building at 69 West Washington Street in Chicago's loop downtown. Cynics remarked that no county worker would still be in his office at 5:00 p.m. on a Friday afternoon, but in fact, several members of the Cook County Office of the Public Guardian worked late, as was their custom.[4] Evacuation information was confusing, and different messages contradicted one another. Evacuees fled to the stairwells, and OPG employees began descending the steps from their 7th floor offices, only to find locked doors on the floors below. What is more, although stairwells are meant to funnel smoke out in case of a fire, the stairs in this building only trapped the smoke inside. Panicked cell phone calls were reported later, but at the time nobody knew of the people locked in the stairwells or even that the doors locked from the inside. Six people died in that fire, three of them longtime employees of OPG.

During the weeks and months that followed, Patrick Murphy made numerous television appearances demanding answers. Why were the stairwell doors locked from inside? Why didn't rescuers look for people in the stairwells? How could the evacuation directions have been so confusing? Who is responsible for the deaths of these people? Meanwhile, the already-overcrowded Roosevelt Road office made room for downtown employees, whose work had not gone away, only their place of work. It would take several months for the smoke, fire, and water damage to be repaired in the downtown office.

Like a family that opens its home to relatives in their time of need, at-torneys shared offices, support staff shared cubicles, and everyone shared computers. Tips on where to park and where to find lunch, as well as how to balance caseloads and address client crises, were shared throughout the now-unified OPG. At one time, some in the Roosevelt Road building envied the downtown office staff for their smaller caseloads and seemingly less dramatic clientele. Juvenile and domestic relations are managed at Roosevelt

Road, whereas adult and estate cases are handled downtown. Some who worked at one office had never met those who worked at the other office. After months of sharing space, however, mutual respect and cooperation grew throughout the organization, while everyone rallied behind Patrick's crusade to resolve someone's fatal mistake.

When the downtown building reopened, a plaque to honor the staff who had lost their lives was hung in the lobby, and the following appears on the OPG website (Cook County Public Guardian, n.d.):

> The tragic events of October 17th have saddened our hearts deeply. We mourn the loss of three of our co-workers who died from smoke inhalation when a fire broke out at the Cook County Administration Building at 69 West Washington Street. Sara Chapman, 38, was an attorney in the Domestic Relations Division of the Public Guardian's Office. She dedicated 10 years of her life working for the Office. She diligently advocated for the rights of children. Maureen McDonald, 57, was a 20-year veteran at the Cook County Public Guardian's office who kept track of finances and arranged funerals for elderly wards. She was an outspoken and meticulous woman. John Slater III, 39, was an attorney in the Domestic Relations Division of the Public Guardian's office for eight years. He was a zealous advocate for his clients. At one point last month he turned down a promotion because he didn't want to lose contact with the families he served.

It is difficult to overstate the passion and dedication of OPG employees. The uniqueness of this office, plus the day-to-day emotion management demands of their regular work, compounded by these deaths and the dramatic organizational changes that followed, made OPG an ideal case for examining emotion work.

The work of the Office of the Public Guardian involves law enforcement investigations as well as social work and client advocacy. Because of this, there needed to be a balance such that the *caritas* function would be complemented by the "tough emotions" involved in macho cultures such as corrections facilities. Thus, the second agency selected for study was a state agency, the Illinois Department of Corrections. Interviews were held in spring 2005 with officials working in several of the department's corrections facilities.

Illinois Department of Corrections

The mission of the Department of Corrections (DOC) is to protect the public from criminal offenders through a system of incarceration and supervision that securely segregates offenders from society, assures offenders of their constitutional rights, and maintains programs to enhance the success of offenders' reentry into society (Illinois Department of Corrections Fiscal Year 2003 Annual Report, p. 1).

Like in many other public service agencies, the work of the department is more complicated than a cursory reference to its agency mission. Numbers tell part of the story. In addition to the headquarters office in Springfield, there are 76 facilities statewide: 27 correctional centers; 7 work camps; 2 boot camps; 8 adult transition centers; 8 juvenile institutions; and 24 parole offices. The DOC houses 46,103 adult and juvenile inmates and monitors about 34,572 adult and juvenile parolees (Illinois Department of Corrections Data, June 30, 2005). The agency provides hundreds of programs and services to rehabilitate offenders, ranging from educational, vocational, and life skills training to substance abuse treatment programs. At any time, more than 25,000 inmates in Illinois prisons require some form of drug intervention, including full clinical treatment (Illinois Department of Corrections Fiscal Year 2003 Annual Report, p. 3). The agency budget for fiscal year (FY) 2005 was a staggering $1,207,504,626. The total work force as of June 30, 2005, was 22,988 (general revenue fund staff, 13,670; adult security staff, 8,427; and juvenile custody staff, 891).

Organizational Climate

Working in Illinois corrections facilities is not for the faint of heart. The prison population in Illinois grew from 36,543 in 1994 to 43,418 in 2003, an increase of almost 19 percent. Another 33,702 offenders are on mandatory supervised release. By the end of 2003, the adult prison population was 38.2 percent over its rated capacity (Illinois Department of Corrections 2003 Statistical Presentation). By FY 2010, the prison population is projected to increase to 48,513. Such overcrowding exacerbates an already high-pressure environment, especially within the facilities where fewer staff are responsible for greater numbers of offenders at a time of budgetary cuts. Working within the facilities can be dangerous. The threat of personal harm is a characteristic occupational hazard. According to the most recent (2003) annual report, person offenders (largely murder, weapon, and assault offenses) and sex offenders account for half the prison population; drug offenders represent about 25 percent of the population. Overcrowding fuels the sense of danger.

Parallel to the annual growth of prison populations, "Corrections is one of the fastest growing areas of employment in the nation" (Quinn 2003, p. 281). One of the greatest challenges to the DOC is in recruiting and retaining high-quality staff members. However, the increase in a better-educated work force often corresponds to increasing levels of job dissatisfaction among corrections employees (Quinn 2003). Survey responses bear this out. One respondent writes, "Been working in the same job for 3 years after getting a B.A. at UIS [University of Illinois at Springfield]. Should be a better opportunity for job advancement with a college degree; after all, the State paid for tuition for this degree. One would think, why is the State wasting money, and a lot of it, for educational costs if they [State] don't reap what they sow?" From another: "I have been stuck in my current position for over 5 years. I have been passed over by people who have less time . . . and were not as qualified for the positions they took. Most . . . were able to get the seniority due to the fact that they were working at a correctional facility doing something else that was not even related. . . ."

The organizational structure, based on military-style chain of command and bureaucratic division of labor techniques (Quinn 2003), encourages a sense of disjointedness within the staff. Evaluations are based on a hierarchical system that rewards record keeping and regulated performance. Election cycles often result in managerial house cleaning, particularly in this agency, where a recent statewide election resulted in a regime change in the executive and legislative branches. Even more recently, investigations into patronage hiring have targeted DOC, among other state agencies. Turnover as a result of political appointments often results in situations where staff members are more experienced with corrections issues and policies than are their supervisors. When speaking of new managerial appointments, one employee commented, "These new bosses have to be taught. . . . They don't want to learn how it's done before making changes. They want changes before figuring out how the system is set up. It seems like the 'new management' cares as little as the last administration." "More paperwork has been added, less promotional opportunities," was a common sentiment. Another respondent summed up the situation:

> Lack of permanent supervisors with any management skill is a major cause of very low morale in my department. They are unskilled in making decisions that best suit the interests of our agency and department. My co-workers and I bring forward issues that need [to be] addressed, and they do not respond until it becomes a crisis. When it's too late, we have to clean up the mess. I have zero confidence in my management, which I think is the cause for our very low morale. It's terrible that filling out this survey is a highlight of my day.

Employees feel that their job skills and expertise are not valued; the fact that they may be able to contribute ideas for improvement of corrections processes and procedures is not acknowledged, much less encouraged. "My biggest complaint is that the people working in the trenches are not allowed to assist in decision making processes which directly affect their work environment." Additionally, the employees themselves feel unappreciated.[5]

"Productivity would improve if upper management took time, on a regular basis, to do walk throughs and talk to employees. . . . Just to say hello [and] thanks for the job you're doing."

Gender discrimination and "chauvinism" are primary factors for job dissatisfaction among female staff. According to the Summary of Work Force Analysis of August 2005, occupational sex segregation defines the workplace. The data for the General Office in Springfield demonstrate that although women make up half of the work force, they are more likely to work as paraprofessionals (97.2 percent of paraprofessionals are women) or as office/clerical staff (65.5 percent of whom are women) with lower wages than their male co-workers. Women remain underrepresented in the officials/managers (41.4 percent) and professionals (47 percent) categories. There are no women in the service/maintenance or skilled craft categories. Supervisors determine the workplace atmosphere and evaluate staff performance, and as with many correctional facilities, sexism remains a problem, especially among older male guards (Quinn 2003). Gender discrimination often has a negative effect on professional advancement as well as on overall job satisfaction for women. One respondent commented: "Another factor for job dissatisfaction for me has been working for 'male chauvinist' bosses. . . . Are we happy about being talked down to and treated inferior? It is the 'all males club' and discrimination is alive and well."

Budget constraints and efficiency initiatives contribute significantly to overall job dissatisfaction. "The stress comes not from the job . . . but by the threat of layoffs, reduced budgets, lack of promotion and staff doing the work of vacant positions." This sentiment is echoed by a co-worker: "I am happy to be employed at the salary I receive but I feel as if I am another number on a chopping block." "I get the most stress from the job because we are required to do more with fewer people due to budget constraints and to a political environment that tries to overcome statewide budget problems by eliminating jobs that are necessary," adds another employee.

Union activities appear to have had little impact until recently. Health care workers at twenty-three state correctional facilities finally achieved success in securing pay hikes and assurances of additional pay increases over the next three years, as well as an increased uniform allowance and long-term disability benefits (Colindres 2005). But the American Federation of State, County, and Municipal Employees (AFSCME), the union that represents the majority of corrections workers, predicts a grimmer future for the rank and file.

"We've lost 15 percent of our staff in the last six years," Local 3567 president Ken Kleinlein said. "We're juggling unmanageable workloads and doing mandatory overtime, but instead of addressing the problem, the state keeps cutting the budget and the department keeps cutting jobs. Last summer they cut our clerical staff, so now we have correctional officers doing clerical work" (AFSCME Council 31, 2005).

Finally, one would expect the work environment to vary depending on whether the Springfield General Office (daytime operations) or the correctional facilities (twenty-four-hour operations) are being examined. One would further expect that differences exist across correctional facilities depending on the security level and whether the institution houses male or female offenders.

It is obvious from this description that the morale among workers in the Department of Corrections is significantly lower than the morale among workers at the Office of the Public Guardian. Whereas DOC workers see management as uncaring and unresponsive, OPG workers see management as they see themselves: committed, engaged, and responsive. Thus, two different work climates with two different types of workers exist in these two sites. OPG is a professional work force that deals with immediate needs of clients but whose actions are constrained and complicated by formal legal proceedings. DOC is a work force subject to the inertia of a large bureaucracy whipsawed by political winds, where workers deal with felons who do not want to be where they are.

Following interviews at both the Office of the Public Guardian and the Department of Corrections, it was clear that workers engaged in emotion work but had no easy-to-understand label for it. We sought a third work force whose work involved "hot" emotions that are not face-to-face, assuming that perhaps they would have a singular term for their emotion work. Police dispatchers who serve as 911 call takers were selected. They were employees of the Tallahassee, Florida, police department and were interviewed and surveyed in June 2005. Their work presents a more remote type of emotion work, in which the worker never has face-to-face contact with citizens and rarely gets feedback on the results of a day's work, yet often engages in "raw" emotion work.

Tallahassee Police Department 911 Call Takers

Jobs that require frontline customer service during crisis situations are emotionally intense. Such is the case for emergency dispatch operators. Of particular interest is the language call takers use to describe their workday and how they perform emotional labor. Interviews reveal how they describe the work they perform and how they exercise emotion management, including that which is required (a) to hold their own emotions in check, (b) to display competence and *caritas*, and (c) to express emotional sensitivity that

25

calms callers. Of particular interest is how dispatchers balance the technical and emotional demands of the work. The research here was gathered from a sample of dispatch officers.

Tallahassee is located in north Florida. The city's population varies seasonally, due to a high college student population and the fact that Tallahassee is the state capital. Once the legislative session is over and college students leave for the summer, the bustling streets turn calm. It is a chameleon of sorts, shifting from a bustling cosmopolitan hub of political action during the legislative session to a quiet small town in the lazy days of summer. The population averages 255,000.

The city employs about 2,800 people and has an annual operating budget of $539 million. It has a council/manager form of government along with a directly elected mayor. The police department employs over 300 full-time employees. The city and its surrounding county enjoy a low crime rate with few violent crimes.

Public Safety Communications Operators, better known as dispatch officers, work rotating shifts and are paid between $21,860 and $50,315 a year. Their primary function is to receive, screen, prioritize, and relay information over a communications system involving multiple lines and channels. A high school diploma plus specialized training is the minimum required education level, although community college and/or certified law enforcement experience is desirable. They are trained to take both routine and nonroutine calls. Call takers wear several hats—they are cross-trained to work as police dispatchers as well as to forward calls to fire, rescue, and ambulance services.

More specifically, dispatch officers are entrusted to operate an entire emergency operations center including a sophisticated communications system that allows contact with the public, police officers, firefighting personnel, other emergency service agencies, and support departments. Operators also use a variety of response techniques over various mediums including radio, phone, and computer. They are responsible for answering 911 fire calls for the entire county and dispatching those calls to both city/county and volunteer fire stations. Further, they are responsible for operating and monitoring several radio frequencies for dispatching police officers and firefighting personnel, as well as for maintaining the status, location, assignment, and safety of each in addition to monitoring various alarms for the governor's mansion, vice, property, panic alarms, and building fire alarms. Finally, they answer nonemergency lines including the telecommunications device for the deaf (TDD) and Crime Stoppers.

Computer skills include use of the National Crime Information Center computer system, which is used for wanted/missing persons, vehicle information, driver license information, entry and cancellation of stolen property, and administrative messages to other local and state agencies in Florida as well as out-of-state agencies. Other computer work includes searching the Criminal Justice Information System for warrants for police officers in the field as they request them, as well as maintaining logs and files such as rotation contract wrecker logs, trespass files, restraining order files, and business emergency contact files.

Dispatch work requires an interesting mix of knowledge and skills. First, dispatch officers must be competent in the hard or technical skills such as the geography of the area, road networks, surrounding area, and major business and residential complexes and locations. This is critical to communicating the information from the caller to the appropriate responder in the most efficient manner. Other hard skills include knowledge of rules and regulations, procedures for public safety dispatching, and methods and procedures for operating radio transmitting and receiving equipment. Additionally, dispatch officers must be familiar with federal, state, and county teletype computer systems; must be able to maintain a variety of logs; and must be able to type.

Second, there are also a number of intangible or soft skills required of dispatch officers as they relate to citizens in crisis. These include the abilities to listen, comprehend, retain, prioritize, make fast and accurate decisions, react quickly and calmly in emergencies, perform multiple duties simultaneously, and effectively communicate orally and in writing with co-workers, supervisors, and the public (City of Tallahassee 2003, p. 377).

This mix of technical and emotional skills makes this occupation a particularly rich arena for emotional labor research. The intensity and criticalness of emergency dispatch work captures a level of complexity not found in other service jobs. During the normal course of an eight-hour shift, a dispatcher may be called upon to bounce back and forth between offering emotional comfort to callers in crisis to answering prank calls to providing basic technical information for standard nonemergency calls. J. B. Davis studied 911 call takers and found that "nearly every call that a 911 dispatcher deals with . . . prompts an emotional response" (2005, p. 75). When dealing with an emergency caller, the level of emotion work rises dramatically and is an important element to minimizing further harm or saving a life. Additionally, all calls are recorded, so any mistake in judgment or procedure is a matter of public record.

The decision to study this mix of organizational sites—Office of the Public Guardian, Department of Corrections, and 911 call takers—resulted from three primary influences. First, although some research has focused on the gendered aspect of emotions and the workplace (Anker 1998; Erickson and Ritter 2001; Guy and Newman 2004; Leidner 1993; Simon and Nath 2004), other researchers, such as Steinberg and Figart (1999a) call for a stop to preconceived notions of gendered jobs when studying emotional labor. Their opinion comes from investigations of nurses and police officers. They concluded that the emotional labor requirement of both these professions were comparable despite gender-specific skill requirements. Second, the selection of these agencies provides the opportunity to query workers at all levels of education and professionalization. Third, these agencies complement one another. At DOC, all of the staff work with clients face-to-face. At OPG, interactions with clients are both face-to-face and voice-to-voice. At the 911 call center, interaction is strictly voice-to-voice. Moreover, the immediacy of emotional labor at 911 is explicit. It comes from the fact that dispatch officers receive calls from people in crisis. At DOC and OPG, there are plenty of times where there is no drama and even times when the work environment is calm and positive.

Stories from the Trenches

For any one of us who has ever felt apathetic toward our government, spending time at a correctional facility, human service agency, or a 911 call center provides a powerful antidote. The quotes that follow serve to illustrate. Their selection is driven by three questions that illuminate the contours of emotional labor: (1) What are the positive aspects of performing emotional labor? (2) What does burnout look like to those in the human service trenches? (3) What are effective coping strategies? That is, what differentiates those who thrive on emotion work versus those who flame out? Answers to these questions have direct implications for all facets of human resource management: recruitment, selection, compensation, training, development, and retention. These stories are the "muscles" that move our story forward.

Positive Aspects of Performing Emotional Labor

As noted above, emotion work has both positive and negative outcomes. Our study supports this conclusion. Respondents describe the positive aspects of their work and, as such, provide a counterbalance to the negative aspects that result in burnout. The intrinsic value of the job itself and the opportunity to serve others represent a powerful motivator for many emotion workers. Engagement with the job is captured by the "bounded enthusiasm" a 911 call taker feels toward her job:

I ask myself [why I keep coming back here] many times. I don't know. It's interesting. It really is interesting. And you know I hate to use the word fun—but it's nice. It's interesting talking to different people. You meet all kinds of people on the phone. People from everywhere—all walks of life, all colors, all everything and it is interesting, you know? And every once in a while you get that call and you think, I don't know if I can do this again . . . you go back to this crazy, up and down thing you have.

A co-worker explains it in these terms:

I taught school . . . for a couple years, I worked in insurance, I did all kinds of stuff but you just—it's just in your blood. I have a real sense of accomplishment. I always have. I just feel like we make a difference. . . . I think it gets in your blood. . . . It's very different from working corrections and being actually locked up—locked down with the people there. . . . Overall I enjoy it. I enjoy helping the people on the phone, you know, I enjoy helping officers, I enjoy helping my co-workers because actually we are the ones that need it the most.

Other respondents spoke about their work in terms of a "dream job," and with a sense of personal and professional accomplishment, of an ability to "juggle twelve balls in the air all at once," and of a "good exhaustion." Here are the words of a correctional counselor who has a caseload of some 200 offenders:

I absolutely love my job and I love being able to calm 'em down when they need to calm down or be stern when I need to be. . . . I just became a counselor a year ago. And I spent 20 years before that doing accounting and being extremely bored and so I find this job just so interesting, and I love every minute of it. . . . [The inmates] are so appreciative for what I do for them and they tell me they are . . . I've just had really good response from the inmates . . . I guess I get some affirmation from them that I'm doing my job. . . . I've got almost 26 years [with the state] and it was all just sitting at a desk doing accounting and not accomplishing anything, not feeling like you were doing anything to influence anybody in a positive way. So now I feel like I am. I know I am. So I'm just so darn appreciative for my life and what I get to do every day.

Taken together, these workers are expressing a "public service frame of mind" (Box and Sagen 1998, p. 196). They are positively engaged with their work, as captured by their expressions of energy, involvement, and efficacy. But there are others who find themselves at the opposite end of the continuum—those who experience burnout. We turn now to them.

Burnout in Practice

Burnout is tangible, palpable, and all too real for many of our respondents. The principal dimensions of burnout are emotional exhaustion (individual stress), cynicism (negative reaction to others and the job), and ineffective-ness (negative self-evaluation). Each of these dimensions is present among our study participants and is illustrated below.

Burnout among correctional staff is legion.[6] The dangerous working conditions and the lack of support from the lay public and their own superiors combine to produce enormous emotional labor demands on these workers. Emotion management is the modus operandi for correctional workers. Not being able to "set it down" takes its toll:

> Our jobs are far more difficult emotionally because you have to overcome your own feelings and their feelings and try to make something happen at the same time. . . . One thing I do really stress for myself is not flying off the handle, but remaining calm and that takes a great deal sometimes out of me. Sometimes I go home at night and I'm just exhausted because I've had to be professional when I sometimes would like very much not to be. . . . All that tension just goes right into you. And it's like you carry it around with you. Because I'm not allowed to shout, scream, yell, carry on like a fool, it just kinda goes around with you.

The all-encompassing nature of people work and a sense that there is little, if any, opportunity to disengage can overwhelm. A corrections officer speaks of the daily grinding pressure that never lets up:

> I think that most of my stress and emotions come out when dealing with inmates and it gets to the point when you're walking on a housing unit . . . they're gonna come up to you, can I have just one minute? No matter where you are. If you're on the walk, if you're on the phone, they'll stand at your door. Can I have just one minute? And it never takes one minute. And it's never just one question. I think that's the part where you begin to say, I gotta get away, you know? . . . they're driving on you and everywhere I go I don't care where it is, if there's inmates around they always want something, always want something. . . .

His co-worker describes the constant pressure she feels:

> Anyone who said that cell phones were going to free us is crazy because now they can get me anywhere I go. I wear a pager. They can find me in church. They can find me at home. . . . There's no laying it down. There's no putting it away. And I think that has been another of the great stressors. . . . I have to physically leave the state of Illinois to put the pager down.

The emotional exhaustion captured in these vignettes is compelling. So too is the hardening of emotions on (and off) the job, and the cynicism that accompanies this dimension of burnout. A call taker explains:

> I had the shooting at the hospital. . . . It was nuts. We've had several others. But you're talking about how do you get to that level? It's like a callous. It's

that callous that allows you to continue. It's not necessarily training. It's the experience. It's the exposure. It's the deadening. . . . My callousness is honestly to the point where I've had to work on having, showing real emotion again.

These sentiments are echoed by a co-worker:

When I first came into this . . . job . . . I used to be a lot more compassionate, a lot more, and I've noticed that. I think the breaking point came the night the officer got shot, and we had to come in and still work and do radio dispatch and I was on phones that night and it was very emotional and trying to answer the phones and these people . . . screaming at you about their party call and you have to be nice . . . and professional . . . but you know at that point in time with what was going on with me personally the only thing I wanted to do was say you know, your call about a noisy party is not that important right now—we've got someone dying you know, can you be a little bit sympathetic and a little bit understanding . . . they were just rude and I think that was my breaking point . . . there's so many rude people that just don't care about anybody else. They're so self-centered, and I became less compassionate from that point on, especially toward calls like that.

Such "hardening" and "deadening" is also expressed as becoming numb to the repeated adrenalin "highs" that accompany so much of high-stakes people work:

I was plugged into the old phone system . . . I had my headset on . . . and I answered the phone . . . you could hear [a] deep breath, and it was like all the gears were starting to just slowly kick in . . . cause this is where shit is about to hit the fan. The adrenalin rush that was with that call—you lose it I think after a while . . . your adrenal gland feels like it just shuts down and things that would wig out a normal person don't affect you. You know, I had to do things like skydiving just to feel a true rush of excitement.

I've changed as a person. It changes a person beyond recognition. I mean from point A to point C I'm not the same person I was when I started. . . . It's because I've seen too damn much. I'm much more cynical than I ever imagined I would be.

Burnout is also manifest in terms of ineffectiveness on the job. An inability to maintain a professional "edge" and balance is one such outcome, as seen in these words of a worker at the Office of the Public Guardian:

When I first started with the office . . . I would actually say, psychologically speaking, I had post traumatic stress disorder to the second degree. . . . If you have no idea, which I had not, how severely kids can be abused and neglected and you have children of your own, which I do, your mind is like crazed almost. Like, how can anybody take an extension cord and whip a child within inches literally of their life? Why would anybody put a child in a scalding bathtub?

More debilitating is a sense of hopelessness and apathy. The absence of concrete evidence of success causes feelings of insignificance, disillusion-ment, and helplessness, which are the hallmarks of burnout (Pines and Aronson 1988). For many of our respondents, regardless of their particular job, there was a feeling that no matter how hard they tried, they could not have a lasting impact on the lives of their clients. This sense of fatalism is expressed by an attorney as he describes the state of a co-worker:

> We can't control what happens to our clients. . . . He's being tortured by this job—he feels out of control—that whatever he does, he can't help these kids. . . . The outlooks for our clients are mostly bleak. . . . Ninety-nine percent of what we do has been done before.

Another co-worker at the Office of the Public Guardian puts it this way:

> At some point you just gotta give up. If they [a client] don't wanna talk to you, they don't wanna talk to you, and you just . . . maybe try again another day. . . . That's really all you can do. And just try not to take it personal. . . . But when you wanna talk to somebody and they don't wanna talk to you, that's like, you know that's not a good feeling, you know it's like a rejection basically . . . you just have to say to yourself they have the right not to talk to me . . . so why am I getting all upset? . . . and the only reason why you get upset is because you want to meet success every time . . . and just realizing that you can't meet success—I mean cause we're dealing in the real world you know. We're dealing with people. If we're dealing with machines, yeah, I would be successful all the time.

For people in human service professions, helping others gives a sense of meaning to life, but not being able to help is stressful. For example, the vicarious involvement in clients' lives can produce overidentification, un-realistic expectations, and finally a painful letdown (Edelwich and Brodsky 1980). Overinvolvement can also upset the delicate balance of "detached concern" and cause a loss of objectivity. An attorney at the Office of the Public Guardian provides an illustration:

> One of my sex abuse clients . . . she's been raped by her father for seven, eight years—was a straight-A student and nobody knew what was going on at home. She finally cried out in junior high school and an aunt had taken her in with her siblings, and she got a full scholarship to the University of Minnesota and I had her in the office—she's been my client for eight years and she called me in May because she's come back after her sophomore year pregnant and, you

know, I hung up the phone and just sobbed and thought, you know, here's—of all the things that are going on in her life and I thought we were on track and that things are better and I realized how emotionally attached I am to [her]. And I've only got 13 clients left and many of them are in my life a long time and I don't know how younger attorneys do this job.

One of the saddest commentaries came from a senior manager at the Department of Corrections whom we interviewed on the eve of his retirement. Here is how he expresses his sense of despondency and loss of trust:

Have I been burned out in my career? Sure. . . . And it's sad. . . . One thing it's taught me that I hate is that I don't trust anyone. I hate that part. I think that hurts everyone too. You can't trust anyone. . . . I know they cheated me. I see that with everyone. Because corrections is a pretty big family . . . you protected each other like a family member and I think all the problems that we have outside of work get solved here at work with fellow workers. . . . That's why I always say you can't trust, you know, I don't trust anyone . . . not like I did before I started working here.

Burnout is characterized by an inability to disengage ("escape") from the work, by an overwhelming grinding pressure, a callousness, an inability to maintain a professional perspective, a sense of hopelessness, apathy, despondency, and a lack of trust. It bears noting that we interviewed those who have either successfully dealt with the threat of burnout or who have not (yet) succumbed to it. Turnover is high, and only those who remain on the job are available for interview.

Every one of the situations in these vignettes may seem extreme, but they are a part of the everyday work life of these public servants and many others in public service. These stories beg the question: Because these workers have such emotional extremes in their jobs, what enables them to get through the day and return the next day?

Coping Strategies

While overindulgence of alcohol or food off the job was a common refrain, our respondents rely upon a number of creative strategies to cope.[7] Taking a "time-out" (by means fair or foul) is one such strategy. The concept of "time-out" is relevant for any work that involves high degrees of emotional or mental stress (Pines and Aronson 1988, p. 189). Time-outs are opportunities for staff to voluntarily choose to do some less stressful, nonpersonal work while others temporarily take over their responsibilities. For example, many 911 call takers report that after a stressful call—a "hot" call—is concluded, they will hand over their station to a co-worker and leave the area for awhile. Some walk around the block, some weep, and some just seek a quiet place to be alone. When they return to their station, they answer the next phone that rings.

> [The little boy] went back in there just to wake the mom up . . . and he said she was sick and wouldn't wake up. Well then his sister goes in there—she's dead. They couldn't wake her up. It was just the most horrible thing . . . I just cried about it—walked around the building. I got out of the building [and] walked around.

This constructive, temporary withdrawal is positive because it allows the worker to regroup and service can be maintained even while the professional is getting a temporary emotional breather (Maslach 1981). A 911 call taker explains how he copes with his work, and offers a description of emotional labor in the process. The challenge is to care and not to care at the same time:

> On the one hand you're supposed to be empathizing and help people deal with it, but once you get to the time that they need you the most, you have to shut your feelings down and deal with the situation. So you have to care and not care at the same time. . . . You're not shutting [your feelings] down, you're just shutting 'em down while you're in crisis mode. . . . I don't know how to tell you how it happens but it's like you just put the brakes on your emotions, you go level, you start to take them level, or try to get what you need to get help to 'em.

The ability to compartmentalize is a complementary strategy:

> He did a really good job on midnights until he took a call and the guy pulled the trigger with him on the phone. It's very rare that happens in this profession that somebody actually pulls the trigger, but . . . after it [he] wouldn't come back. . . . Those who can compartmentalize do this job better than those who cannot. . . . You gotta learn to step away. . . . I probably still absorb more than I should today but . . . getting over the bad ones, you've gotta put 'em in a box.

When physical distancing is impossible, workers use emotional withdrawal as a respite from the stressors of their work. Negative "absence behavior" (Nicholson 1977) and "time abuse," such as taking longer breaks, calling in sick, spending more time on paperwork, leaving work early, and tardiness, are all examples of withdrawal by means of spending less time with clients (Pines and Aronson 1988). An employee of the Department of Corrections provides an example:

> This staff member has called in sick all week. She is always giving me excuses on why she can't be on her unit at the time she's supposed to be there . . . there's

an issue that I have with staff and that issue is the use of time . . . I mean they're calling in at the last minute—just won't come to work. . . . [Discussing another worker:] He's never here. He's always calling in. He's always trying to find a way to get off from work. . . . The counselors that give me the biggest problems are those that don't come to work.

Withdrawal is accomplished more dramatically by emotionally "shutting down." A respondent from the Department of Corrections explains:

I just call it closing down. I shut down the emotion . . . I try to shut it down and just be very professional with them. I cope by shutting down. . . . When I have to deal with them and when they get too emotional with me . . . I shut down.

Other respondents cope by means of a behavioral transformation that consists of putting on *emotional armor:*

When I know I've got to deal with the ladies [inmates], I do prepare . . . and the day of my call line when I get up from that desk with my paperwork and I start walking out [through the double gates] my personality goes to change and I just become a different person and I am the empress . . . I become Mrs. [Smith], the professional . . . I mentally do that cause I'm leaving the office . . . and I feel it—I know I'm doing it. I think I've learned to do it on purpose when I know I'm going out to face them.

Another emotional laborer, a 911 call taker, puts it this way:

It's just when I come in here I'm—it's like you put on a coat of armor, you know, you just, you have to be kinda tough.

Another strategy is a reliance on "gallows humor" as a relief valve. One of the ways staff reported they dealt with burnout was ventilating feelings through humor. They spoke of making fun of their clients as a catharsis. A worker at the Department of Corrections explains:

We use humor a lot. . . . They wouldn't find anything we say too funny because there are times you know when you're referring to one of them—our field services rep's favorite thing is when she gets really angry she calls 'em the bags. The bags—sort of between "hag" and you know the other words. And she'll say the bags—and we laugh about it . . . so that's how we play it off . . . it just lightens the load.

A 911 call taker describes her strategy:

It's just, you know, kind of a philosophy. Once you put the phone down . . . you might laugh at it . . . I'll say, hey, I just had this guy—just a little venting type thing—I had this guy who said this guy beat him up and ha ha ha we laugh about it and go on to the next call, so it's kinda like you just venting with your next door neighbor or something like that about the situation.

Peer support provides an outlet for the frustrations and anguish that arise from emotion work. Familiarity with each other's work demands allows co-workers to understand and empathize with their peers in ways that friends and family cannot. Such empathy relies on the trust that arises from sharing emotionally searing work experiences. The intensity of the collaboration can become central in workers' lives and in some cases takes on a significance equal to family-based relations. As workers explained at all three agencies, supportive work-based relationships become ends in themselves, making work worthwhile. From an organizational performance standpoint, sup-portive peer relations—especially the helping and interpersonal facilitation processes—generate performance outcomes that all take pride in. This creates an esprit de corps that is motivating. A 911 call taker tells this story:

> We had a co-worker and her baby was at daycare. We get a call from this daycare center and it was her baby . . . I didn't know how to tell her. Because at that point the baby was still alive but I didn't know how to tell her that she needed to get to the hospital. So I just got another co-worker to go with me to help me tell her, and after she got to the hospital the last thing I heard her say was, "Lord, please help my baby!" And I mean that's been years—I'm still emotional and, you know, you just don't ever know.

Why do some emotional laborers stay and others leave? We believe that a big part of the answer lies in the fact that these workers may experience both engagement and burnout in their jobs. There is a dual relationship with one's job and the highs and lows of performing "people work." Coping strategies may allow the worker to "just get by," or they may provide their own reward for the job.

The next chapter juxtaposes what we know in theory about the effect of emotion work with what those who actually perform it have to say. Testi-monies from workers in the three agencies inform the discussion.

Notes

1. Cook County, Illinois, Office of the Public Guardian website: www.publicguardian. org, accessed December 25, 2006. OPG perceives itself and operates more as a dynamic advocacy organization than as a rule-bound county bureaucracy, which is reflected in its choice of Internet extensions for its website, "org" rather than "gov," and its relationship to the primary county sites: www.co.cook.il.us and www.cookcountygov.com.

2. Cook County Info Center, www.co.cook.il.us/index.php, accessed December 25, 2006.

3. Cook County Public Guardian P.T. Murphy, personal communication, August 13, 2004.

4. In fact, OPG job descriptions state clearly: "More than 40 hours per week are required to perform the essential duties of the position."

5. In fact, our study was met with skepticism from DOC staff, who said they suspected that we were "really" part of an effort by the state to determine which jobs would get cut.

6. See, for example, Gerstein, Topp, and Correll (1987), and Maslach, Schaufeli, and Leiter (2001).

7. Coping is the link between stress and adaptation (Pines and Aronson 1988). It can be either constructive, as in seeking a "detached concern" (Lief and Fox 1963) that manages job stress by creating some distance for the worker without psychological removal (such as taking a time-out), or counterproductive, as in emotional disengagement and withdrawal, cynicism, or rigidity (Golembiewski and Munzenrider 1988). Moreover, coping in itself does not imply success, but effort.

— 2 —

The Disconnect Between
Public Administration
Theory and Practice

Emotion work is instrumental in bridging the "how" and the "what" of government. It turns our attention to the *caritas* function that is at the heart of public *service*, and the means by which this work is performed.

> Once a month I do the death review. . . it's my least favorite thing to do . . . literally it's an entire afternoon of hearing about one dead baby after another dead baby. . . . I can say there've been plenty of times where I've thought I have to quit this job. This is making me nuts . . . but somehow I always come back . . . it makes a difference that I am there and that is worth it all, and how could I ever survive in a job where, you know, I'm . . . making widgets. . . . (worker at Office of the Public Guardian)

In order to situate our research and to explicate the meaning of public service work, this chapter examines the development of the field of public administration and identifies values that are commonly cited. Next, we examine theories of caring in other disciplines by referencing works in sociology, feminist economics, psychology, nursing, education, and social work. The focus on caring illuminates the disconnect between the actual performance of public service and the theoretical development of public administration.

While a framework of caring is implied (indeed essential) in an understanding of the practice of public administration, it is not articulated. Instead, twin values of rationality and efficiency predominate. With the notable exception of the recent work of Camilla Stivers, Cheryl King, O.C. McSwite, and a handful of others, there is a vacuum in the literature on both a theory of caring and on the value of service and relational tasks. Caring as a value has not moved into the mainstream of public administration discourse. Without a place in the paradigm, the concept of relational work and its essential component, emotional labor, is absent. This chapter situates emotional labor in the theoretical underpinnings of public administration generally, and gendered bureaucracies more specifically.

Caring

The void in the public administration literature on the *caritas* function and the concept of emotional labor as a theoretical construct stands in marked contrast with the rich treatment of "caring" in other disciplines. Most fundamentally, this research stream has addressed the dichotomy between the "rational" aspects of organizations and the role of emotion in organizing, developing, and leadership. A second stream of research focuses on rules governing the expression of emotion, generally in service-based occupations such as counter clerks, caseworkers, counselors, law enforcement officers, and regulatory officials.

The words of workers in the Office of the Public Guardian, Department of Corrections, and 911 call centers underscore the pervasiveness and significance of relational work in public service. To a large degree, emotion work is fundamental to the provision of public services and is the mainstay of the caring professions.

In reflecting on the shape of this chapter, we were reminded of a question that had been asked of one of our doctoral students at the completion of formal coursework: If you had to choose between the value of efficiency and the value of responsiveness (the Hamiltonian responsiveness *to the people*, not responsiveness in terms of timeliness), which would you choose? Without hesitation, the student responded "efficiency." The initial surprise (shock) at the response is tempered by the subject of this chapter. To choose "efficiency" is to view public administration from a "how" perspective, from a (scientific) management approach. "Responsiveness" begins to suggest a competing approach—that of "what" should government be most attentive to? Jane Addams puts it this way: "[Municipal reform efforts led by business groups] fix their attention so exclusively on methods that they fail to consider the final aims of city government" (Addams 2002 [1902], p. 99). The paramount issue for governments, Addams held, was not how they should be run, but what they should do (Stivers 2008). The Bureau Movement's approach to running government agencies came increasingly to be seen as a matter of "management" and management expertise, legitimated by Taylorism (Taylor 1911). McSwite suggests a competing approach: we have to turn to making a world "by developing the kinds of relationships with each other that allow us to figure out what we want to do next" (1997, p. 261).

Nevertheless, the (conventional) intellectual heritage of our field is replete with references of "how" to "do" government better. The reinvention movement is merely the latest in a long line of reform efforts focusing on methods and techniques. For example, Van Riper characterizes the administrations of Grover Cleveland and Ronald Reagan as pursuing "how to do it" not "what to do" programs (1983, p. 487). Missing from much of the conventional history of our field is any significant debate on "what" government should be engaged in. To quote Waldo, the "formal analysis of organizations without regard to the purposes that inspire them [is] but a tedious elaboration of the insignificant" (1948, p. 211).

This brings us to an important point: the concept of *emotional labor* and the concomitant values of *caring* and *service* represent a powerful lens through which to view our foundational heritage. This perspective has the potential to further complicate the conventional founding narrative of our field, a narrative already made suspect by the work of Paul Van Riper, Camilla Stivers, DeLysa Burnier, Cheryl King, O.C. McSwite, Ralph Hummel, Hindy Lauer Schachter, Jong Jun, Robert Kramer, and a handful of others. Emotion work illuminates the missing links in our field—namely, an ethic of care and relational tasks. Administration is not just rule-governed elements in our attempts to design effective governance processes. It is also an interpersonal subjective process, but the latter appears only fleetingly in our theories (Stivers 2005, p. 38). Despite Van Riper's call for a "reapplication of our long-standing and general social ethic on a pragmatic and truly caring basis" (1983, p. 489), "caring as it relates to public administration remains an elusive concept. Little has been written about care explicitly as a value or practice within the scholarly community of American public administration" (Burnier 2003, p. 530). Whether by omission or commission, such inattention flies in the face of actual practice, as the words of our interviewees demonstrate.

Emotion Work and Caring Defined

Stivers makes reference to leadership as having become public administration's "phlogiston—the mysterious substance that, prior to the discovery of oxygen, was believed to be the ingredient in substances that made them burn" (2002, p. 62). The same term can be accurately applied to the concept of emotion work. Most public service jobs require interpersonal encounters, often in emotionally wrenching circumstances. Listen to a social worker as she speaks about the nature of her work: "We have to develop these relationships . . . in order to get our clients to . . . tell us the deepest, and darkest, and whatever's going on—right? . . . [We] have to develop . . . rapport."

Relational skills are essential for job completion but have only recently come under scrutiny as prerequisites that make a difference in the performance of public programs (Guy and Newman 2004, p. 289).

Emotional labor requires that workers suppress their private feelings in order to show the "desirable" work-related emotion. Unlike physical labor, this is "invisible" work: it is not measurable and it can rarely be seen, touched, or heard. Jobs that require emotional labor have three distinct characteristics in common: first, they require person-to-person contact with the public; second, they require workers to manage the emotional state of another person; and third, they allow the employer to exercise a degree of control over the emotional activities of employees (Hochschild 1983, p. 147). In short, the focus is on an emotional performance that is bought and sold as a commodity. A correctional officer in charge of a women's prison puts it this way:

> Being a correctional officer, it's just not about security. It's a lot of emotional needs from the individuals that are incarcerated . . . we have days when we may not be having a good day, but I still have to maintain that level of professionalism. . . . Professionalism is when you go in on a unit for the day and you have women that will literally curse you out and they start with the rolling of the eyes, you know, just because you came in . . . throughout the evening it may progress to having words with this individual due to her behavior . . . and being able to maintain that level of professionalism is when you have to bite your tongue and still . . . remain in control of the situation. . . . You have to be able to go and still have—what's the word I'm looking for?—some kindness in your heart, pretty much.

Emotion work and caring are bound together by definition and practice. Not all emotional labor is caring labor, but caring labor is a type of emotional labor (Himmelweit 1999, p. 34). Care, derived from the Latin *cura*, denotes concern for, commitment to, and attending to others (Leininger 1988, 136). Caring is most fundamentally a *relation*, a commitment to an attitude that keeps one responsive to others (Brabeck 1989, p. 87). Caregiving challenges the division between reason and emotion (Abel and Nelson 1990, p. 5). Referencing Heidegger, King and Stivers (1998, pp. 38–39) state that "*care* is what makes possible that connection, that being-in-relationship. . . . Care is that attentiveness or concern that enables us to orient ourselves toward and connect with things and people in our world and to be aware of those connections . . . *care*-ful relationship."

41

Caring has been variously defined as that which "refers to the direct (or indirect) nurturant and skillful activities, processes, and decisions related to assisting people in such a manner that reflects behavioral attributes which are empathetic, supportive, compassionate, protective, succorant, educational, and otherwise dependent upon the needs, problems, values, and goals of the individual or group being assisted" (Leininger 1988, p. 115); the mental, emotional, and physical effort involved in looking after, responding to, and supporting others (Henderson 2001, p. 131); a concept encompassing that range of human experiences which have to do with feeling concern for, and taking charge of, the well-being of others (Staden 1998, p. 147); and it "involves stepping out of one's personal frame of reference into the other's" (Noddings 1984, p. 24). Caring for another "is the meeting of the needs of one person by another person where face-to-face interaction between carer and cared for is a crucial element of the overall activity" (Kittay and Feder 2002, p. 163). A correctional counselor provides an illustration of how he performs emotion work, compared to how a female peer performs the same function:

> My education is from the school of hard knocks. She has a master's degree and [is] a very learned lady. She does things one way and I do things another way and we work very well together. There's no problems . . . she tells me to go over and talk to [the offender]—trying to get a little cuddle—not physical cuddle, but little emotional cuddle and some of her [offenders] will come over to me when she's not there.

How does this work fit within the conventional script for the founding of public administration? How does "work" become defined in this founding narrative? We now turn to these questions.

Administrative *Science* or Public *Service*?

Who cares when administrative science and public service are treated as one and the same? Perhaps Richard Green, for one: "Our conceptions of the foundations of public administration matter a great deal. They act as broad premises from which we develop roles, functions, and practices. They shape the image of public administration in the eyes of the public, and thereby affect its legitimacy" (Green 2002, p. 556). While Green's purpose is to argue for our nation's founding period as the source of modern public administration, specifically Alexander Hamilton's theory of public administration, his general premise holds true for the field. "It matters if public administrators view themselves as technicians trained in a universal science of administration versus being socialized and educated for service in an administration tailored to a specific political culture and regime structure" (p. 556). Our point is that it matters when public administrators view themselves, and are perceived by the public, as merely dispassionate cogs in the machine of government versus being viewed and treated as public servants engaged in care work or "soulwork" (Kramer 2003, p. 6). Kramer says it best:

> Governance is more than the machinery of public administration, and more than the machinery of impartial cost-benefit analysis. . . . Human relationships are at the heart of governance . . . all public service is people service. . . . You have to communicate with people at an emotional level. . . . Human relationships are the DNA of governance. (2003, p. 2)

In reviewing the intellectual heritage of public administration, attention to the *science* of administration and the cult of efficiency trumps attention to the relational aspects of public *service*. Indeed, discourse on the field's development can be characterized as a testament to the values of rationality and efficiency, scientific principles, objectivity, and generic management processes. Excluded from much of this discourse is any reference to a service orientation and the value of caring.

> At its inception, public administration paid homage to the "god" of science. . . . The developing field of management science prescribed principles of management that emphasized efficiency over all else. In its purest sense, the god of efficiency . . . is simple, clear-cut, and short-sighted. (Guy 2003, pp. 643, 647)

In revisiting the traditional canons of our field through the lens of emotion work and the *caritas* function, the prominence of the principles of science (connoting disinterestedness) over service (connectedness) is undeniable. Even a cursory review of our literature supports this position. From Woodrow Wilson to New Public Management, the *business* of government and the marketization of public administration have served to sanctify the values of (technical) efficiency and (objective) rationality.

A few salient examples serve to reinforce the point. In his essay of 1887, Woodrow Wilson asserted the need for business-like and expert methods. In 1903, Frederick Taylor's *Shop Management* fueled the fledgling Progressive-era movement. Taylor's assertion that scientific research could improve efficiency and rationality became an article of faith of the Bureau Movement (Schachter 2004, p. 44). In 1909, Frederick Cleveland, a leader of the New York Bureau of Municipal Research, wrote that "Science is a codification of exactly determined commonsense . . ." (Cleveland 1909, p. 176). "Administration must therefore become a science in order to eliminate confusion . . .

about the best method of accomplishing tasks" (Stivers 2002, p. 42). In 191?, the beginnings of the management science perspective came with the addition to the Civil Service Commission of a Division of Efficiency (Van Riper 1983, p. 482).

In the 1920s, "bureau men" were the standard-bearers for the ideals of economy and efficiency. They believed that a rational and scientific approach was essential for the eradication of social problems (Baines, Evans, and Neysmith 1998, p. 34). In 1926, Leonard White asserted that "The study of administration should start from the base of management. . . . It assumes that administration is still primarily an art but attaches importance to the significant tendency to transform it into a science" (White 1926, p. ix). In 1927, William F. Willoughby published his *Principles of Public Administration: With Special Reference to National and State Governments of the United States.* In 1937, the Brownlow Commission argued that "Real efficiency . . . must be built into the structure of government just as it is built into a piece of machinery" (Brownlow, Merriam, and Gulick, p. 2). And Gulick and Lyndall Urwick's *Papers on the Science of Administration* provided the first anthology directed at the idea of administration as a universal process (Van Riper 1983, p. 481). King and Stivers provide a summary: "Since the Progressive era, public administration has moved in an increasingly instrumental, managerial direction, valuing the application of scientific methodology to the resolution of public issues and building an identity of neutral expertise" (1998, p. 106).

Missing from much of this conventional narrative is the language of pragmatism, experience, caring, responsiveness, "publicness," and a service orientation. Attention to an ethics of care and those relational tasks that are captured by the concept of emotional labor are rendered largely invisible. The concepts of neutral competency and "care-ful" concern are fundamentally at odds. The experiences of Jane Addams and her cohort and their attention to healing social ills "up close and personal" stand in stark contrast to the rational detachment of administrative science and the perspective put forward by the "bureau men." The following contemporary vignette, from an employee of the Office of the Public Guardian, illustrates the "personal" in sharp relief:

> You do get emotional—you know, you can have attachments especially if you're starting to see kids over and over and over. And then you get to know the foster parents and stuff like that. . . . You're putting a face to everything, especially like the little boy whose brother died. You know, he remembers his brother. He was there most likely when it happened and he talks about it in spurts but because of his age, you're not gonna get, Daddy did da . . . da . . . da . . . , you know? But he's doing good.

The contributions of female scholars and thinkers, whose work emphasized care relations, were ignored for decades. That these "lost" women (such as Mary Parker Follett and Laverne Burchfield) are beginning to be found serves to underscore the fissures in our founding narrative (see Burnier 2004). It also calls into question the conventional wisdom of what it means to "work."

Theories of Work

Our understanding of what it means to work derives from our disciplinary roots, and is founded on Wilsonian, Tayloristic, and Weberian assumptions. For the most part, theories of work and caring are treated as unrelated concepts. According to Himmelweit, "The dichotomized picture—which places home, care, and women on one side and the workplace, paid labor, and men on the other—needs adjusting to remove the distorting dualism that leaves no room for care to cross the boundary into the workplace" (1999, p. 28).

To show the contrast between traditional notions of public administration and the actual role of emotional labor in public service, Kramer (2003) describes Luther Gulick's work of seventy years ago. Gulick advanced the merits of a mechanistic, dehumanized, and emotionless model of administration, asserting that public administrators "are supposed to be smooth running machines—transmission belts for carrying out the will of the people . . ." (p. 140). Compare this view with the practice of administration in a social service agency:

> The office has not really done evaluations. We don't fill out timesheets, we don't fill out worksheets . . . one of the things you don't do is you don't hire people in this office who are rigidly committed to schedules or who say, you know, this is how my day is scheduled and I have to do A, B, C, D. It doesn't work here . . . we put that . . . right up front. If you can't handle that, don't come because the best made plans around here go up in smoke on a weekly basis.

The Weberian model of "man as machine" and "the dominance of a spirit of formalistic impersonality, '*sine ira et studio*,' without hatred or passion, and hence without affection or enthusiasm" (Weber 1922, in Boone and Bowen 1987, p. 16) requires that public administrators become "souls on ice" and conduct relationships "without sympathy or enthusiasm" (Thompson 1975, as cited in Kramer 2003, p. 14). Hence, a rational division of labor, hierarchical control, performance standards, selection and advancement based on technical competence, formal record keeping, and communication are ingrained in the way we think about job classification and performance evaluation. A correctional officer provides an illustration:

> It just depends on what your job is. I mean, if you're the detail officer, you drive around and pick up property and deliver meals. OK, well he does that in a timely manner so he's gonna get a good mark on that. But put him on a housing unit and let him run a house by himself. Dealing with all the issues of 145 inmates isn't the same. Because it's more emotional running a house with 145 inmates than it is out there driving a truck with two guys.

Second, the nature of bureaucracy itself shapes, if not predicts, the character of the work that is performed. According to Weber, "Bureaucracy develops the more perfectly, the more it is 'dehumanized'" (1968, p. 975). In his scathing critique of bureaucracy, Ralph Hummel decries the Weberian orthodoxy. He asks: "Is not a public service bureaucracy, especially, set up to provide public service?" (1994, p. 31). Hummel explains:

> [T]he psychological experience of bureaucracy is this: . . . Bureaucrats are asked to become people without conscience. . . . Those who submit become people without heart. . . . Bureaucrats are asked to leave their emotions at home. Yet all that human beings do—in relating themselves to other people, the objects of their work, the working itself—carries with it feelings . . . we feel for those who are our clients—compassion or disdain . . . and so on. . . . As a result, unconscious feelings silently accompany all our relations with people and things at work—at times distorting, at times supporting our ability to get work done. (1994, p. 112)

As the emerging body of work on emotional labor attests, the expression and management of feelings and emotions gets "disappeared," to use Joyce Fletcher's (1999) term. It does not fit the prevailing pattern of "work." In the same way, caregiving fits uneasily into bureaucracies. The conflict between the universalism of bureaucracies and the particularism of caregiving is difficult to reconcile (Abel and Nelson 1990, p. 12).

As noted in Chapter 1, urbanization created a dichotomy between home and work, with each domain evoking different behaviors. The separation of the roles of men and women, with men designated as the primary workers in the public world and women as the primary workers in the private domain of the household, spills over into the recognition and valuation of skills in the labor market (Baines, Evans, and Neysmith 1998, p. 52). Norms that underlie the work ethic reflect a capitalist economic structure that privileges the work done in the public and "productive" market and renders invisible the relational work women do in the home (ibid., p. 47).

> Having entered the private realm of the home, caregiving becomes invisible. It runs on a different clock than the world of employment. Both these characteristics make it difficult to see it as work when the definition of work is so firmly market-related. It is, after all, work that isn't seen and isn't valued except when it isn't done! (Baines, Evans, and Neysmith 1998, p. 239)

Reliance on "market value" for establishing the value of a job further cemented the status quo because emotional labor and relational tasks fall outside these commonly understood parameters of work. The feminist economist Nancy Folbre says: "I've worried aloud about economists' overconfidence in that abstraction called 'the market'" (2001, p. 231). Such notions simply assign a dollar value to cultural understandings of worth. They do not recognize that jobs "require workers to have emotions as well as muscle and brain" (Himmelweit 1999, p. 34). The emphasis on tangible, testable skills suppresses, or "disappears," behavior that is inconsistent with industrial era standards, even when that behavior is directly related to organizational goals. A counselor provides a window into the reality of this work:

> [W]e see a variety of clients ... those [who have been] severely sexually abused ... the mother may have been poisoning the kids when they went for visits ... this little girl had been raped by her stepfather from ages nine to twelve. I mean very bad ... this is all in the same week, mind you. ... God, I just had a bunch of bad cases ... you're back to ... this emotional up and down because it's like wow—that was just really intense and sad, you know?

To summarize, the market's "objective" approach to task elements and to performance evaluation rests on an ideology of work that is buttressed by norms suited to industrial but not service jobs. Traditional administrative language is the language of scientific management—span of control, hierarchy, authority, and division of labor. A conception of administrative practice that is relational rather than controlling has a very different vocabulary.

Theories of Caring

A necessary first step toward any discussion of a relational aspect to administrative work requires us to discard the notion of government as machine. Luther Gulick provides this perspective:

> If, instead of a machine model, we think of government as an organism, a living organism, we have a totally different and more accurate and constructive understanding of a government organization. ... The staff are no longer cogs, they are suborgans, each with its own life, health, interrelations, and work to do. (1976, p. 9)

47

Gulick's change of heart—from his early guiding metaphor of government as machine in the late 1930s to government as a living organism some four decades later—is revealing. The language of an alternative—and more complete—administrative theory is gaining voice and has its own vocabulary. This language is relational and involves caring, vision, collaboration, courage, and intuition. The care perspective emphasizes values such as attentiveness, responsiveness, and the importance of relationships and emotional connection. These "unscientific" words are not new, but they are relatively new to administrative theory (Regan and Brooks 1995, p. xi). Caring specifically involves the development of a relationship, "not the emotional servicing of people who remain strangers" (Himmelweit 1999, p. 35). Moreover, the caring construct enables us to move beyond the assumptions that underpin the traditional dichotomies of women's work: paid/unpaid, public/private, and formal/informal (Baines, Evans, and Neysmith 1998).

This relational language was the mother tongue of the women of the settlement houses and city clubs. Stivers (2000) provides the context: She argues that, at its founding, the field of public administration faced a choice between two divergent paths: that advanced by the science of the bureau men, and that of the care orientation of the settlement women (see Schachter 2002 for a critique).[1] "De facto rather than deliberately, American public administration chose one and rejected or forgot the other" (Stivers 2005, p. 27). Gender dynamics at the time resulted in a bifurcation between what could have been complementary impulses of systematization and caring. Male reformers felt the need to make public administration masculine by making it "muscular"—that is, scientific and businesslike (Stivers 2002, p. 8). Stivers explains the decision as follows:

> My argument is that at least part of the reason for public administration's preference for scientific administration over the values that animated municipal housekeeping—for efficiency over caring—was the threat to municipal reformers posed by the gender accusations of party politicians: specifically, the risk to their masculinity that lay in associating themselves with women's benevolent activities. (2000, p. 125)

Stivers's more recent work "explores the road less taken: public administration based on ideas of home. . . . [H]ome offers a relational reality for public administration. This reality serves as an alternative to prevailing understandings based on efficiency, control, and competition" (2005, p. 27). The ontology of home is associated with nurturing and caring. These values were reflected in the work of the settlement residents and club women (2005, p. 35). Recall that, in contrast to the bureau men's vision of the city as a business, the settlement women viewed the city as a home, and the community as one great family; accordingly, their reform efforts came to be known as "municipal housekeeping," and their work as "public motherhood" (Stivers 2000, p. 9).[2] The Woman's City Club, for example, characterized its work in terms of "'the Links that bind the Home to the City Hall.' The home and all life within the city were inextricably chained to city hall—female concerns about food inspection, factory safety, and clean air" (Flanagan 1990, p. 1048).

Jane Addams, founder of Hull House in Chicago, lived this reality. From a practical foundation, she articulated a pragmatic view of administration informed by ideas of home and community, and rejected the notion that efficiency was the key to effective administration. She used "family" as a metaphor for the wider society in order to argue for a notion of governance rooted in the kind of caring and nurturing that was seen as typical of the home, with the concomitant commitment to treat people with the kind of respect and care due real human beings, as opposed to abstractions (cases) and statistics (Stivers 2008).

While Burnier has stated that "the voice of care is yet to be heard within public administration" (2003, p. 538), the voices of Stivers, Addams, and others (including Burnier) represent an emerging appreciation. Follett's organizational thinking anticipates the care perspective's emphasis on relationality (Burnier 2003, p. 536). Hummel and Stivers are critical of government for becoming "a specialized enterprise increasingly devoted to the exercise of technical rules and procedures, whether or not these take care of real-life problems. Reason, especially instrumental reason, overwhelms care" (1998, p. 29). They advocate developing a "politics of care" that would be marked by attentiveness and connectedness (p. 38). Jong Jun lists a number of virtues that a civic-minded administrator should attempt to embody, including being "caring and compassionate" (1999, p. 224). Such traits are routinely expressed in the delivery of public services. A clinical services supervisor provides an example:

> The lady was in our health care unit and she has seizures . . . and she says . . . I refuse to take my medication . . . and I asked her why. Well she says, well the inmates always know that I go to Med Line and they think there's something wrong with me . . . and I just basically asked her, you know, why are you worrying about what they're thinking of you because you're dealing with a medical situation that's going to affect your life forever. . . . You don't need to worry about what those individuals out in the unit are gonna think about you. . . . So you need to think about yourself, and it's one of those times when you start talking about emotions . . . well, she started crying . . . saying that, you know, I've never had anybody explain that to me before and actually take a caring role with just myself.

This vignette points public administration in a direction in which care becomes a guiding value. To the extent that the care perspective could become an alternative theoretical framework for public administration, our theoretical base would need to shift away from that of bureaucracy and the marketplace and toward that of relationship and consideration for the "other" (Burnier 2003). Gender dynamics imbue any such shift:

> Theorists may extol the virtues of the responsive, caring bureaucrat who serves the public interest, but the argument will face uphill sledding until we recognize that responsiveness, caring, and service are culturally feminine qualities and that, in public administration, we are ambivalent about them for that very reason. (Stivers 2002, p. 58)

If the language of caring resides on the margins of public administration literature, how does it fare in our sister disciplines? Even here, the record is uneven. Leininger asks why so little attention has been given to caring by humanistically oriented scientists and caregivers (1988, p. 4). Hirschmann and Liebert (2001, p. 71) ask: Why have thinkers worked so hard to keep care in the background? One could speculate that the answer to these questions may be found in their own founding narratives.

In her review of the nursing literature, Leininger notes that caring and emotion work are a sine qua non of the nursing profession. Yet, prior to the mid-1970s, there had been virtually no specific focus on phenomena related to caring and their relationship to nursing care. According to Leininger:

> Although nurses have linguistically said that they give care and they talk about nursing care activities, still there has been virtually no systematic investigation of the epistemological, philosophical, linguistic, social, and cultural aspects of caring, and the relationship of care to professional nursing care theory and practice. (1988, p. 3)

Leininger concludes that caring has permeated the discourse on nursing (1988, p. 18). Yet despite recognizing that the field of medical work contains "emotional zones" (Bolton 2000, p. 580), given the dominant medical (scientific) model of cure and its professionalization, caring values remain submerged.

Emotional labor, caring, and the emotional engagement/detachment continuum are concepts with implications that reach into public service just as they reach into nursing practice. There are multiple occupations in which these characteristics are equally recognizable, including teaching, counseling, casework, corrections work, consumer affairs work, and many others. For example, a relational orientation is part of the discourse in teaching. Regan and Brooks understand care to be the essence of education, and argue that teaching needs to be infused with the "maternal values of caring, compassion, relationship, and collaboration" (1995, p. 6). Feminist scholars such as Carol Gilligan in psychology, Nel Noddings in philosophy, and Nancy Folbre in economics enter the care discourse from their own disciplinary perspectives. Gilligan's (1982) articulation of an ethic of care introduced us to her "voice of care," with a general concern that "no one be hurt" (Burnier 1995).

This voice resonates in the numerous quotes taken from the interviews we conducted with staff at both the Office of the Public Guardian and the Department of Corrections, as well as 911 dispatchers. No one denies that their emotional labor is real work. What could be more real than dealing with the most vulnerable members of our society—advocating on behalf of abused children and elders; counseling adult offenders as they transition back into society; or eliciting information from the victim of a crime in progress? Listen to a warden characterizing his work:

> I think my job is dealing with people every day . . . I think that it [emotional labor] does [relate] a lot with [my job]. I think it does a lot with everyone's— emotional labor, but I don't think you really—you don't come into a prison setting and think that. I don't think anyone does . . . I think that [I'm engaging in emotional labor] every single second of my day. . . . I think the toughest part about my job is you have 1,900 inmates, and you have 400 staff. You know, you gotta go out and talk to those inmates.

As the warden intimates, emotion work is practiced and lives depend upon it. Why, then, does it remain outside the scope of "real work," formally invisible and uncompensated? Can neutral (dispassionate) administration take care of basic human needs that are never experienced in a neutral way (Hummel 1994, p. 14)? These are questions that elude the obvious. Workers' own words, and their responses to survey items, provide a closer look at the obvious. The survey responses listed in the figures help to reveal actual public service practice. These data were collected from the workers who completed the survey.

Table 2.1 shows the response rate across the three agencies as well as the breakdown by gender, marital status, and race. Demographic characteristics presented in Tables 2.1 and 2.2 demonstrate that the respondents include representation from all educational and experience levels as well as a variety of mid-range incomes. The prevalence of women in the sample is characteristic of the work performed by the Office of the Public Guardian (social casework), and it reflects the usual overrepresentation of women in the "street-level" ranks.

Table 2.2 shows the educational level of all respondents. Educational

Table 2.1

Characteristics of Sample

	Office of the Public Guardian	Department of Corrections[3]	911 Call Takers	Overall
# of responses	139 out of 270	135 out of 324	34 out of 40	308 out of 634
Response rate	51.5%	41.7%	85%	48.6%
Women	106	77	22	205 (66.8%)
Men	33	57	12	102 (33.2%)
Married	50%	58%	50%	161 (53%)
Race: White	52%	90%	70%	217 (71%)

Table 2.2

Education and Salary of Respondents

	(%)
High school or GED	4.6
Technical training	2.6
Some college	20.8
2-year associate's degree	10.4
Bachelor's degree	17.6
Some graduate school	7.2
Master's degree	9.8
Law degree	25.7
Doctoral degree	0.7
Other	0.7
Salary of Respondents	
< $20,000	0.3
$20,000–$29,999	9.3
$30,000–$39,999	14.6
$40,000–$49,999	32.5
$50,000–$59,999	21.5
$60,000–$69,999	9.3
$70,000–$79,999	7.9
≥ $80,000	4.6

background of the respondents ranged from GED to doctoral degrees, with 61 percent having at least a college degree. This is consistent with public service jobs in general, in that they require higher levels of education than private sector jobs. There were 77 lawyers among the respondents, and all 77 of them worked for the Office of the Public Guardian. Other educational groups were distributed more evenly across the three agencies. Salaries were in ranges characteristic of street-level professionals and managers.

First, the vast majority (79 percent) of workers report that they prefer working with people. With this high proportion in mind, examine the following charts that display how respondents answered the survey items.

Figure 2.1   **Frequency with Which Workers Are Called Upon to Engage in Emotion Work**

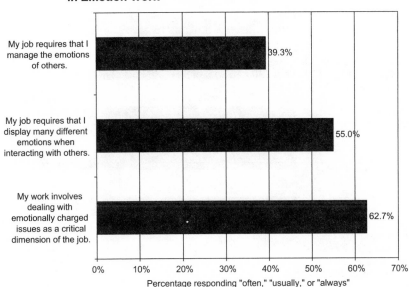

Each of the figures reveals a perspective on how workers practice emotion work: Figure 2.1 shows the frequency with which workers are called upon to engage in emotion work. Figure 2.2 shows how workers rate their level of ability to engage in emotion work, and Figure 2.3 shows how often they are called upon to suppress their actual feelings while expressing a different feeling.

Figure 2.1 demonstrates that the majority of workers must perform emotional labor, either in terms of dealing with emotionally charged issues, or displaying many different emotions when interacting with others or managing the emotions of others. Figure 2.2 shows how workers rate their ability to engage in emotion work. In other words, this figure shows the level of efficacy that workers experience in terms of being to able to perform the emotional labor aspects of their jobs. The bar chart shows that three-fourths of workers rate themselves as good at calming people down and almost as many rate themselves as good at dealing with emotional issues.

The responses show that workers are called upon to exercise various forms of emotion work, ranging from practicing common courtesy to calming people who are agitated or upset to intense degrees of guiding people through trying circumstances. How does such work affect their workday? The answer is that it requires workers to perform not only the cognitive tasks

Figure 2.2 **How Workers Rate Their Ability to Engage in Emotion Work**

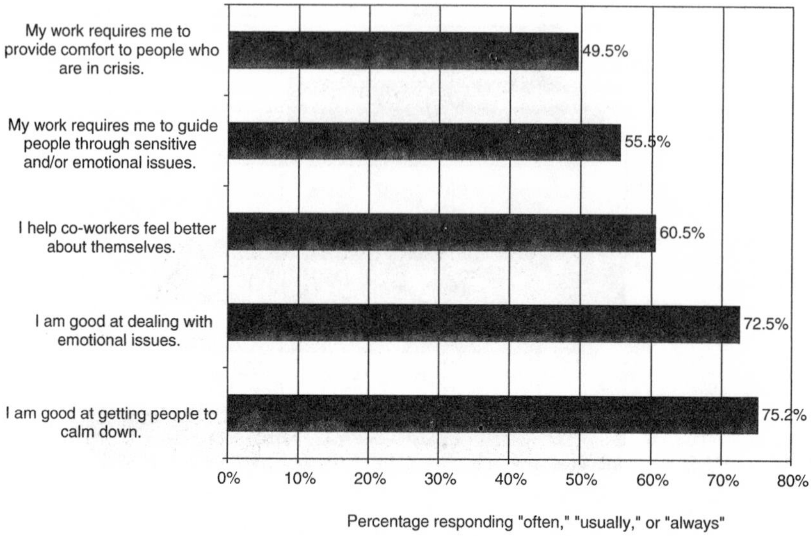

Percentage responding "often," "usually," or "always"

required by their job but also the emotional labor tasks. More challenging than these requirements is the task of suppressing one's own feelings while expressing a different feeling. This is the work that actors perfect on the stage. To the degree that workers must perform this on a daily basis, it is obvious that it is a skill that is closely associated with performance of other duties as well. Figure 2.3 shows the frequency with which workers must hide their own emotions. In fact, the ability to suppress one's own emotions while expressing a different one may often be necessary in order to complete those duties that are listed on the job description. Almost three-fourths of workers report that they must be "nicer than nice." A little over one-third must totally suppress their true feelings in the performance of their job.

These figures show that emotion work is no stranger to public service jobs. In fact, most workers are called upon to exercise it, although to different degrees. By self-report, workers say that they vary in their ability to perform emotion work and they vary in the type of emotion work that they perform.

Dwight Waldo noted that the issues public administration practitioners and scholars wrestle with are issues of "human cooperation." There are few, if any, questions in public administration that are simply technical (Stivers 2000, p. 135). A social worker comforts a frightened child, a paralegal calms a teenage client, an investigator becomes a chameleon in order to gain the trust of informants, a public attorney engages in crisis

54

Figure 2.3   **The Degree to Which Workers Suppress Their Own Emotions**

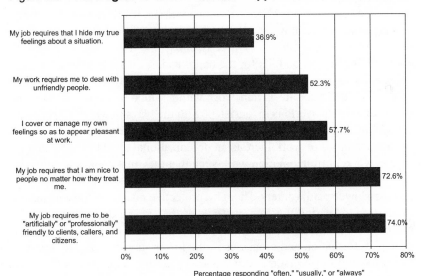

Percentage responding "often," "usually," or "always"

intervention, an administrator rallies her staff, while another acts as a surrogate mother to her charges. Theirs is not work of a "neutral expert" simply "doing the job" as a technician. Their work is relational in nature and involves considerable emotional labor demands. Yet much of their work, and that of others who engage in emotional labor and caregiving, is treated informally. As Chapter 1 demonstrated, it is not part of any formal job description, nor does it appear on performance evaluations. Nor is this work measurable or documented. Much of the work in the caring relation is "uncharted."

The "rich and knotty texture" (Fisher and Tronto 1990, p. 40) of this emotion work—dealing with death, intimate tending, working with clients who are unlikable, resentful, recalcitrant, or hostile, interacting with the most needy and vulnerable members of society—illuminates the chasm between the daily practice of public service and the official rhetoric of management efficiencies. Technique cannot triumph over purpose when dealing with people's lives.

Human service cannot be converted into a commodity to appease the number crunchers. Conceptual dichotomies such as public/private and efficiency/democracy cannot be sustained when we examine actual practices (Stivers 2002, p. 127). Care as a value and practice is inextricably tied to everyday judgments that clients, citizens, and administrators make about what it means to do a job well or what it means to be a good administrator

(Burnier 2003, p. 541). Emotional labor captures these practices. In the words of a caseworker at OPG, "You go home and it's like, wow, I've really accomplished something . . . you can't beat this . . . feeling. . . . Here you see the fruits of your labor . . . I directly impact the lives of our clients from doing my work here and it's for the better and . . . it's a euphoric feeling." What is needed is a realignment between the actual practice of much of public service and the theoretical framework within which it resides. When what we observe in the world is inconsistent with the ways in which our theories require us to talk and think, it is time to amend our theories.

In some types of work there is an organizational shield of sorts that insulates workers from emotion work such that they make jokes and dismiss it, or such that higher-status workers invoke a "status shield" and leave the caring to lower-paid workers. Though a protective maneuver to avoid having to perform the caring function, it sterilizes the citizen-state relation. Organization and status shields work this way: While the higher-status worker collects information and processes it, the lower-status worker is supposed to interact with the person in crisis and explain the implications (Stenross and Kleinman 1989). For example, the physician may administer the test but leaves it to the nurse to explain the implications of the results. The admissions committee may deny the applicant but leave it to the program assistant to deliver the news.

Job skills require more than knowledge. A quick survey of workers in any department usually yields rapid identification of the nurturer who is great at smoothing ruffled feathers and getting people to work together. It is equally easy to identify those who are missing in action when emotion work is required. For instance, directors rely on secretaries, and male police officers rely on female officers. Gender and status shields collude to foist emotion work disproportionately on certain segments of the work force.

Conclusion

The purpose of this chapter was to illuminate a missing link in the theoretical development of public administration and to insert emotion work and theories of caring into the canon. While the literatures of related disciplines are replete with references to a framework of caring and emotion work, with several notable exceptions this is not the case within public administration. The lexicon of our field remains dominated by the vocabulary of the industrial era, bureaucracy, and the market. Factory hands, rigid controls, scientific principles, reengineering, restructuring, reinvention, public entrepreneurs, and management expertise all spring to mind. This is the language of "how" government should best work. Any dialogue is more likely to revolve around how public administration can achieve scientific status. It is less likely that debates question the appropriateness of science as a goal and guiding value of our field (Stivers 2000, p. 131). What government can and should do receives less attention. Following the lead of the Progressive era social reformers, government would focus on improving the conditions of people's lives and "working to put science to the service of life" (Stivers 2000, p. 136). After all, public servants do this every day.

The work of government is people work with all its foibles. The formal language of our field misses the mark when applied to care-centered and emotion work. "If we want public administration scholarship capable of speaking truth to power, it must speak in a language that is meaningful" (Guy 2003, p. 652). Relationship, rapport, interaction, compassion, service, intervention, connectedness, and *soulwork* comprise the vocabulary of this relational administrative perspective.

Public service theory has focused on the practice of democracy, citizen participation, and majority rule, but has rarely reached down to embrace the citizen-state interchange. Even more rare is the acknowledgment of caring in this exchange. Perhaps for reasons similar to those expressed by nursing theorists, it may not be "politically astute to be the primary interpreters of a construct that is both gendered and devalued" (McEwen and Wills 2002, p. 45).

We live in a service economy. Service with a smile, long the mantra in the private sector, is gaining ground in the public realm. A customer-service orientation is bound up with care and emotion work. So, too, is helping those who are in dire straits. The Oklahoma City bombing, 9/11, earthquakes, floods, and tsunamis bring care work and emotional labor to the fore in tragic relief. The daily emotion work of those in the human services is no less taxing, no less demanding, and deserves our attention.

To conclude, viewing public administration theory through the lens of emotional labor and the values of caring and service has pointed up the missing links in our founding narrative, and explicated what it means to "work" in the process. A focus on emotional labor in practice, including care work, underscores the (human) nature of public work. Indeed, it puts us in a public service frame of mind (Box and Sagen 1998). The most important challenge facing public administrators is not to make their work more efficient but to make it more human and caring. The goodness of fit between the foundational values of rationality and efficiency, and the actual practice of public administration, comes up short. It is time to cut the cloth to fit the pattern.

CHAPTER 2

Notes

1. Schachter's argument is that settlement women belonged to a community of discourse close to scientific management. As part of this community they championed rational investigation of work routines, the use of expertise to solve social problems and institutionalize government services for the poor, and the importance of efficiency —understood as maximum use of all administrative resources (2002, p. 565; also see Schachter 2004).

2. For a detailed account of the contrast between the perspectives of the (male) City Club and the Woman's City Club, Chicago, circa 1913, see Flanagan (1990).

3. One of the respondents in the Department of Corrections did not indicate gender. Thus, the sum by gender is one less than the total sum of respondents.

— 3 —

Governance, Demanding Publics, and Citizen Satisfaction

The power to remove a citizen's freedoms does not exist in the business sector. This issue—power—makes public service different from service in business settings. A corrections officer at a prison puts it this way when speaking about families of prisoners when they come to visit:

> We have some that will come in and they're already angry that their family is here, but we're not the reason that they're here. They committed the crime, the judge sentenced them, and we're just here to do a job. . . . They think you owe them something. You know, [a visitor] said, "Well, the customer's always right," and I said, "Well maybe at Wal-Mart, but you know we're not at Wal-Mart. This is a prison, and visiting is a privilege."

This chapter shows how emotion work is required in order to deliver services that only government can provide. We also disentangle emotion work from cognitive/analytic performance and relate its performance to citizen satisfaction. A prison guard explains it this way:

> I have got to maintain control and a lot of times that's when you do have to bring on the toughness because you have to let them know that you run that unit; if you don't, they will see that in you and that will cause them to run over you. . . . Being on a women's unit, we also deal with their families; I even interact with children so, it's like, I can be this real tough guy one moment working in a housing unit but when I work in a visiting room or when I'm working the reception desk, then I have to be this tender, gentle guy.

An appreciation for emotion work well performed came of age as a result of the focus on citizen satisfaction and service quality. Citizens expect service

59

with a smile from retail sales clerks and they expect it from government as well. There is little argument about the relationship between public performance, productivity, mission accomplishment, and citizen satisfaction.

As discussed in the previous chapter, the early influences of objective scientific efficiency still shape public management today. But if two decades of reinventing government and attention to performance management have taught us anything, it is that industrial-era norms fail to accommodate the service economy. As if in a time warp, institutional blinders perpetuate traditional notions of work, making it difficult to see how current practice contributes to the invisibility of emotion work. Anticipating the response of others and communicating *affectively* as well as verbally are mainstays of most public service jobs. This is especially the case in health and human service professions, public education, paraprofessional jobs, most support positions, and over-the-counter transactions between government clerks and citizens. It is also required in many forms of confrontational work, such as police investigations or program audits. This is labor-intensive work that directly influences mission accomplishment. Here we let an investigator's words demonstrate his experience of emotional labor:

> I have the ability to be able to turn off my emotions and at the beginning it was a rude awakening. I can recall the first time I found a child under a child protection warrant and I went out with the police to take custody of the child . . . There was the crying and the screaming and all that and at first it was very difficult. . . I remember I felt extremely emotionally torn and questioned myself quite a bit. . . . Over time I've turned that off—I guess you can say I've grown cold to it.

The buildup to an appreciation of emotion work has been slowly advancing. Eighty years ago, in a 1925 essay, Mary Parker Follett presaged this concept in her discussion of "power with" in contrast to "power over" others in a work setting (1942 [1925]). Now we arrive at a time and place where Follett's prescription and Peter Drucker's (1980) emphasis on the transition from industrial workers to knowledge workers converge. Both saw glimmers of how work would change and employees would be called upon to exercise skills not yet standardized by traditional treatments of the employment environment. Neither moved from a focus on cognitive skills, but both saw that the nature of work was changing and that person-to-person communication would be a big part of the change. The element of emotion work was not articulated in their writings but, especially in Follett's work, it can be inferred as subtext. The words of a woman who works in the records office of a correctional institution demonstrate this new reality—the convergence of emotional intelligence, emotional labor, and cognitive work:

> We have a lot of families calling, asking us about when so-and-so is gonna get out. A lady called this morning and wanted to know when her sister was getting out. You get people on the outside telling you little fibs and lies about things—and to me that's frustrating because that's not the truth and they'll twist around what you just told them. Maybe they misunderstand, I'm not sure, but you know it's a different type of person that you're dealing with out there. They're under stress and tension and they've got issues in their lives going on and they're trying to fix 'em and we're just kinda the sounding board, you know? We're the middle person.

With performance honored more often by silence than by reward, emotional labor affects worker morale, recruitment and retention, citizen responsiveness, and public perceptions of government. It is a human capital issue that affects intrinsic and extrinsic rewards, job satisfaction, and on the dark side, burnout. It is also a subject that directly affects the perceptions that citizens have of government as a result of their one-on-one interactions with officials.

Demanding Publics

An agency's stakeholders can become "demanding publics" and stress workers in the performance of their duties. These demanding publics require a range of responses. Emotion work is on a continuum, with its simplest expression occurring in superficial service exchanges, where "the customer is always right." This is the case that most closely mirrors emotional labor in business establishments. The worker is required to be upbeat and positive in the face of criticism and complaints. The "complaint desk" job requires far less personal involvement than the case in which extreme, deep-seated affective responses must be masked in order to deal with cases of personal tragedy. For example, caseworkers experience this when they must remove a reluctant child from her family or when first responders arrive at a disaster scene. As described by a 911 call taker:

> Sometimes you have those nights where you just pick up the phone and everybody's mad, everybody wants to curse at you. To them, their problem is the most important problem in the entire world regardless if somebody's just been shot, if somebody's gotten in a serious vehicle accident. If somebody is complaining about noise at a neighbor's party, their call is the most important thing and they demand that you get somebody out there right this minute.

Citizen Satisfaction

In an environment where understaffed public services must meet the same "customer" expectations as business establishments, positive exchanges become

61

a benchmark for performance. When citizens meet friendly street-level bureaucrats, they are more likely to have a positive assessment of services rendered and of public services in general. Just as citizens like their own congressman but revile Congress as an institution, citizens may complain about government, per se, but rate a particular agency—or worker—positively.

Employees who are sensitive and skilled at the relational side of face-to-face public service help to humanize government. Because higher performance is the goal of the nation's agencies, emotion work should be recognized and built into job descriptions and reward systems. It is a human capital issue that directly affects the perceptions that citizens have of government.

The goal of citizen satisfaction is met through maintaining a work environment that rewards positive exchanges between citizens and the state. And this requires workers who are capable, experienced, motivated to perform, and who take pride in their work. The subject of job satisfaction is an important variable in this equation. There are two sides to emotion work. On the constructive side, it gives meaning to the exchanges that occur between workers and citizens, leading to job satisfaction. On the other side, too much of it with too little reward contributes to burnout. Looking first at the constructive aspect, the comments below describe how workers express the rewarding aspects of their jobs: "Nobody's getting rich here and it's not like you get any kind of reward from it. People hang in here because they think it's important and they feel like what they do matters." On the other hand, emotion work can result in burnout if the employee fails to develop coping mechanisms. The following comments demonstrate this:

In my first year, I did not take a day off—I worked Thanksgiving—I worked every holiday, thinking somehow that if I gave it enough, I would solve all this stuff. That's just not true, so I have learned. I've actually started playing the piano again, which I haven't done in 30 years.

I come in early, I stay late. But when I leave here I really do have the ability to put my work behind me. I don't like to take work home because I like to keep the separation. I can feel when I need to be away from here for a little while and I try to pay attention to that and to honor that because I know that if I do that then I will be refreshed and better able to do my job and be more productive.

You're constantly balancing all of those things and ultimately you have to put it into little pockets because otherwise you can get overly stressed and become ineffective. We talk about that a lot and it doesn't do to get over the top with it because then you stop being effective.

Another difficulty in delivering public services "feelingly" occurs when the citizen simply does not understand capacity limitations. This produces a mismatch between citizen expectations and practical reality. It complicates matters and makes the work of public administrators more difficult. For example, a call taker for the police department says this: "Citizen expectations can be difficult to deal with: People call—then call back in and are like well why haven't y'all solved my crime yet? We don't solve crimes in an hour like they do on TV, you know."

Constructive work environments foster a camaraderie among workers that enables them to develop "inside" jokes. In cases such as this, effective workers learn how to make light of the situation. Here a co-worker in the focus group responds: "Yeah, there are several calls per day that make you realize that the gene pool is really, really shallow."

Rational Work versus Emotion Work

There is a rich, emerging body of work on the subject of emotional labor in sociological and organizational literatures. Much of it addresses the dichotomy between cognitive/analytic, or "rational" work, and emotion work (Shuler and Sypher 2000; Domagalski 1999; Fineman 1993). For instance, there are arguments that rationality is the norm while emotion is no more than a disruptive influence on efficiency and effectiveness (Tracy and Tracy 1998). In order to accommodate emotion in the workplace, Putnam and Mumby (1993) advance an ideal they call "bounded emotionality," which parallels Herbert Simon's notion of bounded rationality. They contend that bureaucracy privileges rationality and marginalizes emotional experience. That is, "emotion is normally juxtaposed against rationality as a marginal mode of experience to be minimized in routine organizational life" (p. 41). We agree with Putnam and Mumby's critique and believe that emotion work has great utility in public service. An instructor in a prison expresses it this way:

> You have to really kinda customize yourself to the situation. It's weird because you're customizing yourself with the interview and the word process. By that same token, you need to be you, so how do you do all that and customize yourself and design your behavior to the setting and read the people—read the body and don't allow any negative signals coming from you that you may be unaware of?

An internal affairs officer explains how some workers are better than others at the emotional labor component of their jobs. His description captures the importance of interacting "feelingly" in order to perform well:

> You gotta know how to approach people to get any information. I've worked with several people on my crew that just don't have the ability like other people do. They don't get information. You gotta use emotions all the time in my work. When maybe you act like you're frustrated even if you're not, I mean.

As long as human resource policies and procedures barely recognize emotion work, it remains ill-defined and lightly dismissed as "good interpersonal skills" or "gets along well with others." This produces a conundrum: The term *rationality* is loaded with positive subtextual understandings about value and appropriateness while the term *emotion* is negatively loaded. As the excerpt above demonstrates, emotional labor is essential for job performance, but it is assumed, rather than acknowledged and compensated. Job applicants who have good emotion work skills are neither singled out for recruitment nor rewarded for their exercise of these skills.

If performance evaluation forms used by the State of Illinois are any indication, only about 14 percent of the instruments identify and rate the performance of emotion work above a perfunctory level (Mastracci, Newman, and Guy 2006). The reality of many public service jobs demonstrates the incompleteness of standard job definitions, recruiting, and selection processes. An investigator at OPG explains:

> The interpersonal relationships, the ability to listen and ask questions and get information without having the kids think there is a right answer—those are good skills that take a good amount of practice. Some people are just talented at it. I'm convinced it is a talent with some people—it's amazing.

The lack of acknowledgment of these skills hides an essential consideration in the selection of staff, contributes to depressed wages for a required job skill, and renders such labor invisible, a "talent" that cannot be taught.

Public administration comes by its obliviousness to emotional labor honestly: Cultural factors gave rise to society's embrace of business values and industrial production modes. Political processes are rooted in Aristotelian logic, which emphasizes a public focus on ways of thinking that highlight the "rational" and minimize other ways of knowing. Postmodern reevaluations of these roots bring a broader appreciation for holistic human behavior. Camilla Stivers (2000, 2005), for example, offers a refreshing perspective on public administration. Building on the worldviews of social reformers of the early twentieth century, she argues that public administration should embrace not only the "business" aspect of administration but also its "home" side. That is, "home" captures values of caring, community, and quality of life. This perspective expands the rightful focus of jurisdictions from transportation, sanitation, and business development to quality of life and communities that nurture and enable human development.

Emotional Labor Versus Emotional Intelligence

To understand the difference between "natural" behavior and emotion work, consider the worker who is "nicer than nice" throughout the workweek, responding to frustrated callers, needy clients, and impatient supervisors. The positive or calming behaviors performed in the course of the workday are performed to get the job done. They are not performed by the worker on her day off. Thus, they are performed as a part of the work and require analysis, skill, and judgment. Suppressing or managing her own feelings requires higher levels of *emotional intelligence.*

Note the quote below from a caseworker. As she describes what it takes to develop rapport with the children in her caseload, she is talking about emotional labor. She must cause the person she is interviewing to trust her enough to provide the information she needs to perform her duties. This requires discerning the motives and proclivities of the client and acting in such a way as to establish a constructive relationship. Although her job description spells out the educational and licensing requirements of the job, the observable or quantifiable "knowledge, skills, and abilities" only get her hired. They do not accomplish her job. The particular skills she needs to perform successfully are not only the "objective" requirements, but also the emotion work necessary to build rapport with clients:

> There are some people you click with—you just have that connection. There are some you don't. A person can rub you the wrong way and be really hard to get to. I try to think what emotional string I can pull to get the person to relax, to calm down, to talk to me. It doesn't work to meet anger with anger. You have to stay professional, you have to stay calm, and to some degree you have to understand. We're dealing with people. If we're dealing with machines, yeah, I would be successful all the time. You know, it's another face, another personality, another person with issues in front of me.

Emotive Work as a Form of Emotion Work

Based on our interviews and surveys, we believe that there is a difference between jobs that require the evocation of a range of emotions and jobs that require less varied displays. For example, jobs that require workers to play a role and exhibit "manufactured" emotions—the police officer who must be tough, the teacher who must be enthusiastic and cheery—fall in one category; jobs that require empathy or compassion fall in another. The former require more "theater" or pretending, while the latter require expressions of authentically felt emotions. We characterize these two types of jobs as being emotive work versus emotion work.

Figure 2.1 in Chapter 2 shows that most workers must display a range of emotions in order to do their work. Over half of all respondents report that they often, usually, or always display many different emotions when interacting with others. Almost two-thirds report that their work involves dealing with emotionally

Figure 3.1 **Continuum of Emotion Work**

| Superficial expression | Empathy | Intense expression/suppression |

◄──►

charged issues as a critical dimension of their jobs. These are high proportions and draw attention to the amount of work that has an affective component. Like a variation on a theme, emotive work is a variant of emotion work that requires the production of emotions, much as an actor is required to do. The worker is required to don the garb of a variety of emotions, whether the desired expression is one of happiness, surprise, distress, sadness, fear, or anger.

The Emotion Work Continuum

Emotion work exists on a continuum, as shown in Figure 3.1, with the range being from superficial expressions of friendliness to true expression or suppression of deeply felt emotions.

Jobs that are most like retail sales encounters involve the left side of the continuum while jobs that involve protective services, human tragedy, and emergencies involve the right side. Being "nicer than nice" to those who call the help line for information about Medicare prescription drug coverage involves one level of emotion work. Empathy, such as that required of counselors, teachers, human service providers, and those who handle frustrated homeowners' calls to City Hall, requires the ability to understand and appreciate the citizen's situation and respond accordingly. The handling of unruly prisoners, aggravated family members, citizens in crisis, and child abuse investigations requires the active suppression of one's own emotions while simultaneously expressing an alternate emotion. The example below demonstrates several levels of emotion work: empathy, emotion suppression, and managing the emotions of the caller.

> Citizens don't realize that just because you're sitting behind a phone and all they're hearing is a voice doesn't mean that you're not feeling what they're going through, because sometimes it is terrifying to us because you can't help but put yourself in those positions. You don't want them to know you are scared, too. I mean that's the bottom line—they're reacting to what you do so you don't have any choice but to try to stay calm.

> And the main thing we have to do is keep them on the line and reassure them that help is on the way. It seems like it's a long time when you're in that position and we're trying to ask them questions and it seems like it's taking forever. We can't just let it be dead silence. We have to incorporate conversation throughout that time while we have that person on the phone to just keep them calm and let them know that someone is coming to help.

Describing Relational Work

Emotional expressions are often characterized in gendered terms and become regarded as either appropriate, meaning masculine, or inappropriate, meaning feminine (Ollilainen 2000). As an example, traditional civil service systems link compensation levels to quantifiable indicators. The goal is to equalize pay scales and make them as objective as possible. The reality is that it makes relational work seem equivalent to inspecting fruit, a task that can be observed and counted. Tasks are delineated as if equivalent because we have not developed a means for appreciating or expressing the nature and type of work involved in emotional labor. The continuum shown in Figure 3.1 is ignored. Language that captures relational work threatens to diminish the predictability—and rigidity—of traditional job descriptions. But having that language would contribute to more accurate job analyses, hiring decisions, and performance appraisals.

In the words of a 911 call taker, "If you can't handle phone calls on a day-to-day basis like a child's not breathing or a child abuse case, this isn't the place you need to be." And in the words of the office coordinator at a prison records office:

> A lot of people can't work in that office because of the high stress in there. The tugging—there's always somebody tugging at you. I don't understand why it doesn't bother me but it just doesn't and the more somebody else will elevate and get hyper, the more pulled back, the more calm I find myself becoming. And I don't feel like I'm telling myself okay, calm down; it's just a habit; it happens automatically. I do mentally, probably, put a wall up around myself because I've got this going on over here and then I've got all these people over here asking, "Where's this file?" I do put a wall up and pull back from 'em and try to stay focused. I'm not really sure how I do that.

Both the 911 call taker and the office coordinator are homing in on the affective demands of their jobs. Though the context of their work differs, the emotion work skills required are similar: they both involve the ability to control one's own emotions while managing the emotions of the other.

Emotional labor is sometimes thought to be inherent in the types of jobs that women perform and less so in the types of work that men perform. Table 3.1 shows results from statistical tests that looked for differences between women's and men's responses to questions about the type of emotion work they perform. Only two items showed a significant difference between women and men in the degree to which they say they perform emotional labor. All others showed it was performed about equally, regardless of gender.

In one instance, the difference occurred such that women reported a significantly higher degree of emotional labor (item: "My work requires me

Table 3.1

Differences Between Women's and Men's Responses on Survey Items

Items	Sample Size		Means & Standard Deviation		t-value	Prob.
	Women	Men	Women	Men		
Q15 I am good at getting people to calm down.	203	102	5.18 sd = 1.16	5.31 sd = 1.12	-.983	.326
Q20 I help co-workers feel better about themselves.	205	100	4.91 sd = 1.19	4.78 sd = 1.28	.886	.376
Q22 My work requires me to guide people through sensitive and/or emotional issues.	205	102	4.69 sd = 1.86	4.15 sd = 1.86	2.424	.016
Q23 My work involves dealing with emotionally charged issues as a critical dimension of the job.	205	102	4.86 sd = 1.93	4.54 sd = 1.89	1.395	.164
Q24 I try to actually feel the emotions that I must display.	198	100	4.03 sd = 1.62	3.84 sd = 1.72	.939	.348
Q25 My job requires that I pretend to have emotions that I do not really feel.	205	101	2.70 sd = 1.52	3.19 sd = 1.48	-2.677	.008
Q26 My job requires that I manage the emotions of others.	203	101	3.85 sd = 1.84	3.85 sd = 1.86	.003	.997
Q27 My job requires that I hide my true feelings about a situation.	204	102	3.84 sd = 1.62	4.04 sd = 1.60	-1.025	.306
Q29 In my work, I am good at dealing with emotional issues.	203	102	5.16 sd = 1.25	5.20 sd = 1.24	-.221	.825
Q31 I worry that this job is hardening me emotionally.	204	102	3.33 sd = 1.74	3.26 sd = 1.90	.316	.752
Q46 My job requires that I am nice to people no matter how they treat me.	204	102	5.31 sd = 1.53	5.25 sd = 1.52	.344	.731
Q48 I help co-workers deal with stresses and difficulties at work.	200	101	4.24 sd = 1.54	4.04 sd = 1.44	1.087	.278

to guide people through sensitive and/or emotional issues"). In the other instance of a significant difference, men report a higher degree of emotional labor (item: "My job requires that I pretend to have emotions that I do not really feel"). It is difficult to interpret what these differences indicate. Perhaps it is that women are more sensitive to the nuances of working through emotional issues. Or, perhaps it is that women are more willing and capable to engage in this sort of exchange, and thus they acknowledge it as work that they often do. What is clear is that both women and men perform emotional labor.

The item where men responded with higher frequency than women—that their job requires that they pretend to have emotions that they do not really feel—is equally interesting. Whether their responses mean that they must pretend more, perhaps in terms of being "tougher than tough" for corrections officials, or whether they simply do not experience the intensity of emotion that women do, or whether they have been socialized to interpret their labor as emotions that are pretended and not actually felt, is not known. Item 24 probes the authenticity with which a worker performs emotional labor. There was no difference between women and men on this item, which indicates that they are about the same in terms of how they try to actually feel the emotions that they must display.

Public Service Jobs versus the Human Resource Management Canon

To ignore the emotion work that is required in public service is to luxuriate in the myth that mission accomplishment is merely a matter of correctly allocating resources, aligning resources with needs, and providing stipulated services. Were it that easy, none of the quotes presented in this chapter would be relevant. In reality, it is not that easy and, if the *service* in public service means anything, it is that the relational component of public service jobs must be acknowledged and accounted for in staffing plans.

Delivering public services is labor-intensive work. Service jobs differ from industrial jobs because they require face-to-face or voice-to-voice interaction and require emotional labor to solicit a desired response from the "other" in the exchange. This work is relational and facilitates cooperation and mission achievement. Workers' words reveal the corners, curves, and twists to emotional labor in public service jobs. They demonstrate the power of emotion work as it contributes to government performance, responds to demanding publics, and seeks to produce citizen satisfaction. As a worker at the Office of the Public Guardian puts it:

My job is for the most part stressful. But like I said, I guess there's good stress and bad stress. You know that good stress motivates you to do all you can and to be all you can. Bad stress is what slows you down. I feel like I've got the good stress. I'm not saying it's like that every day cause you know I have my bad days too, but my job is stressful.

The stakes are high in public service. Emergencies and statutory and constitutional obligations do not stop just because workers are on holiday or the budget is too spare to afford enough workers. It is not unusual to hear workers complain that although an agency's mission emphasizes service, staffing is too light to provide the hands and feet necessary to respond quickly.

When staffing is inadequate, work that is intense by its definition becomes doubly stressful. And, staffing plans that fail to take into account the nature of the work that must be performed put unnecessary stress on workers. This increases the burden for those who are stretched thin, trying to accomplish their jobs. A 911 call taker says:

It's also stressful not to have enough officers on the street because we're all customer service oriented no matter what anybody might tell you. We want to help people but it worries us to have calls for service where people have legitimate problems and you don't have any officers to send them. All you can do is just tell the sergeant that this is a call and I don't have anybody available.

It is also not unusual to learn that new employees are trained in the technical skills of the job but not in the emotion work skills. Only 58 percent of workers that we surveyed responded that their job training prepared them to do their jobs well. A focus group discussion among 911 call takers yielded this:

You learn over time how to handle the feelings and new employees don't have that. They don't have that level of experience so they haven't had a lot of exposure so they haven't been able to teach themselves. [Another focus group participant:] I think a lot of people come to work here based on what they see on television. It's a whole different atmosphere than what you expect. I used to take a lot of it to heart, and I got very negative for a period of time. . . . [Another participant:] A guy called up and said, 'I know this line is being recorded; just send an officer to my house.' And he hung up. He said that he was gonna commit suicide, and he said he had failed to do it the day before but that was his birthday so he chickened out. But he said, just send somebody out here. He gave me his address and everything and when they got there, he had done it. [Another participant:] I had to talk to a five-year-old today because his parents were beating each other half to death in the next room. I heard the mother screaming and crying and the father screaming and yelling and I heard things banging around and I'm having to talk to a five-year-old who's completely and totally calm. The general public doesn't understand that kind of a call.

Below are four facts that capture the disjuncture between the reality of public service jobs and traditional human resource practices.

1. Typical job descriptions fail to capture the emotional labor required by the job.

Drawing from the Office of the Public Guardian again, the following description is given of the recruitment process for lawyers. It demonstrates the shallowness of formal job descriptions and how informal processes during the interview fill in the gaps:

> We have unique job descriptions that spell out formal job requirements, such as licensing, and so forth. But in the interview [with lawyer applicants] we often talk about the social work aspect of our job—as if the social work aspect somehow encompasses what we are trying to say with potential employees—that there is a lot of the job that is more emotional, more hands on, more involved with a client.

In other words, the job description describes the formal requirements of the job but fails to delineate the emotional skills and abilities that will be required of incumbents. This failure to accurately specify the nature of the work means that the job description details only the cognitive tasks required by the job. It is left to informal person-to-person communication to explain the emotion work requirements.

Another aspect of emotional labor is the necessity to turn affect off and on as circumstances warrant. The excerpt below captures the thoughts of an investigator:

> You know, you've gotta get your game face on; you've gotta get your job done. I just have the ability to turn myself off emotionally and not let my personal feelings become involved. I wouldn't call it acting—I just, uh, can be flexible with my personality out on the street. . . .
>
> You've really got to care to do this job and to continue to do it; you can't really measure that in a job application—you know, you either do or you don't have that—and you can tell right away who has it and who doesn't. . . . In the office is one thing but how they react to people out on the street and how they're able to communicate, that's the key. You've got to be able to communicate to people from every walk of life.

2. A one-dimensional focus represents a vestigial understanding of "work."

To perform challenging public jobs, sophisticated levels of emotional intelligence are required and job incumbents must suppress their own emotions

71

while engaging in intense transactions. The following examples from the Office of the Public Guardian demonstrate the emotional suppression that is required.

> [Interviewer:] Now have you had times when you've known that you're not in the frame of mind to be meeting with a client? [Interviewee:] I think I would just try to make it seem as though I'm fine. If I don't call in sick, then I'm fine.

> [Another Interviewee at OPG:] We had this horrible report on a child who tortured two cats, kittens actually. As awful as it is, you have to have a strong enough constitution that you have to deal with whatever is there and at the same time not be so blunted that it doesn't matter anymore. If you begin to think that every house should have green plastic bags with dirty laundry and garbage all over the place and you begin to think that is the norm, you're in deep trouble and you need to leave. I think you have to be able to still be appalled and annoyed and shocked without going over the bend with it.

Because individuals vary in their ability to "still be appalled and annoyed and shocked without going over the bend," rank-in-person systems work better than rank-in-job. The whole person must perform the job. This requires that the candidate-as-whole-person be evaluated for employment and the employee-as-whole-person be appraised for work performance and rewards. Doing so, however, means that relying solely on observable task characteristics is insufficient.

3. "Market value" reflects traditional biases. Thus, it assigns worth to those competencies that have traditionally been rewarded. It does not assign value to emotion work.

Compensation schedules minimize relational work because we have not developed a means for appreciating or expressing the nature, skill, and type of work involved in it. In an ideal situation, a human resources (HR) system maintains effective linkages between job descriptions, employee manuals, performance appraisals, and compensation schemes. Developing language that captures relational work and emotional labor expectations would diminish the rigidity of traditional job descriptions, contribute to more accurate job analyses, and produce more accurate measures of market value. Moreover, job analysis that identifies and labels, rather than ignores, emotional labor will contribute to a better understanding of the phenomenon and to an overhaul of the job description/compensation connection.

One correctional officer believes the ability to change one's emotional response should be included on the job application. When asked what he would call it, he said:

Um, I don't know. I guess I would call it "Can you emotionally adapt?" . . . I think it should be on the job application because some of my co-workers are not designed for this job and I'm not saying that because I think I am; I'm just saying that a lot of times you might have somebody with a totally negative attitude all the time, and it kinda rubs on other people or they just may be too lenient all the time—always letting inmates run all over them.

4. Home versus work dualism creates a Procrustean logic. It denies, or "cuts off," emotion work—the feeling function— once the worker leaves the home and enters the workplace.

This results in denial that emotion work exists on the job. Attending only to cognitive skills, the employer sees only one dimension of the applicant's performance. Compensating cognitive skills but not emotive skills depresses the earnings of those performing emotion work.

Facts one through four inhibit recognition of emotional labor skills. Standard human resource procedures that have stood the test of time include formal job descriptions based on objective analysis of tasks performed; screening tools that evaluate job applicants' ability to perform requisite tasks; performance appraisals that "objectively" evaluate worker performance; and compensation schedules that are linked to knowledge, skills, and abilities (KSA) that are observable or quantifiable. However, the lag between industrial-era norms and the contemporary service economy results in job descriptions, performance appraisals, and pay scales that fail to capture all the skills required in the employment environment.

Implications for Mission Accomplishment

Service initiatives at the federal, state, and local levels have brought greater emphasis on "service with a smile" in the state-citizen encounter. These initiatives, heralded as a "customer-friendly" approach, are not well understood. There is little argument about the linkages between public performance, productivity, mission accomplishment, and citizen satisfaction. Job descriptions, performance appraisals, and pay scales still are crafted in terms that accommodate industrial production rather than in terms that accommodate the *relational* work required in transactions between officials and citizens.

Once one sees emotional labor as compensable, one also sees the short-comings of traditional reliance on "market value" for setting compensation rates. As we move further and further away from organizations designed to operate assembly lines, we must devise new structures that capture today's work and skill requirements. From an institutional standpoint, job descriptions that ignore the emotional labor component of a position fail to reflect

73

a comprehensive job analysis. Those elements of HR systems that need to change to accommodate the performance of emotion work include job analysis, job description, classification and compensation, employee development, selection, retention, and promotion. As currently constructed, all of these impede a richer appreciation for emotional labor.

Formal organizations are established to minimize randomness, to focus the work of their members on a singular mission, and to coordinate everyone's efforts. They do this by privileging abstract rules and impersonal decision making. They are not created to emphasize caring.

To exercise emotional labor in the context of caring, employees must look at the task holistically. Caring relationships cultivate mutuality and connection and thereby assume trappings—loads, if you will—that consume worker energy yet enrich both caregiver and receiver. In the words of theologian and philosopher Martin Buber, "Relation is mutual. My *Thou* affects me, as I affect it. We are moulded by our pupils and built up by our works" (1958, pp. 15–16).

As Chapter 2 demonstrated, public administration has been criticized for being more technicist and less caring in its purposes and processes (see, for example, McSwite 1997 and 2004). DeLysa Burnier (2003) makes the case that care is a latecomer to public administration and encourages an administrative approach in which care would take its place as a guiding value, alongside principles of cost-efficiency, fairness, and justice. If such were the case, she argues, citizens' actual knowledge of themselves and other citizens' situations would inform administrative decision making and practice. By extension, this requires that those responsible for others' well-being be sensitive to, and take into account, the real needs that citizens have. This would also require that care move from a private concern to a public concern. As a result, the economics of care would be altered such that it moves from being underpaid and undervalued to being a skill worthy of remuneration on the same basis as other essential work skills that are exercised well by some and not as well by others.

Conclusion

This chapter has emphasized the service aspect of governance and the elements of the HR infrastructure that must change to recruit for it, train for it, and reward it. Anticipating the needs of others and communicating *affectively* as well as verbally are mainstays of public service occupations.

Ironically, public service—that conglomeration of professions, crafts, and occupations that provides services for the greater good—trails industry when it comes to understanding the elements in a service exchange. For example, while marketing does not involve face-to-face or voice-to-voice interaction, its intent is to elicit feelings and manage others' emotions. Marketers recognized these elements long ago. When was the last you time you saw an advertisement for a beer or a car that highlighted the actual attributes of the product? Marketing is about instilling a feeling and eliciting pleasant emotions that, in the consumer's mind, then connect to the product.

Emotional labor skills are the ghost in the room. When job candidates are interviewed, when the ability to work well in teams is required, when knowing how to work amid conflict is important, and when jobs have high burnout rates, no one mentions it, for it has no name and it is not tangible. Human resource principles and processes are thus constrained by vocabulary and by the way we think about work versus nonwork behavior. Just as the English language provides one word for snow and the Inuit language provides multiple words, we need multiple job performance words to capture emotion work. We need to capture the "feeling" nature of public service. This is the key to governance, demanding publics, and citizen satisfaction.

— 4 —

I'll Know It When I See It: Emotional Labor, Verbal Judo, and Artful Affect

Emotional labor is something of a black box—the phlogiston theory of service work. We notice it after the fact and somehow it "just happened." It defies quantification, categorization, predictability, and analysis. Antecedents are subtle and nuanced. A paralegal at the Office of the Public Guardian explains how she performs it to work with "high-maintenance" attorneys:

> A high-maintenance attorney will be [someone who] needed something done yesterday, asks "How come it's not done now?" and "How come you didn't read my mind?" I say, "Ok, we need to treat this at an adult level which means we should be able to look at each other and talk to each other and not go crazy."

Asked to explain how she assesses the attorney's communication, she says: "I just sense it; when somebody's in the office with me it's the body language; when on the phone it's different. You have to do it from what you're getting out of the person's voice."

A correctional officer describes an interaction with a prisoner:

> She was very irate [about a misunderstanding with a teacher] and she had gotten to the point that she really didn't care. She was ready to snap at anything and anybody who came her way. I basically calmed her down and I talked to her. All she had to do was apologize to the teacher. By my getting her to

76

realize that, she was real appreciative. That really made me feel good because it's almost that it could have gone totally the other way, where she coulda hurt somebody or she could have hurt herself.

A 911 call taker describes her work this way:

We answer 911 and regular business phone lines and you never know from one ring of the phone to the next what it's gonna be, what's gonna happen or who's gonna be on the phone, and I mean you have to be ready for whatever. . . . You can get a wrong number all the way to "I killed my mom."

How can employers recognize the effort and skill that go into calming someone or suppressing one's own horror? What do workers do when they perform emotional labor? Do they themselves even know? It is to these questions that we now turn.

We need a term that captures this activity more clearly than the oft-used "emotional labor" and with less stigma than the word *emotional* brings. Why? The use of the word *emotional* in emotional labor evoked adverse reactions from many interviewees (e.g., "working in a prison, you just can't get emotional"), so much so that we found the term to be a hindrance. Many workers we interviewed, especially those who worked at the Department of Corrections, recoiled from the suggestion that emotion enters into their workday. As interviews proceeded and people described their typical workday, they surprised themselves with the affective texture of many of their descriptions. To be emotional, in their view, indicates weakness, which can threaten their own or their co-workers' safety.

Few of our interviewees grasped the notion without a lengthy description. The concept was clearer once we explained it using Ronnie Steinberg's definition: "Emotional labor is relational work. It involves managing the emotions of others to achieve a desired state of mind or a desired course of action in them. It also involves managing one's own emotions to project the appropriate emotions for the situation at hand" (1999, p. 149). But we learned that, in the field, the phrase can occlude understanding and impede further communication on the topic. One of the most significant challenges to our research has been to identify a less provocative word or phrase that has construct validity. Even interviewees who intuitively grasped the concept were stymied when we asked them to suggest a term. Linguists call the word-development process "neological creativity" (Batuji 1974), and that is what we turn to next.

This is the not the first time that a term was needed before workplace behaviors were formally acknowledged. For instance, sexual harassment was rendered illegal by Title VII of the 1964 Civil Rights Act, but it was not until its definition was codified almost a decade later that plaintiffs were able to prevail in court (see *Williams v. Saxbe* 1976).[1] Prior to the definition, the construct was so poorly understood that plaintiffs had difficulty convincing a judge and a jury that they had been wronged. Similarly, emotional labor is a poorly understood construct with ill-defined boundaries and requires extensive explanation. A more comprehensive understanding of job demands and work performance will be possible if a definition can capture its essence and boundaries.

To begin this process, we review other disciplines that have examined emotional labor, draw from their definitions, identify components of emotional labor, and employ parts of an occupation database to refine the concept. Our goal is to provide a comprehensive examination of emotional labor across disciplines and to provide clarity about what it is. Words can take us only so far, so we also use statistical analysis of survey data. By cross-matching other literatures, workers' own experiences, and findings from surveys, we develop a broader definition that embraces the multiple dimensions of emotional labor. We close the chapter introducing a term that avoids the negative "baggage" that accompanies emotional labor—*artful affect*.

Finding a Name for It

Etymology—the study of word provenance—is fascinating. Some words are ancient, while others are new. In the English language, for example, "town" dates back to 601 CE, while the earliest documented use of the word "Internet" was 1974 (*Oxford English Dictionary* Online 2006). Words are invented to communicate concepts as the need arises: in the Early Middle Ages, a term was needed to describe a defined space where once-nomadic people lived; in the twentieth century, a word was needed to describe a new communication space. Scholarship and practice need a commonly held word or phrase for emotional labor so that it can be incorporated into discussions of human capital development. The concept is central to public service delivery.

To this end, we seek to manifest emotional labor as a recognizable and measurable facet of public service work. This is necessary because unless it is operationalized, it remains an atheoretical black box: "I'll know it when I see it." Without a valid construct, scientific research cannot proceed and management practice cannot benefit.

Perhaps the most thorough documented acknowledgment of an employer's responsibility to recruit, train, and manage workers' emotional efforts is from the United Nations High Commissioner for Refugees (UNHCR) in their partnership handbook (2003, pp. 320–323):

78

Team leaders need to be particularly observant of individual reactions during an emergency. . . . It is important to recognize that it is impossible to take care of others if you do not take care of yourself. . . . Stress defusings and debriefings are ways of protecting the health of staff after crises. . . . [Debriefings] aim to integrate the experience, provide information on traumatic stress reactions, and prevent long-term consequences, including Post Traumatic Stress Disorder, and help staff manage their own personal reactions to the incident. If a debriefing or a defusing is not offered spontaneously after a trauma is suffered, request one. Information on individual consultations for UNHCR staff members and workshops on stress-related issues can be obtained from the Staff Welfare Unit, HQ Geneva.

The United Nations has long recognized its responsibility to prepare aid workers before placing them in volatile situations and to support them when crises occur. As the above passage demonstrates, UNHCR team leaders and supervisors are instructed to monitor the emotional barometers of their staff. The UN recognizes the importance of emotion management to its mission and provides support through institutionalized management tools and through the Staff Welfare Unit. Relief workers must address the stress they feel when they work with victims of violence, but also when they become victims themselves. Increasingly, UNHCR aid workers not only care for victims of conflicts, but they also have become targets of violence. Aid workers cannot be placed in unfamiliar and unstable contexts without intensive training to prepare them for situations that extend beyond their programs' stated objectives. Nowhere else have we found such a comprehensive acknowledgment of emotional labor in public service delivery alongside an institutionalized management practice that addresses workers' on-the-job emotion management responsibilities.

Conceptual Development

The concept of emotional labor has arisen primarily in six areas of study: social work, nursing, sociology, criminology, and recently in applied psychology and public administration. Curiously, government employs large numbers of social workers, nurses, counselors, and law enforcement personnel, but rarely do these disciplines emphasize the public *service* context within which these professionals practice. Each discipline has crafted its own terminology to capture the emotional labor construct, leaving cross-fertilization for another day. Table 4.1 lists various disciplines and the terms of art that each uses.

Vicarious traumatization and *compassion fatigue* emphasize negative outcomes of emotional labor. *Verbal judo* focuses on process and involves persuasion strategies and tactics to defuse tense situations or gain voluntary

Table 4.1

Terminology Across Disciplines

Discipline	Terminology	Primary Literature
Social Work	Vicarious Traumatization	Pearlman & Maclan (1995)
Nursing	Compassion Fatigue	Figley (1995, 2002); Stamm (2005)
Criminology	Verbal Judo	Thompson (1983, 2006)
Sociology	Emotional Labor	Hochschild (1979, 1983)
Applied Psychology	Emotional Labor	Diefendorff & Richard (2003); Glomb, Kammeyer-Mueller & Rotundo (2004)
Public Administration	Emotional Labor/ Emotion Management	Guy & Newman (2004)

Sources: Verbal Judo Institute (verbaljudo.com); *Social Science Abstracts* (firstsearch. oclc.org).

compliance (Thompson 2006). The terms used in sociology, psychology, and public administration are more general. Sociologists have examined both the hard and soft emotions used to bring about desired outcomes, as has research in public administration. The emotional labor construct has been inserted into professional practice only on a limited basis, however. For example, Steinberg's (1999) emotional labor scales reformed evaluation practices for nurses in Canada, and Thompson's (1983) techniques have been incorporated into law enforcement training.

Thompson's tactical communication training courses have been conducted with dozens of law enforcement agencies across the country, as well as with a handful of other public and private entities. Coincidentally, one of those private companies is Delta Airlines, which was also the focus of Hochschild's (1983) original analysis of flight attendants. Similar to the deep acting that Hochschild describes, Thompson recommends creating emotional distance between self and situation through the use of imagined scenarios (Verbal Judo Institute 2006):

1. Never show your Personal Face, only the necessary Professional Face; and
2. Treat the other as you would want to be treated, under identical situations.

Similarly, Delta flight attendants were told to imagine irate passengers as fearful children or perhaps as someone who is traveling to a funeral. Reactions to "irates" were mitigated when they empathized with this invented character. Some of the Department of Corrections employees whom we interviewed understood the importance of the "professional face." One woman explains: "I shut down the emotion; I try to shut it down and just be very professional with [inmates]. I just won't . . . allow myself to get too involved." On many levels, verbal judo, a technique that focuses on defusing tense, dangerous situations, captures this strategy:

> The principles and tactics taught enable graduates [of Verbal Judo programs] to use Presence and Words to calm difficult people who may be under severe emotional or other influences, redirect the behavior of hostile people, diffuse potentially dangerous situations, perform professionally under all conditions and achieve the desired outcome in the encounter.
> Officers are trained to know that it is always *show time*, and thus they are able to put on a face to meet the faces they meet and find the right words for the right person at the right time. They know that police work is a performing art, and they know they are there to represent the law rather than themselves. (Verbal Judo Institute 2006, emphasis in original)

How better to describe the role of emotional labor in public service? It is a *performance art* allowing public servants to represent the state. Steinberg (1999) also emphasizes the psychological condition of clients when assessing the extent of emotional labor involved in an occupation. Studies of emotional labor have involved a predetermined desirable outcome that one's efforts are intended to bring about, and that outcome involves accomplishing some aspect of the job. The public servants in our analysis also uphold policies enacted by lawmakers, and they too represent "the department, the city, [and] the state" rather than themselves in their professional capacities. Some law enforcement agencies have incorporated emotion management into their officer training and evaluation.

Criminologists have evaluated the effectiveness of emotion management training and have generally found a positive correlation between training and officer performance (Davis, Mateu-Gelabert, and Miller 2005; Johnson 2004; Traut et al. 2000). The key component of emotion management in any literature is its role in getting the job done: workers would not need to engage in these mental and emotional gymnastics if not for the employment expectations that they must meet in order to do their job.

The very foundations of emotional labor connect it to a firm's bottom line. Hochschild's flight attendants were required to display pleasantness, whether they truly felt pleasant or not, and to elicit positive feelings in passengers for the purpose of getting repeat business. Bill collectors studied by Sutton (1991) were required to display intimidating and threatening behaviors. Whether or not they truly felt mean and intimidating, or whether they empathized with debtors' situations, their job was to elicit negative and fearful feelings in delinquent payees for the purpose of encouraging repayment and benefiting creditors' bottom lines.

This essential skill that an employee must use to be effective—emotion management—should be operationalized and recognized so that managers and administrators can hire, train, and reward employees for the work that they really do. To maintain order, prison guards must create an air of authority, even if they are afraid of some prisoners. Social workers and investigators in the Office of the Public Guardian must build trust so that children who have been victims of abuse will confide in them and tell their stories. Failure to suppress their personal feelings is likely to prevent social workers and investigators from obtaining the information that they need. Operators at 911 call centers must create a sense of calm in order to obtain the information that they need to help callers who are in crisis situations. Ultimately, the intimidated prison guard, the disgusted social worker, the panicky 911 operator, and the empathic bill collector fail to do their jobs.

Quantifying Emotional Labor and Testing Hypotheses

To model emotional labor, we used the comments gained through interviews to shape our survey instrument and to test hypotheses. We also used the U.S. Bureau of Labor Statistics' database of occupations and job descriptions—O*NET[2]—to verify that our choice of occupations accurately captured emotion work in public service. Our rationale for selecting specific job descriptors as emotional labor components is based on the similarities between them and other definitions of emotional labor (Steinberg 1999; Pearlman and MacIan 1995; Stamm 2005). These components are measured on a standardized scale from 1 to 100, indicating the degree of importance of each descriptor to successfully performing the tasks demanded by each occupation. Results from searching the O*NET database for the five major occupations we surveyed are shown in Table 4.2.

O*NET ranks both the level of a skill or ability required and the importance of that skill to the job. Importance ratings indicate the degree of importance of a particular descriptor to the occupation. The possible ratings range from Not Important (1) to Extremely Important (5). Descriptor average ratings are standardized in O*NET to a scale ranging from 0 to 100; for example, an original Importance rating score of 3 (the middle of the range) is converted to a standardized score of 50 (the median of the 0–100 scale). As Table 4.2 demonstrates, our five major occupation categories score far above average on most of the emotional labor items.

Corrections officers and jailers rank highest in face-to-face contact—a key component of emotional labor—as well as dealing with others, dealing with angry and aggressive people, and encountering conflict. Both probation

Table 4.2

Ranked Importance of Emotional Labor (EL) Components in Occupations Surveyed

EL Component	Corrections Officers & Jailers	Child Support, Other Investigators	Child, Family, & School Social Workers	Probation & Corrections Treatment Specialists	Police, Fire, & Ambulance Dispatchers
Active Listening	82	85	80	96	97
Contact with Others	96	73	95	88	94
Monitoring	76	30	76	89	48
Social Perceptiveness	80	55	75	92	56
Coordination	69	45	62	78	60
Persuasion	68	35	58	78	36
Negotiation	62	30	59	83	38
Dealing with Angry People	94	70	55	93	94
Frequency of Conflict	84	75	54	90	88
Service Orientation	50	35	74	72	57
Responsibility for Others' Safety	84	20	40	70	63
Dealing with Aggressive People	85	60	32	83	59
Face-to-Face Interaction	99	73	96	94	79

Source: Authors' O*NET database searches (onetknowledgesite.com), December 20, 28, and 30, 2005; January 18, 20, and 26, 2006; and March 28, 2006.

and correctional treatment specialists and child and family social workers rank very high in these areas as well, and monitoring and social perceptiveness are also highly important to these positions. These additional dimensions can be explained by the nature of the relationships that treatment specialists and social workers must build with clients, compared to the relationships between offenders and prison guards. Active listening is the most important skill for effective police, fire, and ambulance dispatchers, as are several of the other emotional labor items. Finally, child support and family investigators rely more on gathering information through face-to-face interactions and contact with others and are less responsible for others' safety as compared to corrections officers.

Interestingly, evidence suggests that highly charged events are not created equal when it comes to the emotional labor required by them. Maddy Cunningham (2003) compared the experiences of social workers who worked primarily with sexually abused clients to those who counseled cancer victims. Her findings are consistent with the *Diagnostic and Statistical Manual–IV* (American Psychiatric Association 1994, p. 424), which indicates that trauma-inducing stress "may be especially severe or long-lasting when the stressor is of human design." Other factors, such as the care worker's own history of abuse and years of experience, affect levels of vicarious traumatization. In other words, there is an interaction effect between the worker's own experience and the perceived experience of the client.

Staff members at the Office of the Public Guardian (OPG) serve children, young adults, and the elderly, and the abuse that their clients have suffered is always "of human design." Guardians ad litem are assigned when children and older adults need legal protection and representation, which comes only after they have been victimized by another person—usually a relative or someone who is close to them. Betrayals of trust on this order diminish the sense of security and faith that care workers have, more so than do traumas caused by natural disasters or disease. The stress felt by counselors, staff members, and administrators at the Department of Corrections is brought about by people—prisoners, their visitors, and co-workers. In some cases, stressors involve budget cuts or changing policies, but those are blamed on supervisors and administrators further up the agency hierarchy, or on the legislature and governor. The acute nature of trauma experienced by Public Guardian workers is often greater than it is for Department of Corrections workers because the OPG's victims are children and vulnerable elderly. DOC staff tend not to view their prisoners as vulnerable or victimized.

The workload of 911 operators is closer to Cunningham's more balanced ideal because emergency calls vary both in their intensity and in the trauma involved. Addressing a call about an auto accident brought on by icy road conditions or about a house fire triggered by lightening can involve less intense emotion management than would a call made amid an unpredictable domestic violence incident, according to Cunningham. The 911 operator would not ask himself "Could I have prevented it?" after a call involving treacherous road conditions or lightening. On the other hand, calls to a suicide hotline—which are often staffed by volunteers and operated by nonprofit organizations—are not brought about by natural disasters. Like 911 operators, suicide hotline workers must build trust relationships, elicit feeling responses, and direct the actions of callers using their voices rather than physical gestures. All the while, the link can be severed at any moment. Both 911 operators and suicide hotline staff are restricted to voice-to-voice contact, and the first goal of each is to persuade the caller to remain on the line. The stakes are high for both. A 911 dispatcher describes the process:

> You just have to see how they react to what you're saying as to which way you're gonna deal with that caller. I mean, sometimes you just have to get the basic information out of them—the address, their name, their phone number, and a little bit about what's going on—weapons, and then you just have to sometimes just listen to them scream in your ear.

Any attempt to model the connection between emotional labor and work characteristics must account for varying contexts. Unlike public guardians, and to a lesser extent corrections employees, 911 operators rarely know the outcomes of their callers' crises. This makes their work all the more stressful. As one dispatcher observes: "You have to deal with all this but you don't really know . . . the outcome of it. There's no closure for us . . . unless the officer comes in and tells us."

Office of the Public Guardian employees build relationships with their clients over several years, and the purpose of their work is to get their clients out of the system and to achieve closure. If an OPG lawyer becomes guardian ad litem for an infant, she may work with that child until the child turns twenty-one years of age. Several OPG interviewees were able to share positive stories about children who graduated from high school and continued on to college. Some former clients kept in touch with their social workers and advocates long after the formal relationship was ended. Some female OPG staffers received Mother's Day cards from their current and former charges. Department of Corrections employees can find out about prisoner outcomes, but they are discouraged from building relationships with offenders. In this respect, the contexts of the 911 call center, OPG, and DOC could not be more different: At the 911 call center, operators seek an immediate trust relationship that will reassure callers and facilitate optimal communication and information sharing between caller and operator. The relationship is measured in minutes and seconds. OPG attorneys and social workers build trust more slowly and reciprocally; relationships can last many years. While offenders might seek friendships with DOC prison guards and administrators because they are among the few people they encounter for years, DOC employees allow those relationships only in limited degrees so that they can maintain control. The potential for violence sustains a necessary environment of distrust between employees and prisoners.

We used factor analysis to generate an index variable "emotional labor" that possesses internal consistency and high reliability ($\alpha = 0.89$)[3] as well as face validity. This alpha level is within the range found by Brotheridge and Lee (2003) in their emotional labor factor analysis, where they used similar components in their survey of service sector workers. The dependent variable—emotional labor—is comprised of responses to the following survey items. Respondents indicated the extent to which they agreed or disagreed with these statements on a seven-point Likert scale:

- My job requires that I display many different emotions when interacting with others.
- My work requires me to guide people through sensitive and/or emotional issues.
- My work involves dealing with emotionally charged issues as a critical dimension of the job.
- My job requires that I manage the emotions of others.
- In my work, I am good at dealing with emotional issues.
- My work requires me to provide comfort to people who are in crisis.

These six statements cover various aspects examined by earlier researchers, including responsibility for others' well-being, adhering to display rules, building rapport, and adjusting one's demeanor as needed (Steinberg 1999; Morris and Feldman 1996; Hochschild 1983), social perceptiveness, coordination, and persuasion (onetknowledgesite.com 2006), and linking those efforts to the job and workplace outcomes (Rafaeli and Sutton 1987; Steinberg 1999; Hochschild 1983; Brotheridge and Lee 2003). For the purpose of identifying the conditions that give rise to the performance of emotional labor, we use the index as the dependent variable and test whether it is a function of occupation, years of experience, gender, and views about work and the work environment. Table 4.3 displays the hypotheses that guided the analyses, our anticipated findings, and the results after performing ordinary least squares (OLS) regression analysis. First, the method for analyzing the models is explained; then the results are discussed.

Table 4.3

Hypotheses Regarding Components of Emotional Labor

Hypothesis	Expected	Result
H_1: Women exert more emotional labor than do men	+	not significant
H_2: Workers with more experience engage in more emotion management than do workers with less experience	+	not significant
H_3: Emotional labor is a function of the job, and not of the jobholder	+	mixed
H_4: Emotional labor involves acting professionally, even if it is artificial	+	not significant
H_5: Emotional labor involves pretending to feel appropriate and necessary emotions	+	$p < .01$
H_6: Emotional labor involves hiding inappropriate or unnecessary emotions	+	$p < .05$
H_7: Emotional labor involves dealing with unfriendly people	+	$p < .01$
H_8: Workers performing emotional labor will feel that they are good at calming people	+	$p < .01$
H_9: Workers performing emotional labor will feel that they are good at helping co-workers	+	$p < .01$
H_{10}: Workers performing emotional labor will worry that work is hardening them emotionally	+	$p < .01$
H_{11}: Workers performing emotional labor will experience a lot of stress	+	not significant

Table 4.4

Comparison of Work Environments

Stressors	Office of the Public Guardian	Department of Corrections	911 call takers
Face-to-face interaction	x	x	
Voice to voice only			x
Need to build trust	x		x
Environment of distrust		x	
Clients as victims	x		x
Clients as criminals		x	
Brief encounters			x
Years-long relationships	x	x	
Lack of closure			x

Estimating the Model

Data were generated from the survey administered at three sites on three different governmental levels: state, county, and municipal. The three sites differ not only in their level of government, but also in some very specific ways that can affect this analysis. Employees at the three sites face very different contexts and stressors, as shown in Table 4.4: face-to-face interaction (OPG, DOC) versus voice-to-voice only (911); building trust relationships (OPG, 911) versus an environment of distrust (DOC); treating clients as victims in crises (OPG, 911) versus clients as criminals (DOC); interactions lasting several minutes (911) versus those spanning many years (DOC, OPG); and commonly dealing with a lack of closure (911) versus having closure (DOC, OPG). These critical dimensions suggest that it may not be appropriate to analyze the data from these three sites in the aggregate.

Running three separate equations suggests that the sites are entirely dissimilar, and we lack evidence of this, given the convergence of our interviewees' descriptions of emotional labor in their jobs. However, increasing emphasis on client- or customer-focused service delivery should be bringing emotional labor to the forefront across all of public service. To overcome any reservations, we first estimate our model using seemingly unrelated regression (Zellner 1962).[4] This respects the differences in the three contexts, while avoiding the stricter assumption that they are unrelated entirely. The procedure allows us to run three equations jointly. Table 4.5 displays the results.[5]

The first three hypotheses are not supported at the Department of Corrections and Office of the Public Guardian, but they receive partial support among the 911 call takers. At the DOC and the OPG, years of experience

Table 4.5

Results from Seemingly Unrelated Regression: Emotional Labor at Office of the Public Guardian, Department of Corrections, and 911 Call Center

	OPG	DOC	911
Must act "artificially" or "professionally" friendly to clients	-0.018	0.037**	0.002
Working with people produces a lot of stress	0.022	-0.016	-0.003
Good at calming people down	0.099***	0.144***	0.023**
Help co-workers feel better about themselves	0.073***	0.009	0.006
Must pretend to have emotions that are not there	-0.012	0.064***	0.015*
Must hide inappropriate feelings	-0.010	0.064***	0.003
Must deal with unfriendly people	0.076***	0.047**	0.037***
Worry that work is hardening me emotionally	0.046***	0.009	0.008
Years of experience	-0.008	0.014*	-0.001
Occupation: Corrections and Law Enforcement	0.010	-0.039	-0.099***
Occupation: Telecommunications	-0.072	-0.137*	0.295***
Occupation: Family Services and Social Work	0.237***	0.168***	-0.061**
Occupation: Legal Services	0.179***	0.229***	-0.067***
Female	0.020	0.023	0.044**
Constant	-1.226***	-1.975***	-0.340
Number of observations	298	298	298
Number of parameters	14	14	14
R-Squared †	0.367	0.376	0.508
Model chi-squared	172.99***	179.80***	307.24***

Note: * p < .10; **p < .05; ***p < .01; † R-squared indicates the percentage of variance explained by the predictors but is not a well-defined concept in generalized least squares.

Table 4.6

Testing for Independence of Three Seemingly Unrelated Equations: Emotional Labor at Office of the Public Guardian, Department of Corrections, and 911 Call Center

	EL at OPG	EL at DOC	EL at 911
EL at OPG	1.000		
EL at DOC	−0.290	1.000	
EL at 911	−0.197	0.067	1.000
	Chi-squared (df=3) = 37.963, p = 0.0000		

and being female have no statistically significant effect on the degree to which emotional labor is performed, while two of the four occupational categories are statistically significant. Few employees in either the OPG or the DOC work in telecommunications, so the lack of significance is not surprising for that variable, but the insignificant coefficient for those who work in corrections and law enforcement at the DOC is unexpected. By way of explanation, however, perhaps these results reflect the reluctance to acknowledge the emotional component of the jobs. Our interviews revealed a resistance to the idea of involving emotions at work. Hypotheses H_4, H_5, and H_6 are supported only at the Department of Corrections, but "working with unfriendly people" is strongly associated with the dependent variable at all three sites (H_7). This evidence also suggests that employees take some responsibility for others: "helping people calm down" is strongly associated with emotional labor for all workers (H_8), and people at the Office of the Public Guardian help their co-workers with their day-to-day issues (H_9). Individually, the models explain sufficient amounts of variance in their dependent variables, but an additional significance test can show whether the data can be run in a single equation using OLS.

We can see if SUR (seemingly unrelated regression) analysis is necessary through use of a Breusch-Pagan (1979) chi-squared test of independence, which creates a correlation matrix of the residuals from the three equations. Table 4.6 shows the results of this hypothesis test.

The results indicate that the three equations are not independent of one another. Chi squared exceeds the critical value for three degrees of freedom, and the likelihood that we would arrive at these findings by chance is minuscule, as denoted by the p-value. This means that the contexts of the three different sites do not differ statistically. In practice, the Office of the Public Guardian employees face different situations than do 911 dispatchers or Department of Corrections prison employees, and 911 dispatchers

Table 4.7

Results from OLS (Dependent Variable: Emotional Labor)

Independent Variable	Slope Coefficient
Must act "artificially" or "professionally" friendly	0.020
Working with people produces a lot of stress	0.003
Good at calming people down	0.267***
Help co-workers feel better about themselves	0.088***
Must pretend to have emotions that are not there	0.067***
Must hide inappropriate feelings	0.057**
Must deal with unfriendly people	0.161***
Worry that work is hardening me emotionally	0.062***
Years of experience	0.005
Occupation: Corrections and Law Enforcement	−0.129
Occupation: Telecommunications	0.086
Occupation: Family Services and Social Work	0.344***
Occupation: Legal Services	0.342***
Female	0.087
Constant	−3.541***
Number of observations	298
R-Squared	0.615
Model F	32.31***

Note: * p < .10; ** p < .05; ***p < .01.

have different relationships with their callers than do employees at the other sites. This chi-squared test tells us, though, that the survey responses across all three sites are not statistically different from one another. This finding allows us to estimate an ordinary least squares model without specifying separate sites. The more parsimonious model is preferred, and findings are displayed in Table 4.7.

The single model performs better than the separately estimated ones, as evidenced by the ratio between explained and unexplained error and other goodness-of-fit indicators. This model accounts for more of the variation in the scores than did the individual estimators and allows us to make stronger claims about emotional labor. The first and second hypotheses are not supported by the evidence. Coefficients for years of experience and gender of the jobholder are not significantly different from zero. Occupations demand emotion management, and while it may be true that the expectations of male and female jobholders differ, our findings show that neither women nor longer-tenured workers "do" more emotional labor. The third hypothesis, however, receives only qualified support. As in the seemingly unrelated regression analysis, effects on emotion management of only two of the four occupation groups are significantly different from zero. An explanation of each hypothesis follows.

H_1: Women Exert More Emotional Labor Than Do Men

In the literature there is a lack of consensus surrounding the role of gender in the performance of emotional labor. It is accepted that caring is one dimension of emotional labor. More specifically, it has been posited that women fulfill, or are expected to fulfill, the *caritas* function more so than men. Chapter 3, however, demonstrated that women and men workers in our sample exercise similar levels of emotion work. That finding is repeated by this analysis. Perhaps if *caritas* were specified as its own measure, findings would reveal a difference. Or, perhaps it is women's and men's differential ability to articulate *caritas* that gives rise to the perceived difference. The likeliest explanation is that workers self-select into jobs they like. This, in turn, accounts for the similarity between women's and men's responses.

H_2: Workers with More Experience Engage in More Emotion Management Than Do Workers with Less Experience

Interviewees often equated emotional labor with on-the-job experience. If this hypothesis is supported by the data, then we would conclude that the performance of emotional labor is inherent in the worker, with those having more experience scoring higher. In fact, we find that years of experience do not have a significant effect on the performance of emotional labor. The following observations from a twenty-six-year veteran in corrections suggest that the perceived relationship between years of experience and emotional labor is more complex:

> I try to enforce the rules the same way with each person; I might have to execute it kinda differently; it just depends on the individual that I'm dealing with. You have your aggressive inmates—who are like hardcore—a little tougher than the other ones, and you can basically tell how they carry themselves as to what type of person they are. So I might have to be a little bit harsher with them when I tell them I need for them to do something. Then there's someone else who is a little bit timid, shy, scared—you can just tell. So I would probably be a little bit more passive with them. It might take me a few minutes longer to explain to them what it is that I want—I've been with the department for 26 years so I have, you know, learned to read the people a little bit better.

Weighing statistical findings of aggregate data against individual reports is both boon and bane. While the expanded view afforded by both illuminates, it also complicates, leaving us in a quandary as to the actual role that work experience plays. According to this vignette, it refines the worker's ability to sense the type of emotional expression that will be most effective.

H_3: Emotional Labor Is a Function of the Job and Not of the Jobholder

Positive and statistically significant coefficients on the occupation variables and lack of support for the first two hypotheses would support the assertion that emotional labor is a requirement of occupations, regardless of whether the job incumbent is male or female, experienced or inexperienced. The results are mixed, with two occupational categories showing significance and two not showing significance. We speculate that the difference in this finding may be due more to a (dis)comfort level among those who work at the Office of the Public Guardian when it comes to articulating the degree to which they engage in emotion work. In other words, the effects of being in child or family social work or legal services increases workers' sensitivity to, and articulation of, the amount of emotional labor they perform. The dependent variable is a standardized z-score of an index variable, so direct translation is not possible. That is, we cannot say "how much more"—just that the level of sensitivity increases as a result of working in one of these occupations. Respondents at the Department of Corrections and 911 call centers may have scored lower on the emotional labor index because of a resistance to expressing their work in terms of its emotion components. This interpretation is consistent with Stivers argument that articulating emotion work represented a "risk to masculinity that lay in associating themselves with women's benevolent activities" (2000, p. 125).

Several variables are included in the model that, according to the literature, should correlate with emotional labor. For instance, employees who engage in emotional labor have to act professionally whether they like it or not, pretend to feel appropriate feelings or hide inappropriate ones as situations warrant, and deal with unfriendly people. The next three hypotheses focus on these and are amplified by workers' words.

H_4: Emotional Labor Involves Acting Professionally, Even If It Is Artificial

This hypothesis is informed by words such as these from an officer responsible for investigating claims of employee misfeasance and malfeasance:

> First of all, when you're working here you're supposed to remain professional at all times. Sometimes you can't. I mean, that's when you gotta have the right frame of mind to do something like this because they're gonna throw anything at you.
> Interviewer: What is that frame of mind?
> Ans.: It's let stuff bounce off of you. Don't take it personal. The stressful

part for me is dealing with the staff because there might be somebody that you've worked with for the last ten years; next thing you know you're investigating him and he could lose his job—and that's happened before. That's very stressful. To be honest with you, sometimes when you're in there and you're dealing with you don't know what, you gotta hold your emotions.

H_5: Emotional Labor Involves Pretending to Feel Appropriate and Necessary Emotions

Take the words of someone who works at the reception desk at a prison:

> You might get an aggravated visitor who comes in and maybe isn't on the list, doesn't understand the rules. I explain things to them, but they can get very rude. You have to bite your tongue. I try to mingle with them when they first come in to see where they are at. You know, I ask them, "How are you doin'?" I start a little small talk, just trying to see exactly where they are.

H_6: Emotional Labor Involves Hiding Inappropriate or Unnecessary Emotions

Now, take the case of an office worker who finds emotional labor to be draining and prefers working with prisoner records, rather than prisoners:

> Within the inmate population, you can't really walk down the hallway because they know that I work in the records office and they swarm to you kinda like a magnet and you really have to stay on your guard because they're needy people and they just wanna hear what they wanna hear. They're manipulative, you know? They'll manipulate you—it's just draining to me to be back there and to be constantly asked questions. It's just tugging. It's just, you give, give, give all day. They just wanna take from you all day long. There's nothing in return. It's very stressful back there; it's such a different environment. You can kind of at least catch your breath up here.

Morris and Feldman (1996) reveal direct associations between the frequency of emotional expression and emotional dissonance, which would lead us to anticipate that a disconnect between genuine feelings and display rules brings about more emotional labor. Therefore, positive and statistically significant coefficients on acting professionally, pretending to feel appropriate emotions, and hiding inappropriate emotions were expected. In fact, that is not exactly what the results showed. While pretending to feel emotions and hiding emotions has a statistically significant effect on emotional labor, acting professionally does not. Just as the words of the correctional officer intimate, acting professionally is consistent with the worker's expectation of appropriate behavior, and therefore seems not to require the degree of emotional labor as when the worker must suppress emotions or pretend to feel emotions.

> On a lot of days there are some times when you feel like you might want to explode because it doesn't seem like you're getting your point across, or whatever, but then what comes to mind is that I am the professional. And that I'm paid to be in control of my emotions. I'm supposed to be a role model here too, you know, and I'm supposed to be in control. I take a few deep breaths and I just deal whatever it is that I have to deal with. I might even step back, you know, depending on the situation. Time allows for me to, you know, walk away, kinda regroup, come back and talk again. I enjoy what I'm doing so, um, a lot of things that other people view as stressful, you know, may not be for me.

H_7: Emotional Labor Involves Dealing with Unfriendly People

Steinberg (1999) links increasing amounts of emotion management with greater frequencies of dealing with unfriendly, angry, and upset people. A positive and statistically significant coefficient on dealing with unfriendly people was expected, and that is what we found.

Estimates of the work attitudes are statistically significant, and signs are in the expected directions to support their respective hypotheses (H_4, H_5, H_6, and H_7). This tells us that the survey items geared toward capturing work aspects that lead to greater levels of emotion management are valid and consistent with prior research.

H_8: Workers Performing Emotional Labor Will Feel That They Are Good at Calming People

This hypothesis was supported. There is a positive relationship between feeling efficacious and performing emotional labor. For example, a 911 call taker speaks about the need to adjust to the peculiarities of each call: "You may have two calls that are similar, but you never have two calls that are alike. What may work with this caller may not work with the other one."

H_9: Workers Performing Emotional Labor Will Feel That They Are Good at Helping Co-workers

Steinberg also defines emotional labor as a sense of responsibility for the well-being of others. The ability to help co-workers feel better about themselves provides another measure of efficacy in regard to performing emotional labor. In fact, this hypothesis is supported by the findings.

H_{10}: Workers Performing Emotional Labor Will Worry That Work Is Hardening Them Emotionally

Finally, two variables are included to examine the relationship between the degree of emotional labor expended on the job and potential markers of burnout. If the coefficient on worrying that their work is hardening them emotionally is positive and statistically significant, then workers who engage in emotional labor are indicating that they worry that their job is hardening them emotionally. This is what we find, and it is consistent with the observation that emotional labor has both an upside and a downside. Under certain conditions, it is stimulating and motivating. Under less facilitating conditions, it leads to burnout. Some evidence indicates that a concern for one's own well-being brings about greater emotional effort: worrying that the job will result in callousness elicits more emotional labor. Perhaps the effort to avoid callousness itself involves emotional labor.

H_{11}: Workers Performing Emotional Labor Will Experience a Lot of Stress

Similarly, if workers report that working with people is stressful, then workers who engage in emotional labor are suggesting that working with people is a source of stress for them. Consistent with the fact that emotional labor can be either positive or negative, these findings are not statistically significant. This means that working with people is not, by itself, a stress inducer. In fact, workers we interviewed and surveyed seem to get their greatest satisfaction from working with people and helping to make a difference in their lives.

Similarly, theory indicates that high degrees of emotion management are brought about by a sense of responsibility for others, and the findings for the last two hypotheses are consistent with theory. Concerns for the well-being of others bring about a greater exertion of emotional labor.

Conclusion

In this analysis we used evidence from regression analysis to pinpoint variables that affect the performance of emotional labor. Findings reveal several aspects of what emotional labor is and is not. The SUR analysis demonstrated that emotional labor is a similar phenomenon across contexts, which is consistent with our findings from qualitative fieldwork as well. The OLS regression results, which analyzed the entire data set, provide several statistically significant estimates, and the model explains a sufficient proportion of the variance in emotional labor. This evidence indicates that a single standard terminology should capture the concept and possess validity across contexts. Emotional labor is demanded in jobs in all three agencies surveyed, despite the variation in the kinds of emotional labor required. Women are no more or less likely to perform emotional labor than men are, but some jobs involve more emotional labor than others. This is consistent with many studies that examine occupations. This causes us to encourage employers to develop human resource management materials that provide guidance in how to select, hire, train, and retain employees when emotional labor is a component of the work.

Targeting the occupation and its demands will improve service delivery more than would targeting individual employees. Therefore, a word or phrase that links emotion management to job descriptions and objectives would improve service delivery, regardless of who is hired and trained. Similarly, years of experience do not dictate high or low levels of emotional labor performed. New employees and long-tenured employees engage in emotion management. This too supports management efforts to include emotional labor in employee training, for it cannot be assumed that the skill will come with time. Although employees work together to achieve the organization's outcomes, emotion management does not lend itself to on-the-job training alone. If no employee is hired, trained, and compensated for it, then the skill will not be acknowledged. Finally, these findings also indicate that higher levels of emotional labor exerted are associated with greater concerns about burnout. This is an issue we address in the next chapter.

A More Comprehensive Definition

After studying the analysis presented in this chapter, we offer this definition to capture artful affect:

> Emotional labor is that work which requires the engagement, suppression, and/or evocation of the worker's emotions in order to get the job done. The goal of this work is to influence the actions of the other. The performance encompasses a range of personal and interpersonal skills, including the ability to evoke and display emotions one does not actually feel, to sense the affect of the other and alter one's own affect accordingly, and to elicit the desired emotional response from the other. The ability to sense the affect of the other is accomplished through intuition and communication. Simply put, emotional labor requires affective sensitivity and flexibility with one's own emotions as well as those of the other.

Terminology

While data demonstrate the constancy of this phenomenon and its potential for verbal standardization, the handful of disciplines that have examined it still use a range of terms. We argue for a common term to advance knowledge in this area, but is that best for practice? Criminal justice practitioners may respond better to the notion of verbal judo than emotional labor, while social workers and children's advocates might shudder at the imagery evoked by verbal judo, as if it suggested their clients were their adversaries. Emotional labor or emotion management, then, might be the appropriate label to shed light on their efforts to elicit behaviors and feelings from their clients and to shield themselves from workplace stressors. Compassion fatigue and vicarious traumatization, on the other hand, are outcomes. Both terms emphasize the damage suffered by employees who exert high levels of emotion management rather than the day-to-day process of engaging in emotion management, which can be fulfilling too.

Both "verbal judo" and "emotional labor" connote processes, while "vicarous traumatization" and "compassion fatigue" connote outcomes. All are dimensions of artful affect. To think of them as totally separate phenomena is wrong. The findings reported in this chapter demonstrate that these facets occur across organizational and disciplinary contexts. For this reason, a common term can be identified and used. Verbal judo is not suitable in an occupation that requires its workers to build trust relationships with their clients, and emotional labor would not suffice in contexts where service delivery demands a certain level of "control over" clients, as is the case in the Department of Corrections or in law enforcement generally. In addition, each term ignores the self-preservation aspects of emotional labor. Boundless empathy and compassion toward clients lead to compassion fatigue and burnout. Distrust and pretending also fail to preserve the self.

We propose the term *artful affect* to help further the process of understanding what public servants do. Artful affect involves managing one's own affect as well as that of the other person in the exchange. Practicing artful affect is both proactive and reactive. It requires the artful sensing of the other's emotional state and crafting one's own affective expressions so as to elicit the desired response on the part of the other. For managers, awareness of artful affect facilitates discussions of, and training for, emotionally reactive situations. Clearly, culturally shaped attitudes about being emotional—as evidenced by interviewees—stood in the way of discussing the issue in depth. *Artful affect* is a more neutral phrase in this respect, and we suggest its use when speaking to employees about their work. It is free from the stigma that the word "emotional" brings, while still capturing the essence of emotional labor.

Notes

1. *Williams v. Saxbe* (1976) established the definition of quid pro quo sexual harassment. The case was brought by a plaintiff who was reprimanded and eventually terminated for refusing to submit to her supervisor's sexual demands. Subsequent legal decisions refined and expanded sexual harassment to include creating a hostile work environment, establishing the definition of unwelcome sexual advances, identifying patterns of harassment, and evaluating charges of harassment. Although sexual harassment had been occurring for as long as both men and women were in the work force, it was not until there was a definition for it that the concept became understandable and plaintiffs prevailed in court.

2. O*NET® Online is an interactive database developed by a consortium funded by the U.S. Department of Labor (onetknowledgesite.com).

3. For more information on the construction of index variables, see Appendix F.

4. Seemingly unrelated regression (SUR) analysis does not assume complete independence of the error structures between the three equations, but we are not assuming that they are the same, either. SUR allows us to assume that the slopes and intercepts of the three equations are not the same, but that there is something systematic in the behavior of the residuals across three "seemingly unrelated" equations. Regression analysis is appropriate because the dependent variable is continuous. The dependent variable in each equation is specific to each site.

5. Occupations are categorized on the survey and include Corrections and Law Enforcement, Telecommunications, Family Services and Social Work, and Legal Services (Administrative is the excluded category). Female is a dummy variable equal to 1 if the respondent is female and 0 otherwise.

— 5 —

Burnout Versus Making a Difference: The Costs and Benefits of Emotion Work

Many public service jobs have high stakes. An oversight may result in loss of life to a citizen or to a co-worker. These jobs are emotionally intense and can take a toll on workers. A 911 call taker recalls the following about a colleague:

> She called one day and said she wasn't coming to work because she couldn't take the stress anymore—making sure she always did the right thing with the person who called. She said she would go home at the end of the day and it would just be overwhelming to her as to "Did I do the right thing for this person; did I forget to do this; did I forget to do that." We've had people sitting there dispatching then all of a sudden just push back, say "I can't do this," get up and walk out and not come back.

For many emotion workers, there is no satisfactory ending to their work. A lack of closure and feedback exacerbates an already stressful job. Is *emotional labor* simply another way of thinking about burnout? Is it merely old wine in a new bottle? What is the relationship between emotional labor demands and burnout? First, we review the broad literature on the theory of stress and burnout, including the pioneering works of Christina Maslach and Robert Golembiewski. We then address the relationship between burnout and emotional labor by examining both positive and negative outcomes of emotion work. We use workers' words to demonstrate these outcomes and present survey data to sketch the big picture. (Note that, throughout this discussion, the terms "emotional labor" and "emotion work" are used almost interchangeably. "Emotional labor" refers to the concept while "emotion work" refers to the performance. This is a subtle difference that, in a context such as this, is almost a distinction without a difference.)

Burnout in Relation to Emotion Work

If emotional labor is as poorly understood as we have argued, then the relationship between emotion work and burnout is also problematic. Assumptions about the negative repercussions of emotional labor have been tempered and challenged by recent work. Numerous studies address the unfavorable consequences of emotional labor,[1] with the most often cited outcome being burnout.[2] Emotional labor can undermine job satisfaction,[3] and has been linked to such problems as generalized stress reactions, substance abuse, headaches, sexual dysfunction, absenteeism, poor self-esteem, depression, cynicism, role alienation, self-alienation, emotional deviance, and inauthenticity.[4] These outcomes are generally associated with the concept of *emotional dissonance*, defined as the mismatch between felt emotions and feigned emotions that are expressed to meet organizational expectations (Zapf 2002).

A few scholars, however, confirm that emotional labor can also produce favorable results, including increased job satisfaction, security, self-esteem, and empowerment;[5] increased psychological well-being; decreased stress, increased task effectiveness; and an increased sense of community.[6] To reconcile these contradictory findings, we take another look at the words and survey responses of workers in our sample. Their perceptions highlight the human costs and benefits of performing the *caritas* and tougher-than-tough functions and, in the process, illuminate the texture of emotional labor in the delivery of public services.

First, a quick review: A worker's emotion management involves either the feeling that is displayed (surface acting) or the private experience of the emotion itself (deep acting). Surface acting involves "pushing down" one's authentic expression of self in favor of an *emotional mask*, while deep acting involves "pumping up" by trying to bring the required emotions and one's true feelings into alignment (Grandey 1998). Accordingly, these management efforts may require evoking and modifying privately felt emotions. They also may require workers to mask, hide, or suppress emotions in order to create a suitable emotional display (Erickson and Ritter 2001). Organizationally mandated "display rules" dictate the degree to which showing and hiding emotions is seen as an expected part of employee performance (Wharton and Erickson 1995).

In the employment setting, emotion work comes in two forms: *other-*

focused and *self-focused* (Pugliesi 1999). *Other-focused* refers to efforts to help others to manage distress, to enhance others' self-esteem, and to mediate conflicts. In contrast, *self-focused* emotional labor taps efforts to suppress or mask emotions and to present a friendly demeanor (p. 136). The measures of self- and other-focused emotion management encompass interactions with clients *and* co-workers. In sum, emotional labor is the effort, planning, and control needed to express organizationally desired emotion during interpersonal transactions (Morris and Feldman 1997).

The Foundational Burnout Literature

The renewal of interest in the symptoms and causes of burnout rests upon a rich literature in the fields of industrial-organizational psychology, social psychology, sociology, management, nursing, and organizational development. Nurses call it *compassion fatigue,* and emergency responders refer to it as *vicarious traumatization.*

The nature of bureaucracy and the values of formal organizations frame this literature. Max Weber, for example, refers to the "dehumanizing regimentation" inherent in organizations (as cited in Argyris 1964, p. 8). A simultaneous emphasis on cognitive rationality and deemphasis on emotions results in emotional expression being viewed as irrelevant and "not work" (Argyris 1964, p. 100). The management of one's own feelings and feelings of others remains out of bounds. This led Ralph Hummel (1987) to characterize workers in large, formal organizations as "truncated remnants of human beings." Now we appreciate the fact that suppression of emotion is an element of emotional labor. Argyris foreshadowed this understanding a generation ago when he envisioned the organization of the future: "The emotionality and interpersonal competence relevant to achieving these . . . activities will now be as important as the values of rationality and intellectual competence" (1964, p. 273).

The term "burnout" was defined as its own phenomenon by the psychiatrist Herbert Freudenberger in 1974 (Paine 1981). Some fourteen years later, Golembiewski and Munzenrider reminded us that burnout is more than "just a darling of pop psychology" (1988, p. 6). By the late 1980s, burnout (or "flameout") was a common expression both in the popular press and in the research literature.

Burnout is an occupational hazard for those in professions that pepper the public service landscape: case work, family assistance, public health, law enforcement, and public education (Ryerson and Marks 1981). It has been variously defined as a psychological syndrome occurring among individuals who do "people work" (Maslach and Jackson 1986, p. 1; Maslach, Schaufeli, and Leiter 2001, p. 397); an affliction of "those who care" (Maslach 1982); the numbing of the inner signals of emotional feelings, reflected in the inability to create or feel any emotion (Maslach 1976); a disease of over-commitment (Freudenberger 1980) or understimulation (Golembiewski, Munzenrider, and Stevenson 1986); and a state of physical, emotional, and mental exhaustion caused by chronic emotional stresses resulting from in-tense, emotionally demanding involvement with people over long periods of time (Pines and Kafry 1981, p. 139). In sum, burnout is an indication of employees' growing inability to adequately manage their emotions when interacting with clients (Zapf et al. 2001).

Not surprisingly, the early work on burnout involved people in "high-touch" jobs where empathy is an important aspect of the job, such as social workers (Barad 1979, as cited in Golembiewski and Munzenrider 1988), law enforcement officials (Maslach and Jackson 1979), lawyers in legal-services offices (Maslach and Jackson 1978), and day-care workers (Daley 1979; Pines and Maslach 1980).[7] As Maslach and Jackson (1981) explain, workers in such professions are often required to spend considerable time in intense involvement with troubled people, and these exchanges become charged with feelings of anger, embarrassment, frustration, fear, or despair. The resulting chronic tension and stress can be emotionally draining, which leaves the worker feeling "empty" and "burned out" (Golembiewski and Munzenrider 1988, p. 12). Maslach, a social psychologist, provided much-needed theoretical and methodological direction by offering a conceptual definition of burnout, referring to it as a syndrome (Einsiedel and Tully 1981, p. 102). Burnout involves a sequential process (Cherniss 1980). To measure this phenomenon, Maslach and Jackson (1981) developed the Maslach Burnout Inventory (MBI). Golembiewski (1981), Golembiewski, Munzenrider, and Stevenson (1986), and Golembiewski and Munzenrider (1988) developed an eight-phase model as a refinement of the MBI. The work of Golembiewski, an early pioneer in the field of organizational develop-ment in public service organizations, explicated the links between burnout prevention, intervention, and overdose (Paine 1981).

Interwoven throughout this early work was a central focus on *relation-ships*—usually between provider and recipient, but also between provider and co-workers or family members. The interpersonal context of the job meant that, from the beginning, burnout was studied not so much as an individual stress response, but in terms of an individual's relational transactions in the workplace (Maslach, Schaufeli, and Leiter 2001).

Now that emotion work is under the magnifying glass, researchers have begun to investigate the relationship between it and burnout.[8] While sev-eral of these studies provide initial evidence for a relationship between the two, some of the findings are equivocal.[9] It has been assumed that there is something unique about the helping professions that makes their occupants more likely to experience burnout (Cherniss 1993; Jackson, Schwab, and Schuler 1986; Leiter and Maslach 1988; Schaufeli, Maslach, and Marek 1993). Several researchers have proposed that it is due to excessive emotional demands (Maslach and Jackson 1984; Pines and Aronson 1988; Brotheridge and Grandey 2002; Cordes and Dougherty 1993). For example, Maslach (1981, 1982) argued that interactions with clients are inherently difficult and upsetting because these are troubled people. She proposed that frequent face-to-face interactions that are intense, emotionally charged, and of long duration are associated with higher levels of emotional exhaustion, which is a key dimension of burnout (Zapf 2002). Such characteristics also define emotion work.

Here is why we should care about the relationship between burnout and emotional labor: Burnout is an issue of primary concern in occupations that involve lots of face-to-face contact—in other words, those with heavy emotional labor demands. The majority of street-level public service jobs can be characterized as high-touch and as requiring emotional labor. References to "soft skills," "interpersonal skills," or simply "people work" affirm that a job requires some kind of emotional labor (Wharton 1999, p. 174). The shift from an industrial economy rooted in the performance of physical labor to a postindustrial economy grounded in the skilled performance of emotion work (Erickson and Ritter 2001), coupled with the increasingly high-tech working world, has produced extraordinary demands for personalized, interactive customer service (Maslach and Leiter 1997).

Burnout is increasingly costly in human and economic terms. In order to "burn out," a person needs to have been on fire at one time. It follows that one of the greatest costs of burnout is the diminution of the effective service of the very best workers (Pines and Aronson 1988), and the resultant loss of productivity. Absenteeism, turnover, physiological symptoms, compensation for health claims, psychological withdrawal, aggression, alienation, depersonalization, and dysfunctional coping mechanisms—such as reliance on drugs and alcohol—combine to raise the price of getting the job done. More important for our study, burnout has been identified as the primary negative outcome associated with the performance of emotional labor.

Costs and Benefits of Performing Emotional Labor

The performance of emotional labor implicates the *self* more directly than other types of work and is accompanied by distinct psychological costs and benefits (Wharton 1999). Emotion work is not negative per se; rather, it has both negative and positive outcomes with *burnout* and *engagement* at opposite ends of a continuum (Leiter and Maslach 2000; Zapf et al. 2001). Emotional exhaustion (individual stress), cynicism (negative reaction to others and the job), and ineffectiveness (negative self-evaluation) are the principal dimensions of burnout. At the other end stands the positive state of engagement with work, with its three dimensions of energy, involvement, and efficacy.

Emotional Exhaustion

Exhaustion is the central quality and most obvious manifestation of burnout. When people describe themselves or others as experiencing burnout, they are most often referring to exhaustion. This component represents the basic individual stress dimension. It refers to feelings of being overextended and depleted of one's emotional and physical resources (Maslach, Schaufeli, and Leiter 2001). In human services, emotional demands of the work can exhaust a service provider's capacity to be involved with, and responsive to, the needs of recipients. Moreover, workers who perform emotional labor under conditions of low job autonomy or high job involvement are thought to be at greater risk of emotional exhaustion than those who have more autonomy or less job involvement (Wharton 1993). This outcome is captured by the feeling of being frustrated and perceiving work as too demanding (Zapf et al. 2001). People feel drained, used up, and unable to unwind and recover. A 911 dispatcher provides an example: "Sometimes dealing with people—one [911] call can drain you. I mean literally drain you, and I try not to let it stress me out, you know? . . . That one call—whether it be a child or a person . . . it's just too much. It's the last straw."

Burnout is manifested as an overwhelming exhaustion and an incapacity to disengage from the job, even in sleep. This condition can be exacerbated by a paradoxical combination of weariness and sleep problems. The content of nightmares is often related to the burned-out state of the dreamer (Pines and Aronson 1988). A long-time manager in corrections puts it this way: "I'm tired . . . I mean I really have to say I just don't want to do this anymore. . . . I don't sleep well at night . . . I dream about this place, and it's not even romantic. It's just work, you know, problems that pop up. . . . I do find I dream about this place a lot. Not every night, but frequently."

Cynicism

We have probably all interacted at one time or another with a service worker who appears to be "absent on the job," going through the motions in a detached, uncaring, even robotic manner. This worker is likely suffering from burnout. People use *cognitive distancing* by developing an indifference or cynical attitude when they are exhausted and discouraged (Maslach, Schaufeli, and Leiter 2001, p. 403). The cynicism (or depersonalization) component protects against the interpersonal nature of the job.

In the helping professions, depersonalization often means treating clients as objects and becoming apathetic with regard to their welfare (Zapf 2002). It results in negative, callous, or excessively detached responses to the very people whom the worker is supposed to be helping (Maslach, Schaufeli, and Leiter 2001). Workers discover in themselves a coldness and nastiness they never knew existed—manifested in the development of dehumanizing attitudes toward the recipients of their services. Often, clients are labeled in a derogatory way and treated accordingly (Schaufeli and Enzmann 1998). Detachment is a means of making clients appear more object-like and less human, and hence more manageable. A 911 dispatcher provides a chilling illustration:

> I didn't know how many times I've said it, and I'll say it again even on the record. I feel kids should come with two options—and they're not options. There should be a shock collar and volume control. . . . See what this job does to us? . . . I'll say that to even a stranger on the street. Kids should come with a shock collar and volume control because that kid needs to have a pacifier in his mouth or [be] told to shut the hell up.

Depersonalization also relates to the notion of reciprocity. In service professions generally, and helping professions especially, there is a built-in nonreciprocal balance of giving. The professional gives, the client takes (Ryerson and Marks 1981). Depersonalization is a way of restoring reciprocity by withdrawing psychologically from clients (Buunk and Schaufeli 1999). In sum, depersonalization means that a person is no longer able to adequately use detachment as a strategy to handle interactions with clients. Instead of adapting to the situation, "detachment becomes permanent and the person is chronically unable to feel what he or she should feel" (Zapf 2002, p. 257).

Ineffectiveness

A work situation with chronic, overwhelming demands that contribute to exhaustion or cynicism erodes one's sense of effectiveness. It is difficult to gain a sense of accomplishment when feeling exhausted or when helping people toward whom one is indifferent (Maslach, Schaufeli, and Leiter 2001). This lack of personal accomplishment is the third dimension of burnout and is the tendency to evaluate one's work negatively.

Reduced efficacy represents the self-evaluation dimension of burnout. It refers to feelings of incompetence and diminished achievement at work (Maslach, Schaufeli, and Leiter 2001). The belief that one is no longer able to achieve one's goals with clients is accompanied by feelings of inefficiency, poor professional self-esteem, and a growing sense of inadequacy (Maslach and Leiter 1997; Schaufeli and Enzmann 1998). The confluence of these dimensions of burnout results in employees who are no longer able to manage their emotions or the emotions of others (Zapf 2002). For those in the helping professions, where the management of emotions is at the heart of the enterprise, burnout is a serious problem.

The Benefits

An individual's relationship with work is also captured by the concept of engagement,[10] the opposite of burnout. Engagement encompasses the dimensions of energy, involvement, and efficacy. Its dimensions are self-explanatory: engagement is defined as a persistent, positive affective-motivational state of fulfillment that is characterized by vigor, dedication, and absorption (Maslach, Schaufeli, and Leiter 2001). Engagement is particularly related to job resources, such as job control, availability of feedback, and learning opportunities. For example, here a criminal investigator speaks about his work:

> I must be just emotionally drained; but by the same token, when we've done something really great here, nothing beats that feeling. You go home and it's like, wow, I've really accomplished something. You know that's why I never got into the corporate world or did anything like that—you can't beat this—this feeling. . . . Here you see the fruits of your labor. . . . I directly impact the lives of our clients from doing my work here and it's for the better and it's just—nothing beats that feeling, it's a euphoric feeling.

In sum, this review points up the ambivalent character of emotion work. That there are both positive and negative consequences of this work underscores the fact that it is a multidimensional construct and far more complex than originally conceived.

Predictors of Engagement Versus Burnout

Because engagement and burnout are best understood as opposites, we view predictors of engagement and burnout as mirror images. Burnout, then, would occur when job control, feedback, and opportunities to learn are absent.

In an earlier paper, we analyzed the relationship between burnout and job characteristics: occupation, extent of emotional labor, quality of job training, career opportunities afforded by the job, worker preference for working with people, and years of experience (Newman, Mastracci, and Guy 2005). That analysis showed that:

- Greater emotional labor demands lead to greater degrees of burnout.
- Workers who enjoy working with people report lower degrees of burnout. We suggest that employees who enjoy working with people will self-select into relationship-intensive occupations, and therefore will be less likely to be stressed by the encounters they have on the job. The selection process could screen applicants for emotion management jobs by gauging their preference for working with people. We do not propose, however, that this self-selection can replace the need for relevant and repeated training courses to prepare workers for their jobs. Tools to screen applicants at the point of hire and to train employees for the emotional labor demands of their jobs appear equally important to avoiding burnout.
- Better training may bring about a lower incidence of burnout. People who report that their training prepared them well for the job-related challenges that they face do not score as high on burnout as those who report that their training was inadequate. If these employees received high-quality training and they feel prepared for a wide range of on-the-job ordeals, then they are not as susceptible to suffering burnout.
- Better career opportunities lead to less burnout. People who believe that their jobs provide good career opportunities and therefore do not feel trapped in their current jobs do not suffer as much burnout. Human resource managers could curtail burnout among their employees with strong training programs as well as by instilling in their employees a sense that the skills they learn are marketable.
- Length of time on the job does not affect burnout rates but youth does. Older workers report less burnout than younger workers. Perhaps this is due to experience or perhaps it is a function of the winnowing process: Either older workers remain in emotion work jobs because they like the work or they have learned how to avoid burnout or the aging process has seasoned them sufficiently that they can handle emotion work. Because number of years of experience is not significantly related to burnout, the truth may be that older workers, through their own life experience, have learned how to cope with emotionally intense situations.

Taken together, the words of the workers and their survey responses provide compelling insights into the nature of emotional labor in practice. Their words illuminate the dual sides to emotion work: extreme personal rewards and extreme personal anguish. The survey data punctuate the discussion, making it clear that emotion work is complex and that there are multiple dimensions to it. Before we can expect managers to develop reasonable prescriptions for ameliorating burnout while capitalizing on the personal satisfaction and fulfillment that accompanies the positive side of emotion work, we need more information. To that end we move now to a deeper investigation into types of emotion work.

Although it has long been thought that "people work" is more suscep-tible to burnout than other forms of work, the converse may be the case. Prior research shows that human service jobs do not necessarily correlate with higher burnout rates (Brotheridge and Grandey 2002). In fact, human service workers reported lower levels of depersonalization and higher levels of personal accomplishment. Brotheridge and Grandey conclude that there is a hierarchy of emotional labor expectations, with human service profes-sionals reporting the highest levels of emotional labor. Surface acting, or faking emotional expressions at work, was related to feeling exhausted and detached, while deeper emotional work was related positively to personal accomplishment.

To probe the nature of emotion work among our sample, we conducted an exploratory factor analysis of survey data. It produced three factors pertaining to emotional labor: the performance of emotion work per se, workers' feelings of personal efficacy in performing emotion work, and the performance of emotion work that requires a worker to put on a "false face" by suppressing his/her own emotions while expressing an emotion different from that which he/she is actually feeling (see Appendix F).

The questionnaire also included items pertaining to burnout, job satisfac-tion, and pride. These factors were used to identify the relationship between these items, emotion work, and burnout. The Pearson correlation matrix in Table 5.1 shows positive correlations between the performance of emotion work, per se, and personal efficacy with the variables of job satisfaction and pride in work. Conversely, "false face" emotion work correlates positively with burnout but inversely with pride and job satisfaction. Additionally, job satisfaction and pride correlate inversely with burnout, as one would expect.

The differences between straightforward emotional labor (emotional labor, per se), feeling efficacious in the performance of emotion work (emotional labor, efficacy), and having to display an emotion one does not feel (emo-tional labor, false face) reveal much about emotion work. The following discussion provides an explanation.

Table 5.1

Correlation Matrix of Indices

	EL, efficacy	EL, false face	Job Satisfaction	Pride	Burnout
Emotional labor, per se	.491**	.442**	.218**	.424**	.285**
Emotional labor, efficacy		.331**	.336**	.345**	.009
Emotional labor, false face			.010	.004	.418**
Job satisfaction				.717**	−.238**
Pride					−.197**

Note: **p ≤ .01.

Emotional Labor, Per Se

This index variable was used in Chapter 4 to test hypotheses about emotion work.[11] Here, it is used to investigate whether agencies vary in the degree to which workers must perform it. Because of the different kinds of work performed at the Department of Corrections versus the Office of the Public Guardian versus the 911 call center, we hypothesized that there would be a difference between agencies because this factor focuses on the degree to which emotion work is required on the job.

H_1: The Agencies Will Differ in the Degree to Which Workers Report That They Perform Emotion Work

In fact, results showed that there is a statistically significant difference across work sites ($F = 61.979$, $p = 0.000$). The 911 call takers report performing emotion work significantly more than the other two agencies. The Department of Corrections workers report the lowest level (mean = 3.678, s.d. = 1.326), Office of the Public Guardian workers report a higher amount (mean = 5.011, s.d. = 1.207), and 911 call takers report the highest (mean = 5.773, s.d. = 0.621). Because of the nonsubtle form of emotion work involved in handling emergency calls, this result is expected. The fact that the analysis confirms that which is expected provides a measure of validity for the survey instrument.

Interestingly, similar results obtained when the three agencies were compared in terms of workers' scores on the Pride in Job factor ($F = 10.814$, $p = 0.000$). The Department of Corrections workers report the lowest level (mean = 5.101, s.d. = 1.166), Office of the Public Guardian workers report a higher amount (mean = 5.582, s.d. = .853), and 911 call takers report the highest (mean = 5.777, s.d. = .794).[12]

This leads to conjecture about whether emotion work gives meaning to one's work in such a way that job performance increases the individual's pride and sense of accomplishment. This interpretation would be consistent with Brotheridge and Grandey's (2002) research. In other words, these findings lead to speculation that emotion work that involves the wholeness of the worker is more fulfilling than jobs that require only cognitive contributions. This interpretation is consistent with Ralph Hummel's criticism of bureaucracy that, in essence, its sterile focus on cognitive tasks sucks the vibrancy out of workers and leaves them "truncated remnants."

Emotional Labor—Personal Efficacy

The next perspective on emotion work involves workers' assessments of their level of skill. Called "personal efficacy," these items query the degree to which workers actually engage in behavior to manage the emotions of others and look at workers' own assessment of their effectiveness.

Unlike emotional labor per se, personal efficacy in the performance of emotion work should not be contingent on the workplace. Thus the hypothesis is that there will not be a difference across agencies. Again, analysis of variance was used to test this.

H_2: The Agencies Will Not Differ in the Degree to Which Workers Report Their Levels of Personal Efficacy as They Perform Emotion Work

Results show that the hypothesis is supported (F = 2.125, p = 0.121). There is not a significant difference between the agencies in terms of the degree to which workers express their ability to perform emotion work. Efficacy pertains to individual differences among workers and is not dependent on organizational context. This is an important finding because it demonstrates that the performance of emotional labor is worker dependent, not work site dependent. In other words, there are individual differences in the skill required to perform emotion work. Some do it better than others.

Emotional Labor—False Face

The third variant of emotion work relates to the requirement that workers suppress their own emotions while expressing another emotion for the purpose of the interaction. In other words, this factor probes workers' ability to act as if they feel one way when they actually feel another way. The items in this index include the following:

- My job requires me to be "artificially" or "professionally" friendly to clients, callers, citizens, etc.
- I cover or manage my own feelings so as to appear pleasant at work.
- My job requires that I pretend to have emotions that I do not really feel.
- My job requires that I hide my true feelings about a situation.
- My work requires me to deal with unfriendly people.
- My job requires that I be nice to people no matter how they treat me.

These items query work requirements, so it is likely that they are context-specific and that there will be a difference between the agencies, based on the types of jobs that workers perform. For the purpose of the analysis, we hypothesize that there will be a statistically significant difference across work sites.

H_3: The Agencies Will Differ in the Degree to Which Workers Report That They Must Put on a False Face and Express Emotions They Do Not Feel

The analysis of variance reveals that the hypothesis is correct. There is a significant difference between the agencies in terms of the requirement to put on a false face and express an emotion that they do not actually feel ($F = 14.365$, $p = 0.000$). Just as they responded in regard to the first hypothesis, 911 call takers report that they perform "false face emotion work" significantly more than workers in the other two agencies. Workers in the Office of the Public Guardian (mean = 4.3515, s.d. = 0.865) and Department of Corrections (mean = 4.428, s.d. = 1.038) report similar levels of this form of emotion work, while 911 call takers report a significantly higher amount (mean = 5.294, s.d. = 0.760). What should we make of this result? The 911 call takers also reported a higher incidence of emotion work, per se. Does false face work simply *come with* emotion work such that measuring one is tantamount to measuring both? It remains for future research to tease out the answer to this question.

Burnout

On the subject of burnout, the correlation as shown in Table 5.1 between false face emotion work and burnout is revealing. Unlike the absence of a relationship between efficacy and burnout, the significant correlation of .418 shows a positive relationship between the two. Thus, it appears that the type of emotion work may be either a motivator, resulting in greater job satisfaction and pride, or a demotivator. However, there may be more levels to this relationship than we currently understand. In theory, the 911 call takers should report higher levels of burnout than workers in the other agencies because they perform more false face emotional labor. Data indicate that is not the case, however. A comparison of respondent scores across the three agencies indicates that there is no difference in the level of burnout ($F = 1.074$, $p = 0.343$).

Pride in Work

Perhaps the absence of higher burnout scores among the call takers is because, as Brotheridge and Grandey (2002) intimate, there are job satisfiers inherent in human service work that mitigate against burnout. Or, perhaps there are mediating circumstances per work site that mitigate the deleterious effect of false face emotion work. To investigate this quandary, analysis of variance was used to look for differences between agencies in the level of pride workers express. Items for this latent variable include:

- My job is interesting.
- I am proud of the work I do.
- I am doing something worthwhile in my job.
- My work is challenging.
- My training prepared me to do my job well.
- I feel like my work makes a difference.
- My work gives me a sense of personal accomplishment.

Results show that the call takers have significantly greater pride in their work than do workers at the other agencies ($F = 10.811$, $p = 0.000$). Closer to the call takers (mean = 5.777, s.d. = 0.794) were the workers in the Office of the Public Guardian (mean = 5.582, s.d. = 0.851). Department of Corrections workers had more variability in their responses (mean = 5.101, s.d. = 1.166) than workers at either of the other two agencies. Perhaps higher levels of pride mitigate the effect of false face emotion work. This is another question that invites more research.

Parsing Emotional Labor

One final analysis was conducted to assess the potency of emotion work's three forms: the work itself, personal efficacy in its performance, and false face work. Table 5.2 displays three analyses. Model 1 uses pride in work

113

Table 5.2

Summary of Regression Analyses for Three Models

	Dependent Variable		
	Model 1	Model 2	Model 3
Independent variables	Pride in Work	Job Satisfaction	Burnout
	4.256**	3.492**	1.589**
Emotional labor, per se	.324**	.130*	.196*
Emotional labor, personal efficacy	.212**	.347**	−.296**
Emotional labor, false face	−.284**	−.198*	.581**
R^2	.274	.145	.233
ANOVA sig.	.000	.000	.000
n	280	267	278

Note: *p < .01; **p < .00.

as the dependent variable, model 2 uses job satisfaction, and model 3 uses burnout. While emotional labor, per se, is the most potent influence on pride in work performed, personal efficacy is the most potent influence on job satisfaction. And, as predicted by Brotheridge and Grandey (2002), false face emotion work is the most potent form to influence burnout.

Job Satisfaction

Another means for examining the essential role of emotion work is through examining job satisfaction. The theory of work adjustment emphasizes the dynamic interaction between individuals and their work environment (Champoux 1991; Lawson 1993). Studies in work adjustment reveal the importance of two concepts: congruence and self-realization. The concept of congruence implies the following: a harmonious relationship between individual and environment, suitability of the individual to the environment and of the environment for the individual, consonance or agreement between the individual and the environment, and a reciprocal and complementary relationship between workers and their environment. According to this theory, workers will seek employment in environments that are congruent with their needs. When they find a correspondent relationship between work and self, they seek to maintain it. As correspondence increases, so does tenure (Dawis, Lofquist, and Weiss 1968). Another way of saying this is that when workers find a work environment that provides greater self-realization, they will stay longer (Karlsson 1990). The term *self-realization* refers to

Table 5.3

Job Tenure

Years in job	≤ 1	1–2	2–3	3–4	4–5	5–6	6–7	7–8	8–9	9–10	≥ 10
% of sample	9.8	10.4	8.1	8.5	13.4	7.8	5.2	3.9	2.9	2.9	27.0

the capacity to develop one's own talents, resources, meanings, and social relations. If emotion work, as a component of individual ability, provides satisfaction and pride, then it would seem that its performance will help to retain employees.

As human capital concerns increase, strategies to retain good workers become more important. If the performance of emotional labor gives meaning to one's work, then recognizing the importance of it is a worthwhile consideration for recruiters as well as for performance awards. In this survey, respondents were asked to report the length of time that they had worked on their job. This is reported in Table 5.3. To assure confidentiality, categorical responses were requested rather than precise length of employment. Analysis of variance[13] was performed to determine if the amount of emotion work, per se, differs based on how long respondents have been on their job. There is not a statistically significant difference. This reinforces the observation that the performance of emotion work endures throughout the tenure of the worker. If not, the incidence of emotion work would be weighted in the early years. In fact, based on the relationship between emotion work and job satisfaction, it is likely that it is a salient, rewarding aspect of the job. In this sample, 27 percent of respondents have worked longer than ten years.

Of the agencies surveyed, 24 percent of respondents at the Department of Corrections and the Office of the Public Guardian had worked there ten years or more. Among the 911 call takers, 50 percent had worked there ten years or more. This is a blunt measure of the relation between emotion work and retention, but it provides enough of a hint to suggest further research: Do those who score higher on personal efficacy in performing emotion work seek out jobs that require more emotion work? Conversely, do those who score higher on personal efficacy tend to leave jobs where there is too little emotional labor expected of them?

Emotional labor and burnout are inextricably linked, but the relationship is more complex than it first appears. This is one of the reasons why gauging emotional labor is so crucial to public management practice: recognizing the emotion management demands faced by employees allows managers to hire the most suitable candidates, train them to excel, evaluate their performance based on the actual skills they use, compensate them for doing so well, and mitigate the ill effects of false face emotion work.

Implications for Human Resource Management

Emotional labor is performed across the organizational spectrum. Its contours are magnified in human service agencies, where burnout and engagement apparently coexist. It is no longer, if it ever was, tenable to deny that emotional labor is "real work." It is skilled work. The mental manipulations that dispatchers have to go through to assess what a caller needs, a reliance on one's "spider sense" when a situation turns dangerous, the skill of an investigator to turn himself into a chameleon in order to elicit information, the ability to remain professional when counseling a sexually abused and poisoned child—these are some of the characteristics of this work. The voices in our study, combined with the rich body of multidisciplinary research on emotional labor, lead us to a primary practical and theoretical implication—namely that this skill must be recognized, acknowledged, and compensated. Selection mechanisms that capture the goodness of fit between job demands and worker characteristics, the development of more accurate and complete job descriptions, and meaningful performance evaluation procedures for human service workers are necessary first steps. As will be discussed in Chapter 7, making emotional labor compensable is the next step. A second implication is to respond to the evidence that emotional labor has both positive and negative outcomes. A focus on both engagement and burnout can lead to workplace interventions that aim to increase worker energy, involvement, and efficiency, and alleviate emotional exhaustion, cynicism, and, ultimately, ineffectiveness.

Job autonomy presents another key point of intervention. Although job autonomy is an important predictor of satisfaction among all types of workers, it is particularly important for workers whose jobs require emotional labor (Wharton 1993, 1999). Autonomy and control over their work, and hence over their emotional expression, becomes a crucial factor in determining which outcome is likely to prevail (Morris and Feldman 1996; Richards 2004). Individuals with high job control would have the possibility to decide whether or not to follow the employer's 'display rule' in a given situation. (The employer's 'display rule' refers to mandates to greet even the surliest citizen with a smile, for example.) Individuals high in control may be able to adapt the display rule to their personality and individual styles, thereby reducing emotional dissonance, whereas individuals low in control may not have this degree of discretion (Zapf 2002).

Another major point of intervention is the redesign of jobs to relieve the emotional pressure on staff members. One way of doing this would be to rotate responsibilities so that the individual could alternate between work intensely involved with clients and lighter administrative tasks (Edelwich and Brodsky 1980). For example, at the DOC, correctional officers and counselors routinely divide their time between interacting with inmates in the housing units and performing administrative tasks in their offices. Administrators can also reduce demands on workers by changing the workload. They can structure "time-outs" that enable workers to temporarily escape from job demands, to "recharge their batteries" for meeting those demands, and to develop more positive coping efforts. Training sessions and workshops organized to discuss and exercise emotion management practices, and protocols that set forth rules of emotional display and expression would serve to legitimize and institutionalize this work.

Relatedly, the job description itself should accurately reflect the actual work that is performed. This point is best illustrated by the experience of 911 dispatchers. Working as a telephone operator for the Tallahassee Police Department requires skills that go beyond simply typing the call transcripts and routinely answering calls. While the job may be characterized as a "glorified secretarial position," the work bears little resemblance in actuality. To paraphrase the fictional Forrest Gump, working in police communications is like opening a box of chocolates: you never know what you are going to get at the other end of the phone. The uncertainty about the nature of each successive call, and the need to make quick judgments and snap life-and-death decisions make this job particularly complex and stressful. The job can be "10 minutes of boredom interrupted by 90 seconds of terror." A supervisor explains it this way:

> When we interview dispatchers or people that have applied for the job, I believe a lot of people, especially the public, [think] this is a typical office job and it's not. They have no idea what they are coming into, other than sometimes watching a show, [Rescue] 911, or whatever show they watch with [William] Shatner on it. They have no idea what we do. And when they get in here and they realize what all we do and what we have to deal with, the volume of calls, the type of calls, it scares them, it scares a lot of people. . . . You have to be able to work with people and a lot of people don't realize that. . . . I think they have no clue what they are coming into the majority of the time.

A final intervention discussed here involves social support on (and off) the job. There is a strong body of evidence that a lack of social support is linked to numerous stress-related outcomes, including burnout (Golembiewski, Munzenrider, and Stevenson 1986). Receiving such support from supervisors is especially important, perhaps even more so than from co-workers, according to the findings of Maslach, Schaufeli, and Leiter (2001). Regardless of the source of stress and the presence or absence of support from supervisors, social support from family, friends, church groups, or co-workers can be a buffer against burnout. An opportunity to "talk shop" and to ventilate feelings with co-workers was a recurring theme in our interviews and an important source of social support.

Attention to social support raises two additional issues that bear on the performance of emotional labor. Social support on the job is an element of the organization's culture. Golembiewski and Maslach (and their colleagues) recognized early on the relationship between burnout and the organizational environment. For example, Golembiewski, Munzenrider, and Stevenson (1986) concluded that the quality of working life (QWL) contributes to the level of burnout. Leiter and Maslach (1988) found that burnout and organizational commitment are related to the interpersonal environment of an organization. Emotion work requirements exist for interactions with both clients and co-workers (Tschan, Rochat, and Zapf 2005). The literature further reveals that interactions with co-workers are cited as the most important sources of job stress and burnout (Gaines and Jermier 1983; Leiter and Maslach 1988). This is consistent with findings from our interviews. Given the troubled populations with which these workers deal, it is somewhat surprising to us that our respondents reported that it was not their respective clients or inmates that made their jobs so emotionally demanding, but rather their co-workers. In addition, each agency "felt" very different to us. That is, the organizational culture of the OPG can be characterized as open, collaborative, and supportive. In contrast, the correctional environment can be characterized by a palpable tension that surrounds the staff. For 911 operators, the milieu varied: each of the three eight-hour shifts reflected a different level of camaraderie and trust.

Conclusion

People skills and emotional labor are integral to service work. As trends indicate in Chapter 8, working in a postindustrial, service-based society *requires* that people become adept at the successful execution of emotion management techniques (Erickson 1997, p. 7). Interactions with the public are required in most jobs, especially as a customer focus is emphasized (Brotheridge and Grandey 2002). Service workers must exercise artful affect. They may not particularly like becoming a one-minute friend to the next citizen who approaches, but that is indeed what frontline work entails (Albrecht and Zemke 1985, p. 114).

Two additional overlapping features of the contemporary public workplace directly relate to the significance of emotional labor and the consequence of burnout. Cutbacks in management and "doing more with less" remain the mantra of current administrative reforms in public agencies. Downsizing in an organization rarely includes reducing its mandate. Fewer people do more work, with no time to catch their breath. Moreover, public cynicism and distrust of government exacerbate the challenges of service delivery. Frontline public servants engaged in human services work bear the brunt of budget rescissions and the seemingly insatiable service demands.

In the helping professions such as family and children's services, social work, corrections, and law enforcement, interpersonal skills and emotional labor are at the heart of service delivery. Emotion work produces benefits, including a heightened sense of personal and professional accomplishment, a more productive interpersonal exchange, and a facility to achieve workplace goals. The downside to the "masks of impression management" is a tendency toward worker stress and burnout (Brotheridge and Lee 2003, p. 377).

Workers ("social servants") can experience both positive and negative outcomes concurrently—exhilaration for a successful work episode on the one hand, and emotional exhaustion and depersonalization on the other. Burnout is a silent partner of many workers in the human services. A number of respondents report that they cope with burnout; others have succumbed to it.

While our study captures a snapshot of worker perceptions of emotion work, motivation, and burnout, the picture that develops shows emotional labor in sharp relief. It is no longer tenable to deny that emotion work is crucial to effective job completion, nor to ignore the costs and benefits of performing "people work." That emotional labor is real work is undeniable. That it remains a part of a hidden workload (Pugliesi 1999) is clear. That emotional labor can lead to burnout is also clear. When the workplace does not recognize the human side of work and the emotional labor required to effectively perform this work, then the risk of burnout grows, carrying with it a high price (Maslach and Leiter 1997).

Further research is needed to tease out the specific tasks that lead to both burnout and engagement. The men and women we interviewed demonstrated burnout in some aspects of their jobs and fulfillment in others. The next step is to examine this dynamic at the "task level" to improve human resource practices. Emotional labor is at the heart of service work; indeed, emotional labor defines public service. We encourage human resource professionals to acknowledge this skilled work, to evaluate it, to compensate it, and to address worker burnout. Those who daily perform the *caritas* and tougher-than-tough functions deserve nothing less. The relationship between emotional labor and burnout has not been settled here, but this chapter and its findings serve to chip away at the conventional wisdom about what is "real" work, and the nature and consequences of emotional labor in the delivery of social services. While the voices here generate waves, the challenge remains to change the direction of the tide.

Notes

1. See, for example, Rafaeli and Sutton 1987; Wouters 1989; Ashforth and Humphrey 1993; Leidner 1993; Conrad and Witte 1994; Waldron 1994; Pierce 1995; Morris and Feldman 1996; Schaufeli and Enzmann 1998; and Pugliesi 1999.

2. See Hochschild 1983; Tolich 1993; Wharton 1993.

3. See Bulan, Erickson, and Wharton 1997; Parkinson 1991; and Pugliesi and Shook 1997.

4. See Hochschild 1983; Sharrad 1992; Pugliesi 1999; Ashforth and Humphrey 1993; Fineman 1993; Seeman 1991; Pugliesi and Shook 1997; Wharton 1993, 1996; Fineman 1993; Tolich 1993; Erickson and Wharton 1997; Leidner 1993; Parkinson 1991; and Sutton 1991.

5. See Strickland 1992; Tolich 1993; Leidner 1993; Wharton 1993, 1996; and Adelmann 1995.

6. See Ashforth and Humphrey 1993; Connellan and Zemke 1993; Conrad and Witte 1994; and Shuler and Sypher 2000.

7. For a comprehensive overview of burnout research, see Maslach, Schaufeli, and Leiter 2001.

8. For example, see Abraham 1998; Adelmann 1995; Brotheridge and Lee 1998; Grandey 1998; Morris and Feldman 1997; Schaubroeck and Jones 2000; Brotheridge and Grandey 2002; Grandey 2000; Morris and Feldman 1996; Zapf et al. 1999; and Erickson and Ritter 2001.

9. For an overview of this literature, see Zapf 2002.

10. According to Maslach, Schaufeli, and Leiter (2001, p. 416), engagement is distinct from established constructs in organizational psychology such as organizational commitment, job satisfaction, or job involvement, and provides a more complex and thorough perspective on an individual's relationship with work.

11. Index scores were computed by calculating the mean value for each of the items. This produced a score for the latent variable so that the three agencies—Office of the Public Guardian, Department of Corrections, and the emergency call center—could be compared. Analysis of variance was performed to determine whether there is a statistically significant difference between the agencies in terms of workers' reports about the amount of emotional labor they perform.

12. As a cautionary note, it is possible that the elevated level of emotion work recorded by 911 call takers is an artifact of the research design. Workers were engaged in focus group discussions on the subject of emotion work immediately before being handed the survey. Much as the workers at the Western Electric plant in Hawthorne elevated their performance during the illumination studies, it is possible that these workers, after participating in the focus group, responded more positively than they would ordinarily. Subsequent research with similar workers in other dispatch centers would address this quandary.

13. ($F = 1.459$, $p = .154$).

— 6 —

Do Human Resource Practices Recognize Emotional Labor?

Well, [a new employee] said that HR informed her that all we did was answer the phones and type on the computer. Well I had a homicide today and this person was shot, and I had a call where this lady was bleeding from a knife in her chest that her boyfriend put there. To do this job, you gotta find people who can take the calls, ask the right questions, input data, as well as handle their emotions and those of the caller. Out of all my 16 years, I could count on one hand the number of times somebody's actually said "thank you" or "you did a good job on that call."

More and more, public agencies are hiring public workers on an "at will" basis. These initiatives are promoted as a means for encouraging workers to be more "customer friendly" to citizens and threaten them with dismissal when they are not. As if in a time warp, however, most job descriptions and performance appraisals are written the same whether they are for service jobs or industrial jobs. The process of job construction—where tasks are lumped together to form clearly defined positions—is designed to deperson- alize work and separate it from the person who performs it. Thus, workers can be treated as interchangeable parts, and any employee with X skill can be expected to perform any job with Y requirements. A corollary to this is that only those tasks that are observable are delineated. This assures an impersonal, objective evaluation process that protects against favoritism due to race, age, gender, kinship, or any other characteristic that differentiates one worker from another. (See, for example, Lytle 1946, p. 287, as cited in Figart 2000, p. 1.)

The singular focus on manifest skills rests on an outmoded ideology of work. Missing from this modus operandi is any mention of *relational* work that involves anticipating the needs of others, caring and nurturing, and communicating affectively as well as verbally. These tasks are a mainstay of jobs in health and human services, public education, paraprofessional areas, most support positions, and work involving over-the-counter transactions between clerks and citizens.

We live in an era when greater responsiveness is required of public workers, yet there is a blind spot in employee performance appraisals that makes emotion work invisible. Rationality, or "left brain" work, remains privileged while relational work remains unmentioned, unrewarded. Here we examine the disconnect between the service exchange that occurs day in and day out in offices across the land and the procedure that is used in all jobs to document and reward performance. We review samples of performance appraisal instruments used by public agencies and demonstrate that the vast majority identifies the performance of emotion work at only a perfunctory level or less. The lack of acknowledgment renders such labor invisible and contributes to depressed wages for those whose jobs require it.

To understand why this matters in public service, consider a citizen's response when a public employee seems cold and uncaring. Such a perception causes the citizen to criticize the services being rendered, whether the job performance is technically correct or not. In sum, emotion work is part of the job that must be done well for citizens to positively evaluate their interaction with the state.

As already discussed, emotional labor does not fit easily into a box. It comprises both soft (feminine) and hard (masculine) emotions. Its purpose is to make citizens feel good or feel bad, depending on the purpose of the exchange. In these terms, the jobs of the mayor's assistant and prison guard can be viewed as opposite poles of emotional labor. One employs a smile and requires its incumbents to be "nicer than natural." The other employs toughness and requires "nastier than natural" behavior. Acting in a neutral manner may also involve demanding emotional labor as one suppresses one's true feelings.

A second stream of research focuses on rules governing the expression of positive emotions, generally among workers in service-based occupations, such as convenience store clerks (Sutton and Rafaeli 1988), flight attendants (Hochschild 1983), food servers (Paules 1991), those in fast-food and insurance industries (Leidner 1993), banking and health care (Wharton 1993), litigators and paralegals (Pierce 1995, 1999), and professors (Bellas 1999). Negative emotions receive specific attention from Sutton (1991) in his study of bill collectors. Taken together, these studies highlight how emotions are commodified by employers.

Jobs and Emotional Labor

Across all jobs, approximately one-third of American workers have employment that subjects them to substantial demands for emotional labor. This means that their work requires personal contact with the public, they are required to evoke an emotional state in the client, and the employer exerts control over the emotional activities of employees (Hochschild 1983). Because of the service nature of public work, the proportion is probably substantially higher in public service jobs. While men and women both are called upon to perform emotion work, they "do" emotional labor differently, with different outcomes. For example, service workers, primarily women, are expected to display nurturance and compassion. Professionals and others in jobs dominated by men are either expected to display no emotion or to express hard emotions such as anger and imply threats in order to induce fear and compliance (Martin 1999). Hochschild explains these differing expectations as follows: "The world turns to women for mothering, and this fact silently attaches itself to many a job description" (1983, p. 170). Because men often find it easier to express emotions to a woman than to another man, they frequently cast women into the stereotypical role of "nurturant mother" (Martin 1999) or confidante. Different role expectations attach to women and men, even within the same occupation (for a discussion of paralegals, see Guy and Newman 2004).

Moreover, women are expected to perform more emotional labor of the *caritas* variety than men, even within the same occupation (Morris and Feldman 1996). Caring work is exceptional or optional for men, while it is obligatory for women (Bellas 1999). For example, in her study of professors, Bellas found that students expected female professors to be warmer and more supportive than male professors, and judged them more harshly when they were not. Teaching and service involve substantial amounts of emotional labor, but are generally seen as requiring no special training and, as a consequence, are rewarded less than administration and research. Hochschild explains this dynamic in the following general terms: "The more she seems natural at it, the more her labor does not show as labor, the more successfully it is disguised as the *absence* of other, more prized qualities" (1983, p. 169). In the same way, many of the skills possessed by nurses derive not from the qualities of being a nurse but from the qualities of being a woman—a statement that clearly renders nurses' skills as invisible by naturalizing and essentializing them (Steinberg and Figart 1999b).

Emotional labor (at least emotional labor that involves the production of soft emotions) does not register on the wage meter (Clayton 2000). Decision makers are more likely to acknowledge the exercise of instrumental skills, which are culturally coded as masculine. The importance of skills culturally coded as feminine is mostly overlooked (England and Folbre 1999). The following description of a woman's work experience illuminates the gender-hinged expectations regarding the performance of *caritas*.

> For the past fifteen years, I have held three different positions in as many agencies where emotional labor is a decided advantage for the role. I once worked for the Department of Children and Family Services doing eligibility determinations for people applying for food stamps, Medicaid, and Aid for Families with Dependent Children. There were approximately 20 employees and two were male, one being the director. The other male and I shared the same responsibilities. This type of work required a tremendous amount of patience and empathy and Greg had problems demonstrating both. He received more complaints than any of the other caseworkers but was allowed to slide more often. I believe that this is because he was not expected to exhibit the same level of emotional labor as his female counterparts. They, on the other hand, were expected to exhibit a high level of empathy and patience with the clients because they were women.
>
> My next job was as a Child Support Enforcement caseworker. In this position, I interviewed clients, ordered paternity tests, and represented clients in court. In my office we had seven caseworkers, of which all were female except one. This position required much empathy and patience with the clients and with the parents who were ordered to pay support. At times they could be quite threatening. The one male caseworker was not subjected to as much bullying as we were. Oftentimes, these women did not want to participate in collecting child support from the father of their child. Jimmy was allowed to intimidate and bully the women into compliance. However, the female caseworkers were required to use other methods of persuasion to get the information out of our clients. Additionally, when we were in court, the judge, who was male, would give more latitude to Jimmy than to the rest of us. He rarely berated Jimmy for not having a case properly prepared, while we would be berated for less.
>
> My current position is as an academic advisor at a university. Students often ask me to help them make important decisions. After I tell them the pros and cons of their alternatives, I usually tell them that they have to make the decision for themselves. Oftentimes they will then ask, "If I were your son (or daughter) what would you advise me to do?" I asked my male co-worker if students ever asked him how he would advise them if they were his child and he said that he has never had that question. I believe this is another instance of females being perceived as capable of emotional labor while males are not expected to provide the same function within the same job.

The question at hand is whether an appreciation for employees' emotive proficiency is incorporated into performance evaluation criteria. Do manifest skills remain privileged, while relational work is marginalized or ignored? To answer this question, we employ an interpretive analysis of employee performance evaluation instruments and processes, with particular focus on the knowledge, skills, and abilities (KSAs) component. Emotional labor constructs established in previous analyses are used; these include communication skills, human relations skills, enabling cooperation, and fostering teamwork (Fineman 1993; Fletcher 1999; Guy and Newman 2004; Steinberg 1999; Steinberg and Figart 1999a, 1999b).

Performance appraisal instruments are where formal recognition of emotional labor would take place, just as such forms appraise workers' proficiency with decision making, accuracy, comportment, and reliability. Our research design presumes that the appearance of key words and concepts related to emotion work skills would indicate recognition of this aspect of job performance. As Deborah Figart (2000) finds, acceptable scores on job evaluations translate into positive outcomes for the worker in the form of pay increases, opportunities for advancement, and at the very least, some measure of protection from dismissal.

Method

Sample

Annual appraisal forms used by Illinois state agencies were requested and evaluated to determine the extent to which they acknowledge and value emotion work. Illinois is a large, diverse state that includes the third-largest metropolitan area in the United States. Its economy is diverse, with a combination of agriculture in the rural areas and mixed industry throughout the numerous municipalities. Based on this fact, we expect these findings to be not unlike those in other public settings. A letter was sent to ninety-eight state agencies requesting that they send copies of their employee evaluation forms to the researchers for a research project aimed at identifying "the range and scope of evaluative criteria across agencies." Forty-nine responses were received, resulting in a 50 percent response rate. From those 49 respondents, we received 73 performance appraisal instruments, because some agencies use more than one form, depending upon the type of position under evaluation—supervisory versus nonsupervisory, for example. Table 6.1 includes an excerpt from a standard performance appraisal form used by the State of Illinois. Raters are asked to rate the employee's performance on each item on a Likert-type scale. This format is representative of appraisal formats in use today.

Threats to Validity

Because emotional labor is a relatively unexplored concept and a work attribute that is only sparingly understood, we are sensitive to threats to validity. This study employed a qualitative methodology guided by systematic, theoretically based prior research (Steinberg 1999). We judged this to be the

Table 6.1

Example of Criteria on Performance Appraisal Form

Part II. General Appraisal of Employee Performance

1. JOB KNOWLEDGE: Knowledge of duties and responsibilities as required for current job or position.
2. PRODUCTIVITY: Amount of work generated and completed successfully as compared to amount of work expected for this job or position.
3. QUALITY: Correctness, completeness, accuracy and economy of work—overall quality.
4. INITIATIVE: Self-motivation—amount of direction required—seeks improved methods and techniques—consistence in trying to do better.
5. USE OF TIME: Uses available time wisely—is punctual reporting to work—absenteeism—accomplished required work on or ahead of schedule.
6. PLANNING: Sets realistic objectives—anticipates and prepares for future requirements—establishes logical priorities.
7. FOLLOW-UP: Maintains control of workloads—allocates resources economically—insures that assignments are completed accurately and timely.
8. HUMAN RELATIONS: Establishes and maintains cordial work climate—promotes harmony and enthusiasm—displays sincere interest in assisting other employees.
9. LEADERSHIP: Sets high standards—provides good managerial example—encourages subordinates to perform efficiently—communicates effectively.
10. SUBORDINATE DEVELOPMENT: Helps subordinates plan career development—trains potential replacements—gives guidance and counsel.

Source: State of Illinois form CMS201, page 2.

most appropriate approach to gauging the level of emotional labor recognition in performance appraisal instruments.

It is unlikely that respondent self-selection is an issue. First, 50 percent of the agencies contacted supplied their forms and this provided a representative sampling of forms used. Second, Steinberg's methodology is sound and has been employed in the past, which mitigates threats to construct validity of this technique (Sloan 2004; Erickson and Ritter 2001). Third, no external event occurred in Illinois to trigger an appreciation or heightened sensitivity to the subject of emotional labor, as was the case in the Ontario nurses' union lawsuit, as Steinberg describes in her 1999 analysis. Fourth, no problem of hypothesis guessing by respondents exists: the letter never indicated what we were looking for, and we did not elaborate in any of the follow-up calls and letters.

Content Analysis

The forms were analyzed to determine the extent to which the largely invisible emotion work components of job classification and compensation systems are made manifest. Ronnie Steinberg's (1999) emotional labor scales were used as criteria to guide the content analysis of these instruments. Steinberg identifies four factors that capture the detailed content of emotional labor (1999, p. 149): human relations, communications skills, emotional effort, and responsibility for client well-being. Human relations and emotional effort are defined along two separate, five-point ordinal scales measuring lowest to highest levels of human relations and emotional effort, respectively (see Appendix D for a summary table). Communication skills are defined to include "writing and speaking skills, including nonverbal skills, reading, listening, and the requirement to use a different language" (1999, p. 151). This definition of communication skills coincides with Guy and Newman's (2004) work, as well. Steinberg defines responsibility for client well-being as "informing, training, advising, counseling, teaching, nurturing and regulating the behavior of clients to ensure their well-being" (1999, p. 154).

Using Steinberg's typology, we developed three categories of emotional labor recognition. Table 6.2 describes each in detail. In the *Perfunctory* category, interpersonal interactions and communication skills are restricted only to job content and work function. *Moderate* recognition involves complex and direct interactions with others, whether subordinates, clients, or other stakeholders. *Advanced* recognition of emotional labor involves an appreciation for the full range of emotional requirements in the workplace, particularly the need to employ persuasion techniques, understand group dynamics, handle emotionally charged issues publicly, deal with dangerous or hostile people, deal with highly sensitive issues, and take responsibility for the well-being of others, whether subordinates or clients.

Findings from Analyzing Performance Appraisal Instruments

Of the 49 agencies responding, 23 use standard Central Management Services (CMS) forms.[1] Human relations and communications skill demands described on the standard forms indicate Level A or Level B recognition of emotional labor. Leadership and Subordinate Development skill requirements on these forms are not only restricted to managerial and supervisory personnel, but also, they only suggest a technically oriented relationship with clients or staff. They do not reach the level required by Steinberg's typology for "hand-holding, reassurance, compassion, empathy . . . resolution of minor conflicts" and dealing regularly with people who are emotionally impaired (1999, p. 155), all of which Steinberg's typology demands.

The table displays the analysis of seventy-three performance appraisal instruments along with characteristic phrases quoted from forms. Findings

127

Table 6.2

Emotional Labor Recognition in Job Appraisal Instruments

Category of Emotional Labor Recognition	Key Words in Performance Appraisal Instruments Characterizing this Level	Corresponding Levels in Steinberg Typology	No. of Agencies	Representative Phrases from Performance Appraisals
None Perfunctory	• Ordinary personal courtesy or polished courtesy • Occasionally deal with clients and/or unfriendly people • Relations with the public reflect organizational image, maintain professional rapport with colleagues, clients • Motivate, mentor, coach, or train employees	Human Relations, and Communications Skills: Levels A & B Emotional Effort/Emotional Demands: Levels A & B*	4 (5.5%) 59 (80.8%)	• Possesses the necessary written and verbal communications skills. • Ability to work with others to attain goals and objectives. • Presents self in dress, appearance, and conduct that meet organizational standards. • Ability to weigh alternatives and arrive at conclusions.
Moderate	• Empathy, compassion, reassurance, hand-holding, considerable patience required • Minor conflict resolution • Deal regularly with people who are emotionally impaired, considerable patience required	Human Relations and Communications Skills: Level C Emotional Effort/Emotional Demands: Level C	4 (5.5%)	• Displays good listening skills and demonstrates the ability to effectively and consistently communicate verbally with co-workers, members, and agencies. • Works well with others, willing to assist co-workers, accepts assignments without complaint. • Shows initiative and drive.

128

Advanced		Human Relations and Communications Skills: Levels D & E Emotional Effort/Emotional Demands: Levels D & E	6 (8.2%)	
	• Understanding, compassion, uncooperative clients, deal with dangerous or hostile people • Use of persuasion techniques, understanding group dynamics, deal with emotionally charged issues in public forums • Coaching/guiding clients through difficult situations; providing comfort for those in considerable pain; deal regularly with dangerous or violent people • Responsibility for the well-being of others			• Is reasonable, respectful, and understanding. • Considers the opinions of others when making decisions about work or the working environment. • Handles unexpected or crisis situations appropriately. • Functions effectively under stress. • Accommodates opinions and ideas of others, controls emotions as to not disrupt, offend, or frustrate others. • Effectively and persuasively expresses self in appropriate fashion to clients, public, media. • Establishes and maintains appropriate rapport with other employees, clients, and the public. • Implements effective strategy, acts appropriately with sensitive information and confidential matters, demonstrates decisiveness and develops creative solutions.

Table 6.2 (continued)

Category of Emotional Labor Recognition	Key Words in Performance Appraisal Instruments Characterizing this Level	Corresponding Levels in Steinberg Typology	No. of Agencies	Representative Phrases from Performance Appraisals
				• Fairly and objectively evaluates performance, clearly communicates directions and expectations, offers appropriate solutions, addresses issues in a timely fashion, sets a positive example for subordinates, anticipates long- and short-term needs of employees, effectively utilizes and coordinates available resources.

*Motivating and training subordinates appears as part of Steinberg's Level C, but since that level also involves "hand-holding, reassurance, compassion, empathy . . . resolution of minor conflicts . . . [and] dealing regularly with people who are emotionally impaired, may work directly with people under the influence of drugs or alcohol," it was determined that the mention of training and mentoring responsibilities for supervisory positions, or maintaining rapport with personal and professional contacts, did not imply the full range of emotional labor described in Level C on Steinberg's scales. If motivating, training, and workplace rapport were mentioned *along with* other aspects of Level C, then the appraisal instrument would be placed in the Moderate category. See Appendix D for detail.

reveal that most agencies pay only the most rudimentary attention to emotion work. Five percent include no mention of *any* form of emotional labor, not even basic elements of interpersonal communication such as "effective written and oral communication skills." Eighty-one percent pay perfunctory attention to it, while about 14 percent give moderate or advanced recognition to it.

Perfunctory

As shown in the table, the forms showed a passing awareness that communication, working with others, and being decisive are important skills. Whether these fall within a distinct category of emotion work is debatable, but these criteria at least acknowledge the importance of the employee's being in relationship with others and being aware of work-related scenarios that extend beyond the employee's immediate situation.

Moderate

This category captures forms that include performance criteria that focus on the employee's ability to collaborate with others in a constructive manner. However, such criteria conflate emotional intelligence with emotion work, as occurs in "accepts assignments without complaint" or "shows initiative or drive." Emotional intelligence and emotion work are different but related concepts, as noted in Chapter 1. Emotional intelligence is the ability to monitor one's performance and to know when to exercise or hold one's affective side in check. To be effective at performing emotion work, one must have emotional intelligence. Expressed another way, emotion work is the application or performance outcome of emotional intelligence. For employers, it is the exercise of emotional labor that is of interest because in relational work, it is the employee's labor that yields the desirable outcome in the public service exchange between citizen and state.

Advanced

It is in this category that emotion work is best expressed among the forms examined. As shown by the phrases in the table, one sees key words that imply the performance of emotion work: "handles unexpected or crisis situations," "controls emotions," "maintains appropriate rapport," "acts appropriately with sensitive information," and "anticipates long- and short-term needs of employees." Criteria such as these acknowledge the work of employees who must be not only cognitively skilled but also emotionally skilled in order to satisfactorily complete their work.

Patterns Revealed

Several interesting elements of these performance appraisal instruments were revealed through this analysis. They concern assumptions about supervisory and nonsupervisory human relations requirements, emotional labor displays, and subjective criteria. First, nearly all incidents of motivating, mentoring, or coaching were restricted only to appraisal instruments for supervisory personnel. Either line personnel are not in positions to motivate or mentor others or if they are, their job evaluations do not reward them for it. For example, the Illinois Office of Attorney General evaluates its attorneys and support staff using two different forms. The attorney form is in the Advanced category because its criteria include persuasive self-expression; appropriate interpersonal relationships with colleagues, clients, and the public; and appropriate action "with sensitive information and confidential matters" (OAG Attorney Form, p. 2). The support staff form, however, only inquires into whether the "employee possesses the necessary written and verbal communication skills" and if the "employee has professional, courteous demeanor, shows respect to other agency personnel, and enhances the image of the Office of Attorney General" (see OAG Support Staff Form, p. 3). Is it possible that support staff never deal with sensitive and confidential material, or that they do not communicate with difficult or upset clients? If support staff do encounter these responsibilities, then they are not rewarded for it in their performance evaluations, for the appraisal instruments do not recognize such work demands nor do they recognize these demands as work. The irony, of course, is that the first contact citizens have with public agencies is via "front desk" workers—clerks, assistants, receptionists.

Emotional display requirements and subjective criteria are implicit in the expression of emotional labor. This leads to the second point: many performance appraisal instruments contain emotional display requirements. Although not the focus of this analysis, emotional display demands from State of Illinois performance appraisal instruments include a variety of phrases on various agencies' forms. For example:

- "Displays a positive attitude to constituents"
- "Models an appreciation of a diverse workforce"
- "Job Stamina: Physical and mental ability to meet job demands"

These elements and others beg for further research on the subject of surface acting and deep acting among public service workers. Recall that surface acting refers to those job performances where the employee engages in a dramaturgy of sorts. Regardless of the employee's true feelings, the job demands are such that s/he plays a role, as if on stage, expressing emotions that are not actually felt. This is surface acting. Deep acting, on the other hand, requires emotive imagery such that the employee actually experiences the emotion that s/he is expressing.

Third, this analysis of state agency performance appraisal instruments reveals several instances of subjective criteria, which also provide the basis for further research. The question that arises is whether items such as these provide a means for evaluating the employee's performance of emotion work or whether they simply fall prey to halo evaluations, in which the rater assigns positive or negative values based on the rater's personal like or dislike for the employee. Examples of subjective criteria from these evaluation forms include:

- "Demonstrates flexibility and willingness to assist by taking on difficult or inconvenient responsibilities"
- "Adequately comprehends the words of others"
- "Asks meaningful questions"

Such items are difficult to operationalize—or deconstruct—in terms that reveal emotion work. In the absence of such, however, they require remarkable levels of insight on the part of the evaluator if they are to produce accurate information.

Finally, two appraisal forms mention emotion explicitly, one in a positive context, the other in a negative one. We note these here to demonstrate different usages of the term in such instruments. The performance evaluation form used by the City of East St. Louis Financial Advisory Authority, an agency of the State of Illinois, begins (p. 1):

1. Generally, how are things going?
   a) What do you like (feel good about)?
   b) What do you dislike (feel bad about)?
2. List three to five accomplishments you feel good about over the past year.

These two questions use the employee's own likes, dislikes, and positive assessments as a springboard for performance appraisal. This approach elicits affect from the employee at the outset and uses it to guide the evaluative process. Although affect is incorporated into the evaluation process, it is used not in reference to emotion work but rather as a means for exploring the employee's reaction to the work performed. In contrast, the State Universities Retirement System of Illinois performance appraisal form explicitly cites emotion at work *qua* emotion work: under "Temperament," criteria are "Is reasonable, respectful, and understanding. Accommodates opinions and ideas of others, *controls emotions as not to disrupt, offend, or frustrate others*" (p. 1, emphasis added). In this case, the employee's use of affective self-control is appraised in the context of emotional labor, per se.

Although not included in the sample, another example of performance appraisals focuses on the service transaction, rewarding supervisors and managers for being responsive to the city's "customers." For example, for supervisors and managers for the city of Tallahassee, Florida, the 2003 form for their performance appraisal included this item among the list of competencies to be rated: "Look Good/Sound Good." This item was described this way: "Uses the 10/5 greeting—smile and make eye contact at 10 feet, offer a greeting at 5 feet." This performance element captures how the worker "seems" to the public. It captured first impression, personal presentation, and tone of voice. With an emphasis on customer service, the evaluation specified that supervisors and managers were supposed to "maintain composure under stressful situations." Under the heading "Leadership and Personal Responsibility," supervisors and managers were evaluated on their ability to "Demonstrate and convey enthusiasm and a positive attitude in achieving organizational goals and priorities." Under the heading of "Teamwork," managers were evaluated on whether they "Participate positively and enthusiastically in a team setting." Under "Interpersonal Skills," the manager was evaluated on "Understands how behaviors impact others. Is considerate and reacts appropriately to the needs, feelings and capabilities of others." Under "Empathy" the manager was evaluated on "Uses best effort to satisfy customer requests, and when we must say no, it is said in a nice manner" (City of Tallahassee 2003). Some of these categories are at the perfunctory level and some rise to the moderate level depicted in Table 6.2.

Conclusion

The purpose of this chapter is to demonstrate the degree to which performance appraisals in public service agencies include an explicit evaluation of the performance of emotion work. The review of State of Illinois performance appraisals shows that performance appraisals include acknowledgment of emotion work to only a limited degree. It is not generally represented in the lexicon of employee evaluations.

Emotional expression and suppression at work generates more questions than answers. For example, a deeper examination of the link between job description and performance appraisals for sex-segregated jobs may be revealing. Is there a differential presence or absence of items pertaining to the gender divide: jobs that require "tougher than tough" versus jobs that require "nicer than nice" emotion work?

Another examination should focus on the relationship between performance evaluation instruments and actual career outcomes with a focus on whether "recognition" translates into "compensation." It could involve a closer examination of how bureaucracy privileges instrumental rationality and marginalizes instrumental emotion work. And, it could be an analysis of managerial or leadership training programs, focusing on the extent to which these programs genuinely recognize emotional labor and relational skills. In addition, further research could examine an agency's job descriptions and link job content to performance appraisal and pay scales. This would reveal the presence or absence of logical links between tasks, emotion work, performance, recognition, and compensation.

Additional research could also probe more extensive comparisons between leadership studies and recognition and remuneration of emotional labor. How might leadership relate to emotional labor, you ask? In a speech delivered at the 2003 conference of the American Society for Public Administration, Alice Rivlin outlined the requirements of successful leadership. Among these she included "unwarranted optimism." What does it take to exude "unwarranted optimism" day in and day out? Is this a form of emotional labor?

Research could also examine the extent of emotional labor recognition by type of agency, using Lowi's (1964) typology: distributive, redistributive, and regulatory. In other words, is agency type related to the degree to which emotional labor or relational skills are necessary or acknowledged? Evidence confirms that bureaucracy privileges rationality and marginalizes emotional experience. Perhaps future evidence will challenge this overall assertion and reveal that "bureaucracy" is not monolithic: differences may exist as a result of the mission of the agency. (See, for example, Newman 1994; Kerr, Miller, and Reid 2002.) We already suspect that self-selection causes some workers to remain in jobs that require emotion work, while others seek other types of employment.

There are many questions waiting to be answered. If public service work is anything, it is service, and service is relational. As government strives to become more responsive to citizen needs and expectations, "service with a smile" is a term often heard. We need to know more about the skills and abilities required to provide "service with a smile" day after day, week after week, month after month. Worker training, development, and retention are important variables in the human capital equation and will benefit from this knowledge.

Note

1. CMS is the Illinois agency that provides human resource services to state agencies. Some agencies use variations of these forms.

— 7 —

Pay Inequity as the Penalty for Emotion Work

Most emotion work goes unrecognized. In the words of a 911 call taker:

> There aren't a lot of thank you's. And that's the problem. That's the one thing that's missing with the job because we are definitely the people who nobody knows about. You hear the bad stuff. . . . We take about 350 calls a day and we make very few errors, but the errors that we make are the ones you hear about. . . . A police officer could go into a situation where there's guns and people who are shooting. If you don't get the right information, someone can get killed. It's a very difficult job; it's extremely thankless because the administration and the people who are governing don't really hear about this type of job . . . we are the people behind the scenes . . . very rarely do you hear someone say, "you know, that group down there is really doing a good job."

A fellow call taker explains the invisibility of emotion work this way:

> We're the lifeline that started the thing, and we told the officers where to go and we gave descriptions and we just worked the call as much as we could and we're the dispatchers—people thank Officer So-and-So—hey, you know, we played a hand in that too, you know, but that all goes back to the recognition that we never get.

To what extent does emotion work contribute to the persistence of pay inequity between women and men? The construct of gender fails to fully explain the continued concentration of women and men in quintessential female and male jobs, respectively. Nor does it fully explain the enduring pay gap between women and men. Perhaps the concept of emotional labor

136

provides a window into the subtleties of this phenomenon. Prior chapters make clear that emotion management is at the heart of "people work," that it is a bona fide occupational skill, and that it remains, for the most part, invisible and uncompensated. We also know from the data presented in Chapters 3 and 4 that gender is not a significant variable in the performance of emotion work in the workplaces studied. This may be because workers self-select, such that men who work in these jobs are more like their female peers. Our hunch is that this explanation is inadequate, however. The bigger question is: Are jobs that require the expression of caring compensated to a lesser degree than jobs that do not require it? To the degree that women gravitate to this type of work, the chicken-and-egg question becomes an egg-and-chicken quandary. Which comes first? Do job requirements attract particular workers, or do workers imbue the job with their preferred work style? Do jobs that require workers to be "tougher than tough" pay more than jobs that require workers to be "nicer than nice"?

Our scope of inquiry is state employees in four states—New Jersey, Oregon, Illinois, and Florida. These four states represent the East, West, Midwest, and South. We begin with an examination of vertical job segregation. Then we turn to horizontal job segregation, and present an overview of the relationship between jobs, emotional labor, and compensation by displaying median weekly earnings of full-time workers by selected occupations that require emotional labor. This categorization reinforces the prevailing "wisdom" of the nature of work for women and men. Horizontal job segregation defines women's work experiences—women remain overrepresented in relational jobs and underrepresented in scientific and technical jobs. Moreover, there is a monetary penalty not only for being female but also for holding a job that involves caring and nurturance. Occupations that involve *caritas* pay lower wages for both women and men, but men in these jobs still earn more than their female counterparts. Labor that generates perceptions of rapport, supportiveness, congeniality, nurturance, and empathy register low on the wage meter. The discounted wage attached to emotion work reflects an assumption that care is a *natural* activity that neither deserves nor requires remuneration. It is possible that "feeling rules" comprise an inherently gendered set of expectations that go hand-in-hand with the person holding the job, so much so that it is inaccurate to examine jobs or job holders alone to capture emotional labor demands.

This view reflects the bias that imbues civil service job descriptions. While the requirement is for emotional performance, its value is low. In order to test this view, we extend the earlier work of Guy and Newman (2004) and examine three selected listings in the Career Service Class for the states of

Illinois, New Jersey, and Oregon. The generic listings are driver's license examiner, food inspector, and social service counselor. We hypothesize that the amount of emotional labor expected of job incumbents will vary dramatically. We expect that the Illinois, New Jersey, and Oregon findings will be consistent with those reported in Florida (Guy and Newman 2004)—that women performing emotional labor are paid less than men performing emotional labor, *even within the same occupation.* Such differential evaluation of work that is performed to advance organizational goals becomes a subtle form of wage discrimination.

Taken together, we find that data from the states support the same conclusion as was found in Florida—and that is that women experience "double jeopardy" in the workplace. The "care penalty" applies to both women and men, but not equally. Given that such jobs are disproportionately held by women, more women than men are so penalized. Further, even though occupations involving nurturance skills pay lower wages for *both* women and men, men in these jobs still earn more than their female counterparts. There is a monetary penalty not only for being female but also for holding a job that involves caring and nurturance. Such labor is either rendered invisible or, when it is recognized, it is characterized either as a natural work function or defined, without justification, as involving low levels of skill and effort. In either case, emotional labor (at least emotional labor that involves *caritas*) is excluded from salary calculations. Decision makers are more likely to recognize the contribution of jobs that involve instrumental skills, which are culturally coded as male. The importance of skills coded as female is mostly overlooked (England and Folbre 1999). "Seeing" the largely invisible emotional components of job classification and compensation systems should enable human resources (HR) executives to more fully comprehend the tenacity of sex segregation and pay inequity in the workplace, and to fashion policy and procedural responses in turn. Making emotional labor visible is a necessary first step in this process. The next step is making it compensable.

Separate but Not Equal

The phrase "women and work" conjures up images that are shaped (even distorted) by the traditional family-wage ideology. According to Schultz (2000):

> Family-wage thinking has left us with a mythologized but misleading image of women as creatures of domesticity—and not of paid work. This view inhabits labor economics, anti-discrimination law, and even some strands of feminist thought. In policy terms, it finds expression in the proposition that

it is women's position within families, rather than the work world, that is the primary cause of women's economic disadvantage. . . . This view is both empirically inaccurate and theoretically counterproductive; it reifies gender-based patterns of labor. (p. 3)

The "appropriateness of place" argument is telling, and rests upon the idealized separation of the private (domestic) and public (market) realms of work. This "distinction between productive workers (men doing 'real' work for wages) and non-productive workers (women supporting, raising, and rehabilitating those real workers)" changed the meaning of the work women and men do (Daniels 1987, p. 404). Despite women's presence in the paid labor force in overwhelming numbers, they still tend to be viewed from a domestic orientation and, as such, as "inauthentic workers" (Shultz 2000, p. 6). Women's conventional roles of wife, mother, daughter, sister, general nurturer, and provider of care and cleanup carry over to the workplace. Occupational sex segregation defines these roles, such that women are segregated into separate-but-less-remunerative occupations and jobs that require traits of support and nurturing. Such traits are deemed to be "natural" and hence of little market value.

Across all sectors of the U.S. economy, women earn about 80 percent of what men earn (U.S. Department of Labor 2005a). Government workers fare less well: national data that compare salaries for full-time wage and salary employees in public administration show the pay gap to be 76 cents, 2 cents less than when business and nonprofit workers are included in the analysis (U.S. Department of Labor 2005a).[1]

Job segregation, the tendency for men and women to work in different occupations, is the easy answer for why women's wages lag behind men's. Though sex-typed work has decreased since 1970, the rate of decline has slowed and job integration is now proceeding slower than it has in the past thirty years (Anker 1998). Over half of all employed women would still have to change jobs to equalize occupational distribution by gender (Jacobs 1989). This, despite the fact that over half (56%) of all college students are women (U.S. Department of Commerce 2005), 55 percent of the legal profession are women, 32 percent of physicians are women, and, in overall numbers, the public work force has moved steadily toward representativeness that is roughly proportionate to the population in terms of gender, race, and ethnicity (Guy and Thatcher 2004; Naff 2001; U.S. Department of Labor 2005b).

On average, jobs for which men are thought more capable pay about 24 percent more than jobs for which women are thought more capable (Guy and Killingsworth 2007). Little is heard about comparable worth, though, because its opponents claim that work performed by women is not comparable to work performed by men. In fact, on its face this argument is correct: women's jobs are different from men's. Does emotional labor offer an explanation? Close to three-fourths of all paraprofessionals are women, and almost 90 percent of support jobs are held by women. Though these jobs require skills of a level comparable to the skills required of craft workers, an occupational category that is 87 percent male, they are compensated at lower rates (U.S. Equal Employment Opportunity Commission 2003).

Compression and Concentration

For the most part, women and men experience work differently. Women are more likely to be compressed into the lower organizational levels and concentrated into female-type occupations. Job segregation occurs both horizontally and vertically. Horizontal segregation—nicknamed the *glass wall*—refers to the distribution of women and men across occupations, such that women are caseworkers and men are highway patrol officers; women hold staff posts and men hold line posts. Vertical segregation—nicknamed the *glass ceiling*—refers to the distribution of women and men in the job hierarchy in terms of status within an occupation, such that women work as assistants and men as directors. Tables 7.1 and 7.2 exemplify sex-typed work in both dimensions.

Table 7.1 provides an example of vertical segregation, using current data from the states of Illinois, New Jersey, Oregon, and Florida. Data for state employees across all job levels in our sample show the average pay gap to be 89 cents, which is 13 cents better than the national average for public workers (IL 93¢; NJ 82¢; OR 86¢; FL 87¢).

Although Table 7.1 presents data from a convenience sample of only four states, the pattern is a familiar one and data from most jurisdictions reflect a similar pattern. Overall, the majority of public workers at the lowest rungs of the career ladder are women (IL 48.2%; NJ 55.9%; OR 54.5%; FL 56.1%). Moving upward, women still represent over half of all workers in the middle tier in IL (63.7%), OR (50.5%), and FL (54.1%). At the top level, which represents policy makers, the pattern turns upside down. Well over half of these workers are male (IL 57.5%; NJ 59.1%; OR 59.2%; FL 61.7%). The wage gap is smaller at this level (at least for NJ, OR, and FL), largely because the women who hold senior management posts are working not in sex-typed posts but in "unisex" positions.[2] It is in these jobs that the Equal Pay Act of 1963 has had the greatest impact. When women work in "men's" jobs, they come close to earning equal pay, though Fletcher (1999)

140

Table 7.1

Comparison of State Workers

	Career[a]		Exempt/Unclassified[b]		Senior Management[c]		Total	
	Men	Women	Men	Women	Men	Women	Men	Women
Number								
Illinois	25,723	23,948	920	1,612	896	615	27,539	26,175
New Jersey	27,060	34,254	6,362	3,492	182	126	33,607	37,872
Oregon	13,097	15,664	2,524	2,572	324	223	15,945	18,459
Florida	37,322	47,679	8,485	10,249	346	215	46,153	58,143
Percentage of service								
Illinois	51.8	48.2	35.9	63.7	57.5	40.7	51.2	48.7
New Jersey	44.1	55.9	64.6	35.4	59.1	40.9	47.0	53.0
Oregon	45.5	54.5	49.5	50.5	59.2	40.8	46.3	53.7
Florida	43.9	56.1	45.9	54.1	61.7	38.3	44.0	56.0
Average Salary								
Illinois	$49,596	$46,320	$78,328	$63,490	$79,452	$68,184	$51,527	$47,836
New Jersey	$54,709	$46,248	$76,129	$70,531	$96,217	$92,636	$58,990	$48,642
Oregon	$40,409	$35,407	$59,770	$51,292	$88,291	$80,057	$44,447	$38,160
Florida	$35,825	$31,825	$56,503	$46,256	$106,284	$104,377	$39,829	$34,632

(continued)

141

Table 7.1 (continued)

Number	Career[a]		Exempt/Unclassified[b]		Senior Management[c]		Total	
	Men	Women	Men	Women	Men	Women	Men	Women
Women's salary per $1 earned by men								
Illinois		93¢		81¢		86¢		93¢
New Jersey		85¢		93¢		96¢		82¢
Oregon		88¢		86¢		91¢		86¢
Florida		89¢		82¢		98¢		87¢

Notes:

[a]Career Service employees represent the largest category of state workers and the lowest skill levels. In New Jersey, Career Service means those positions and job titles subject to the tenure provisions of Title 11A, New Jersey Statutes. In Oregon, Career Service means those positions and job titles in the Classified Service as defined in Oregon Revised Statutes 240.210.

[b]In Illinois, Exempt employees include staff attorneys, legal or technical advisors, engineers, physicians, healthcare administrators, registered nurses, resident administrative heads of charitable, penal, and correctional institutions, and confidential assistants. In New Jersey, Unclassified Service means those positions and job titles outside of the senior executive service, not subject to the tenure provisions of Title 11A, New Jersey Statutes, or the NJ Administrative Code rules unless otherwise specified. In Oregon, Select Exempt means selected positions and job titles in the Unclassified Service as defined in Oregon Revised Statutes 240.205 and includes those defined in state policy as Management Service. Select Exempt also includes legislative employees defined as Exempt Service in Oregon Revised Statutes 240.200. In Florida, Selected Exempt employees are all managers, supervisors, confidential employees, and certain professionals such as physicians and lawyers.

[c]In Illinois, this includes those in policy-making positions and in upper management. In New Jersey, Senior Executive Service (SES) means positions in state service designated by the Merit System Board as having substantial managerial, policy-influencing, or policy-executing responsibilities not included in the career or unclassified services. The SES does not include cabinet or subcabinet positions. In Oregon, Senior Management means positions and job titles in State Unclassified Service as defined in Oregon Revised Statutes 240.205 and designated as Executive Service under state policy. Also, Senior Executive excludes appointed or elected department directors, appointed or elected officials, as well as lawyers, licensed physicians, and dentists employed in their professional capacities. In Florida, workers in policy-making positions and others in upper management are in the Senior Management Service. This category contains appointed department heads.

142

argues that emotional labor is still expected of them there, over and above that which is expected of men. To the point of our argument, it is sex-typed jobs that penalize women the most. These jobs require more "natural," that is, unpaid, tasks that are missing from the job description's list of required knowledge, skills, and abilities (KSAs).

The bottom section of Table 7.1 represents the amount of money that women earn for each dollar earned by men in that category and state. Among senior management, women come much closer to parity. Because the number of women in that category (IL, n = 615; NJ, n = 126; OR, n = 223; FL, n = 215) is so small, parity at that level does little to change the overall pay ratio.

Now we turn to horizontal segregation. Table 7.2 illustrates jobs that are found in one form or another in civil service rosters and that possess three characteristics: they require voice or facial contact with the public, workers are required to evoke an emotional state in the client, and the employer exerts control over the emotional activities of employees. We add that some jobs, especially those of confidential aides and secretaries, require emotional labor not so much for contact with external constituencies but for internal "customers." Though the worker is not required to meet the public, she is required to engage in emotional labor to meet the demands of her superior and of constituencies within the agency.

As the table shows, among these jobs, it is the rare occupation that employs equal numbers of women and men. In a number of these occupations, there are fewer than 50,000 men across the nation who hold these jobs (for example, teachers' aides and child care workers). Given the range of jobs and interests of workers, the concentration of women and scarcity of men calls attention to the difference that gender makes. Postal workers who staff counters in post offices are the exception.

Within each occupational category other than postal clerks and receptionists, women earn less than their male counterparts, regardless of women's representation. While women comprise 31 percent of all physicians, they earn 52¢ for every $1.00 their male counterparts earn. In occupations such as insurance adjuster, appraiser, examiner, and investigator, where women outnumber men (66.5% of total), they earn 71¢ for every $1.00 their male counterparts earn. Even when women appear to have an advantage—that is, working in a traditionally female job with mostly other women—they still do not fare as well as men. More than 90 percent of registered nurses are women, but female nurses earn 13 percent less than male nurses. We attribute this disparity to the different role expectations of women and men and the different exchange value between the performance of women's "natural" skills and men's. Daniels puts it this way:

143

Table 7.2

Median Weekly Earnings of Full-Time Wage and Salary Workers by Selected Occupations Requiring Emotional Labor

Occupation	Number of Workers (in thousands)	Percentage Total Female	No. Men	No. Women	Median Weekly Earnings ($)		Percentage Wage Gap
					Men	Women	
Insurance Adjusters, Appraisers, Examiners, Investigators	257	66.5	85	171	952	677	71.1
Human Resource Specialists	612	67.8	198	415	952	755	79.3
Social Workers	620	76.1	148	472	720	689	95.7
Counselors (Community & Social Service)	513	65.9	175	338	832	689	82.8
Clergy	351	13.4	304	47	795	a	—
Lawyers	621	33.5	412	208	1,710	1,255	73.4
Teachers (Elementary & Middle School)	2,206	80.3	435	1,772	917	776	84.6
Teachers (Secondary)	1,013	54.8	458	555	955	824	86.3
Teachers' Aides	545	91.7	45	500	a	373	—
Physicians	555	31.2	382	173	1,874	978	52.2
Registered Nurses	1,800	91.7	148	1,651	1,031	895	86.8
Therapists, Physical	121	57.9	50	70	955	900	94.2
Health Service Occupations	1,985	88.4	230	1,755	453	402	88.7

Occupation						
Protective Service Workers (Police)	654	12.7	571	83	845	841	99.5
Protective Service Workers (Corrections)	370	28.9	263	107	654	558	85.3
Waiters	799	67.3	261	538	399	327	82.0
Child Care Workers	413	93.7	26	387	[a]	334	—
Cashiers	1,355	75.0	339	1,016	380	313	82.4
Clerical Supervisors	1,441	69.5	440	1,001	792	636	80.3
Telephone Operators	55	90.9	4	50	[a]	459	—
Receptionists	847	93.9	52	795	454	463	102.0
Postal Clerks (except Mail Carriers)	162	45.1	89	73	761	778	102.2
Secretaries, Stenographers, & Typists	2,657	96.7	87	2,570	598	550	92.0

Source: U.S. Department of Labor, Bureau of Labor Statistics, Employment and Earnings, January 2005, Table 18, *Median Usual Weekly Earnings of Full-time Wage and Salary Workers by Detailed Occupation and Sex, 2004 Annual Averages,* pp. 50–56.

[a]Data not shown where number of job occupants is less than 50,000.

145

The closer the work to the activities of nurturing, comforting, encouraging, or facilitating interaction, the more closely associated it is with women's "natural" or "feminine" proclivities. Such activity is not seen as learned, skilled, required, but only the expression of the character of style of women in general. (1987, p. 408)

Table 7.2 also demonstrates that women's wages are clustered toward the lower end of the wage spectrum while men's are clustered higher. The highest-paid occupation for men is physician ($1,874 per week, amounting to $896 more per week than female physicians). The highest-paid occupation for women is lawyer ($1,255 per week, amounting to $455 less per week than male lawyers). The earnings gap between women and men is relatively narrow for social workers (95.7 percent), but even here, wages vary by gender. With the two noted exceptions (postal clerks and receptionists), women performing emotional labor are paid less than men performing emotional labor. Interpersonal and caring skills are not seen as *natural* for men. Accordingly, men receive more credit for showing these skills (Daniels 1987, p. 409). This suggests that "all emotional labor is not created equally"—that emotional labor is recognized, valued, and rewarded when it is performed by men (even in female-dominated occupations) and devalued when it is performed by women. It gets "disappeared" because it is "natural."

Skill-based Jobs

Based upon our interviews and surveys at the Cook County Office of the Public Guardian, the Illinois Department of Corrections, and the Tallahassee, Florida, Police Department, we conclude that the concept of emotional labor is far more complex than we originally thought. Far from being a matter of attitude, the expression of emotion management is highly sophisticated and nuanced. This is to say that emotional labor is a bona fide occupational skill that should not be taken for granted. That it is real work is undeniable. From a cursory review of the literature on skill-based jobs and pay, the skill of emotion management is conspicuous in its absence. Yet if emotional labor is so crucial to effective job performance, especially in "people work," then why does it remain outside the scope of traditional KSAs? It is to this that we now turn.

As the previous chapter has demonstrated, the emotional management skills required of relational work are not captured by traditional performance appraisal instruments. Working for the service sector requires the mastery of skills very different from those required in industrial production—not surprising given the differences between knowledge work and production work. Service workers "manufacture social relations" (Filby 1992, p. 37), not widgets. As organizations flatten, frontline service providers are required to exercise judgment and discretion, and work is performed in teams. Nevertheless, the entire human resource management infrastructure, including a reliance on standard operating procedures and scientific management pay practices, remains as if in a time warp.

Emotion work is not well understood in human resource management, yet those who employ relationship skills are patently familiar with the effort, knowledge, and skill that it takes to do this kind of work well. "Having a good attitude" may be a necessary prerequisite to emotion management, but it falls short of capturing the complexity of emotional labor skills. These skills include developing rapport with an abused child in order to elicit information; remaining professional in the face of hostile taxpayers; patiently explaining to an applicant why he failed his driver's license test; applying one's game face, be it stern or sympathetic, in order to effect a successful outcome; governing one's emotions when confronted with a delicate situation; and the ability to multitask in intense, dangerous, chaotic environments.

Recent reform initiatives, such as skill-based pay (also known as pay-for-knowledge, multiskilled pay, and competency-based pay) and pay-for-performance, have the potential to move us closer toward a new way of thinking about identifying and paying for emotional labor. These new pay approaches depart from the traditional link between pay and the job by focusing on pay and the worker, which is congruent with new post-bureaucratic structures (Heckscher and Donnellon 1994). Traditional pay relies on paying people for the jobs they do rather than the skills they possess. Skill-based pay shifts the focus by paying for attributes (KSAs) of individuals, and represents a radical departure from traditional job-based pay that compensates employees for the job they hold (Shareef 1994).

Under skill-based pay (SBP), compensation is based on the range, depth, and types of skills that employees are capable of using, rather than the job they are performing at a particular time (Lee, Law, and Bobko 1999, p. 853). The focus is on skill acquisition rather than recognition of existing skill sets. According to Shareef, "SBP allows employees an opportunity to learn those skills that are needed (or will be needed) by the organization and to be compensated for this skill-acquisition" (1994, p. 62). Skill-based pay is best applied to "knowledge workers, managers, and service situations where the strategy calls for one-stop service and a high level of customer satisfaction" (Lawler 1995, p. 17). It fits best in high-involvement environments (Lawler 1986) and where performance depends on good coordination and teamwork among individuals (Lee, Law, and Bobko 1999, p. 869).

Emotional labor is, by definition, required in "high-touch people work." To the point of our argument, the challenge for human resource managers is to ensure that *emotional labor skills* are included in the repertoire of skills being examined and then to recognize, label, and compensate them accordingly. For example, teachers who use good questioning techniques, stimulate higher-level thinking, provide counseling, and diagnose needs should be compensated for those skills (Feldhusen 1984). The police officer "who can understand the dynamics of groups and community problems" and "who understands psychology is better able to understand the complexities of the human mind. These skills are good for police work" (Webber 1991, p. 123). The movement toward community-oriented policing represents a radical shift from traditional policing—from a focus on crime fighting to a focus on problem solving; in other words, a focus away from police *force* to police *service* (Martin 1999). Such service is interactive and relational. It requires emotional labor.

In order for the potential of new pay approaches to be fully realized, emotional labor skills must be incorporated into the discourse. Shaw et al. hint at this imperative in the conclusion to their study of skill-based pay plans: "We hope that this study leads us toward the adoption of more nuanced approaches to compensation and HRM [human resource management] dynamics" (2005, p. 17). We agree that such approaches must take into account that complex work systems rely upon more abstract sets of skills (Lee, Law and Bobko 1999, p. 858). KSAs required of the contemporary work force are both cognitive and emotional. Skill-based and knowledge-for-pay systems, as well as the more recent pay-for-performance orientation, can help us think about the goodness of fit between skills and compensation. Paying emotional laborers for their knowledge, skills, and competencies is the next step in the evolution of skill-based pay systems. It is no longer tenable to rest on the argument that "To date, there are no well-developed systems for determining the worth of individual skills in the marketplace" (Lawler 1995, p. 17). In order to close the gap, and to align pay systems with a service economy, emotional labor must first become economically visible; it must then be compensated.

The Penalty for Caring

Both men and women engage in emotional labor. Hochschild (1983) estimates that approximately one-third of American workers have jobs that subject them to substantial demands for emotional labor. Moreover, of all women working, over one-half have jobs that call for emotional labor (Hochschild, 1983, p. 171). A female correctional officer captures the emotional demands of her job this way: "With the men, it's like you're the mother, you're the doctor, the nurse, the teacher, the counselor, the chaplain, everything. . . .

I just tell them what I would tell one of my children to do, and a lot of it is like mothering, it's like that. 'Cause there are some [offenders] that are more needy than others."

Women are overrepresented in relational jobs and underrepresented in scientific and technical jobs. The discounted wage attached to women's emotional labor reflects an assumption that care is a *natural* activity that neither deserves nor requires remuneration (Schultz 2000; England and Folbre 1999). Women who come up short in their emotional labor skills fare poorly. Who wants to be treated by a cold nurse, taught by a confrontational teacher, assisted by a gruff clerk? Unlike "men's" professions, where expressions of anger are tolerated and autonomy is expected, women's work is rooted in interpersonal exchanges that require supportive behaviors.

Emotional labor has been characterized as an oxymoron in its linking of emotion, a negatively valued experience, to labor, a positively valued means of production (Putnam and Mumby 1993). This view reflects the bias that imbues our civil service job descriptions. While the requirement is for emotional performance, it is worth little. The jobs described in Figure 7.1 provide a comparison. They are current listings in the Career Service class for the states of Illinois, New Jersey, and Oregon.[3] We have italicized specific mention of tasks and KSAs that require relational work.

As these job descriptions illustrate, the amount of emotional labor expected of job incumbents varies dramatically from the little that is expected of the agricultural inspector to the maximum amount expected of the social service counselor. While the agricultural inspector earns almost as much as the social service counselor, there are fewer qualifications for the job and fewer different kinds of demands on those who have the job. Other than the standard taglines—"to maintain harmonious working relationships with meat processing industry personnel" (IL), "to deal courteously and effectively with others in complex situations concerning the certification of agricultural products" (NJ), or "to maintain harmonious working relationships with both agency staff and personnel from industry being served" (OR)—there is little requirement to engage in emotional labor. As shown in Table 7.3 on page 158, there are 108 jobs in this category (IL, n = 79; NJ, n = 21; OR, n = 8), and only 16 percent of them are held by women.

Conversely, both the driver's license examiner and the social service counselor require significantly more emotional labor; almost two-thirds of all driver's license examiners are women, and almost 80 percent of the social service counselors are women. This comparison between job qualification, job description, salary, and gender provides an example of how emotional labor is discounted, or "disappeared," to use Fletcher's terminology, and remains "invisible work" (Daniels 1987, p. 405).[4]

Figure 7.1 **Comparison of Selected Jobs in Three States**

JOB 1

State of Illinois
Public Service Representative[a]
Pay: $2,160–$3,380

Qualifications—2 years of general office experience.

Examples of Work Performed

Administers road examinations to applicants for all classes of drivers' licenses. *Serves as information clerk directing applicants and public to proper areas of the facility to receive service.* Administers and grades written driver examinations. *Explains incorrect test responses.* Performs office clerical tasks.

Knowledge, Skills, and Abilities

Knowledge of office methods, practices and procedures/basic bookkeeping procedures and techniques. Ability to maintain records of some complexity/*to deal tactfully with the general public and to maintain satisfactory working relationships with other employees/to communicate both orally and in writing.*

State of New Jersey
Examination Technician, Division of Motor Vehicles[b]
Pay: $2,343–$3,178

Qualifications—Two years of clerical experience or one year of experience in administering oral, written, or performance examinations; possession of a valid New Jersey driver's license.

Examples of Work Performed—Examines documents presented by applicants to determine their authenticity and validity. Administers oral/written examinations and scores tests using standard methods. *When applicants fail road tests, explains the reason(s) for failure and what methods should be used to correct the deficiency.* Operates vision-testing machines. Prepares records and reports of daily activities. Maintains essential records and files. *Interviews and transacts routine business with persons who visit or telephone the center to insure good public relations.* Types driver's licenses and reports. Assists with the planning and revising of clerical procedures and office routines.

Knowledge, Skills, and Abilities—Knowledge of modern office methods, practices, and routines/of examining documents and records for authenticity and accuracy. Ability to operate standard equipment/to evaluate the driving abilities of both new and experienced drivers/to learn to operate specific machinery used in the issuance of licenses/to administer and score routine tests/to give clear concise directions and information to applicants as to testing procedures/*to work effectively and courteously with the public*/to maintain essential records and files/*to deal courteously and effectively with diverse types of persons and to explain accurately, clearly, and convincingly the reasons for approval or rejection*/to perform the basic mathematical calculations necessary to prepare required reports/to learn to utilize various types of electronic and/or manual recording and information systems used by the agency.

State of Oregon
Job: Transportation Services Representative 1[c]
Pay: $2,067–2,847

Qualifications—None listed.

Examples of Work Performed—Customer Assistance—explains compliance requirements to help customers understand agency policies and procedures/explains the application of transportation licensing and permitting laws/questions customers, as needed, to determine appropriate service; responds to requests for information verbally and in writing/reviews forms from the customer for compliance with policies/retrieves information from computer records/reviews documentation to determine authenticity/gives and scores motor vehicle tests/takes photographs of customers for licenses/does vehicle identification and inspections on vehicles. Administrative Duties—Computes and collects fees/accounts for documents and monies received/balances receipts daily/makes bank deposits/keeps inventory of supplies/prepares reports. *Relationships with others—has daily in-person contact with the general public/communicates with customers who may be displeased, hostile, frustrated, or confused/explains policies, procedures, and laws.*

Knowledge, Skills, and Abilities—Knowledge of proper grammar and sentence structure/of rules, policies, and procedures/of business arithmetic/in verbal communication. *Skill in questioning people to get accurate and complete information/in dealing with displeased, frustrated, confused, or hostile customers/in concurrently performing multiple tasks/in doing detailed work under conditions of heavy workloads, time limitations, and noise*/in using a computer/in collecting money and making change.

JOB 2

State of Illinois
Meat and Poultry Inspector[d]
Pay: $2,964–$3,737

Qualifications—High school equivalency, preferably with courses in algebra, biology or chemistry + successful completion of an agency approved meat and poultry inspection training program + valid IL driver's license.

Examples of Work Performed—Inspects live animals and/or poultry prior to slaughter for the presence of diseases/inspects carcasses, incises organs and glands of slaughtered meat producing animals and/or poultry to determine their fitness for human consumption/assures the appropriate branding and identification of carcasses/identifies suspect animals/conducts daily inspections of slaughtering and processing procedures/prepares reports on operations and conditions/maintains records on inspections performed/performs processing inspections of a variety of fresh, smoked, cured or cooked meat and poultry products/performs calculations to ensure that proper amounts of chemicals and water are introduced into the product/ submits product samples for laboratory analysis.

Knowledge, Skills, and Abilities—Knowledge of the methods and techniques of antemortem and postmortem inspections involving meat producing animals and poultry/of laws, rules and regulations governing the inspection and processing of meat and poultry products/of the use of additives and preservatives. Requires ability to exercise sound judgment in the determination of wholesome meat and poultry products/to conduct antemortem and postmortem inspections of animals/to remove, dissect and analyze parts of animals for signs of obvious disease/*to express ideas clearly and concisely in order to explain regulations and inspection results*/to tolerate exposure to unpleasant odors in slaughterhouses/to use safety practices around dangerous meat cutting machinery/*to maintain harmonious working relationships with meat processing industry personnel/to adapt to and tolerate humane slaughtering and destruction of animals.*

State of New Jersey
Agricultural Products Agent 2[e]
Pay: $2,672–$3,639

Qualifications—One year of experience in commodity storage or agricultural production, processing, marketing, or inspection which shall have included official grade determination, some form of official agricultural quality control work, or regulation enforcement + a valid driver's license + heavy lifting.

Examples of Work Performed—Inspects egg-breaking plants and processes to ensure compliance with USDA regulations/conducts shipping point and/or terminal market inspections of fruits, vegetables, shell eggs, fish and fisheries products, red meat, and poultry on the basis of USDA standards and certifies their quality, grade, etc./prepares technically accurate official state/federal certificates/collects samples of animal feeds/inspects and grades poultry products/test-weights poultry products to certify compliance with a contract agreement/grades fruits and vegetables/makes special field visits and investigations of licensed milk dealers/examines records of milk dealers, processors, etc./*explains and interprets the provision of basic law and regulations*/provides assistance to milk dealers in the preparation and interpretation of various required reports/reports irregularities in the milk industry/prepares and presents training for Agricultural Products Agent Trainees/acts as a state/federal witness for the state at hearing and in court and gives testimony under oath/reviews storage facilities/takes inventory/conducts exit conferences with responsible agency administrators to review deficiencies and suggest corrective actions/responds to natural or manmade disaster situations in which commodities must be provided to feed those individuals affected/attends job related conferences/publicly addresses small groups to inform and update recipient agency program requirements.

Knowledge, Skills, and Abilities—Knowledge of marketing practices and perishability of products being graded/or common types of violations and evasions of regulations/storage and inspection protocols. Ability to understand, analyze, and apply official state and federal regulations governing inspections and grading of agricultural products/to explain scoring defects and tolerance and laws/to organize assigned work, analyze inspection and grading problems, and develop effective work methods/to prepare reports and correspondence/to maintain essential records and files/*to deal courteously and effectively with others in complex situations concerning the certification of agricultural products*/to publicly address food service personnel/*to explain program requirements to new applicants*/to learn to utilize various types of electronic and/or manual recording and information systems used by the agency.

State of Oregon
Shipping Point Inspector 2[f]
Pay: $1,907–$2,595

Qualifications—Two years of experience as Shipping Point Inspector 1 or three years of experience in a commercial fruit or vegetable growing, grading, or marketing enterprise. U.S. Department of Agriculture license to inspect fresh fruits and vegetables + good eyesight and sense of smell to detect irregularities in fruits, vegetables, or nuts.

Examples of Work Performed—Sampling and Inspections—directs the selection of representative samples from cartons or storage bins/interprets federal and/or state standards for particular commodity being inspected/inspects sample for compliance to grade taking into consideration shape, size, color, and any physical deterioration. Documentation and Compliance Assurance—prepares certificates of grade/enforces compliance with state and federal laws pertaining to packing, inspection, labeling, transportation, sales, or quarantines. Coordination—coordinates work of grading crews in processing plants and inspection stations/assists in planning work and assigning personnel/*trains agricultural workers and new Shipping Point Inspectors. Relationships with others—daily in-person contact with personnel, managers, and/or owners of fresh produce packing houses or processing facilities and with other inspectors, aides, laborers and the District Supervisor.*

Knowledge, Skills, and Abilities—Knowledge of OR and U.S. fresh fruits and vegetable grade standards/of arithmetic. Skill in the use of inspection tools/*in coordinating personnel at job site/in communicating orally and in writing.* Ability to *maintain harmonious working relationships with both agency staff and personnel from industry being served*/to impartially render decisions regarding fresh fruit and vegetable grades and condition/to work with honeybees as required/to perform heavy manual labor/to distinguish color, texture, or visible defects in products inspected.

JOB 3

State of Illinois
Child Welfare Specialist[g]
Pay: $3,207–$4,738

Qualifications—Preferably requires a master's degree in social work; or a master's degree in a related human service field + one year of directly related professional casework/case management experience related to family preservation, family re-unification, adoption, youth development, counseling and advocacy services or a related field OR a bachelor's degree in social work + one year of directly related professional casework/case management experience OR a bachelor's degree in a related human service field + 2 years of directly related professional casework/case management experience. Requires a valid driver's license.

*Examples of Work Performed—Conducts interviews with clients to obtain the necessary information for an assessment of the conditions, needs and issues/determines needs and placement of children/*participates in administrative case reviews/prepares court reports and testifies in court hearings/recommends permanent plan for the child/ *conducts studies of relatives' homes/provides direct service intervention/*maintains client records/*recommends decisions for adoption, aftercare to birth families, and post adoption referrals and services/serves as an "ambassador" to the community/*offers public speaking and public relations services/serves as a liaison to various community organizations.

Knowledge, Skills, and Abilities—Knowledge of the principles and techniques in the child welfare field/of DCFS [Department of Children and Family Services] rules and regulations/of child growth and development. *Ability to resolve problems in a calm manner as they arise—often in a hostile environment/*to prepare complex written and oral reports.

State of New Jersey
Family Service Specialist 2[h]
Pay: $3,533–$4,843

Qualifications—Bachelor's degree + 1 year of experience in social work. A Master's degree in Social Work, Psychology, Guidance and Counseling, Divinity, or other related behavioral science area may be substituted for the indicated experience + valid driver's license.

Examples of Work Performed—*Conducts investigations for abuse and neglect referrals/interviews children and family members/takes appropriate action to seek court intervention, police assistance, or removal of the child from an unsafe environment in accordance with statute*/organizes a service program for family and/or child/*assists in identifying and meeting problems of personal, emotional, and economic adjustment/maintains cooperative relationships with public and private agencies*/prepares formal reports of all alleged abuse and neglect cases/provides testimony to juvenile courts/*gathers evidence of abuse and neglect,* prepares affidavits and depositions/ *processes children for adoption placement/visits homes of client and families to plan and implement corrective measures to problems of parent/child relationships/conducts investigations to identify problems leading to family disintegration/screens and evaluates applicants for foster and adoption care/personally provides counseling and advice to children and families regarding alcoholism, drug abuse, etc./plans and conducts group activities for children and their families/assesses alleged abuse and neglect referrals through telephone or in-person interviews and provides recommendation for assignment to a service unit.*

Knowledge, Skills, and Abilities—Knowledge of the economic, social, emotional, and other problems of abused and neglected family members/of counseling and interviewing techniques/of the signs of child abuse and neglect. Ability to interpret and apply laws and rules to specific situations/to collect and analyze data and evaluate the social relationships of individuals and families and take appropriate action/to conduct field visits/to prepare case histories/*to interview persons who may be emotionally upset or antagonistic, and obtain information/to remain calm and decisive in emergency situations and make immediate and critical decisions based on agency policy and perform judiciously under pressure.*

State of Oregon
Social Service Specialist 1[i]
Pay: $2,846–$3,955

Qualifications—Requires a criminal history check and a record free of founded abuse referrals + some positions require the willingness to travel to client homes, private care facilities, foster homes, or court hearings and to work extended or weekend hours as necessary. Requires at a minimum a bachelor's degree in social work/human services or a related field, or a bachelor's degree in a non-related field and a year's related experience. May require written and verbal bilingual language skills.

Examples of Work Performed—*Foster care certification*—evaluate foster home applicants/assess applicant's ability to deal with multiproblem children and understanding of child abuse and neglect. *Adoption Services*—evaluate adoptive parent applicants/assess applicants' ability to deal with complicated parent-child relationships/counsel child and selected family to prepare for the placement. *Liaison Activities*—screen referrals for appropriate placement in substitute care programs/resolve differences between agency staff and providers. *Parent*

Training—conduct group sessions to help change behavior and alleviate family problems/testify in court as needed. *Substitute Care*—gather information to assess family situation and determine appropriate substitute care for child. *Family Service*—maintain ongoing contact with service providers to monitor and assess client's progress/provide individual and family counseling to improve quality of life for children and prevent the need for placement outside the home. *Permanent Planning*—observe home conditions and assess problems and needs of families where children have been removed from their home/decide whether to replace the child in home or pursue other permanent placements. *Family Therapy. Sex Abuse Therapy*—conduct individual intake interviews with family members affected by sexual abuse to assess treatment needs/conduct specialized interviews with victims/plan, prepare, and conduct therapy treatment programs. *Protective Services*—investigate reports alleging child abuse or neglect/interview children and parents to collect evidence/conduct risk assessment/identify specific needs of family and provide individual and family counseling to rehabilitate the family/assemble case narrative and reports and testify on abuse/neglect cases in court hearings. *Relationships with others—employees are in regular contact, in person and by phone, with clients, medical professionals, mental health workers and attorneys.*

Knowledge, Skills, and Abilities—Knowledge of behavior management techniques/of early childhood development and family dynamics/of family counseling techniques/of conflict resolution and crisis intervention techniques. *Skill in interviewing to gather data needed to assess needs of individuals and families/in providing counseling to clients/in communicating on a one-to-one basis and in groups to provide information, advice, and give assistance/in conducting social service assessments/in communicating with angry, disturbed, and aggressive clients/in obtaining information on abuse from young children.*

[a]*Source:* State of Illinois, Office of the Secretary of State, Department of Personnel, 2005.

[b]*Source:* State of New Jersey, Department of Personnel, 2004d, http://webapps.dop.state.nj.us/jobspec/56440.htm.

[c]*Source:* State of Oregon, Department of Administrative Services, Human Resource Services Division, 2005d, www.hr.das.state.or.us/hrsd/class/0331.htm.

[d]*Source:* State of Illinois, Department of Central Management Services, 2005c, www.state.il.us/cms/downloads/pdfs_specs/26070.pdf.

[e]*Source:* State of New Jersey, Department of Personnel, 2004, http://webapps.dop.state.nj.us/jobspec/33892.htm.

[f]*Source:* State of Oregon, Department of Administrative Services, Human Resource Services Division, 2005c, www.hr.das.state.or.us/hrsd/class/5451.htm.

[g]*Source:* State of Illinois, Department of Central Management Services, 2005b, www.state.il.us/cms/downloads/pdfs_specs/07218.pdf.

[h]*Source:* State of New Jersey, Department of Personnel, 2004a, http://webapps.dop.state.nj.us/jobsspecs/62152.htm.

[i]*Source:* State of Oregon, Department of Administrative Services, Human Resource Services Division, 2005b, www.hr.das.state.or.us/hrsd/class/6612/htm.

PAY INEQUITY AS THE PENALTY FOR EMOTION WORK

To be successful, workers who engage in emotional labor must be aware of their own emotions and manage them, motivate themselves, recognize emotions in others, and respond to them in such a way that the relationship achieves the intended goal. Such skills are not merely natural expressions that occur spontaneously; they are neither "extraneous nor trivial" (Daniels 1987, p. 411). The KSAs required of the Illinois Child Welfare Specialist hint at this work: "Ability to resolve problems in a calm manner as they arise—often in a hostile environment." The following vignette gets us closer to the complex nature of this work:

> We have to develop these relationships . . . in order to get our clients to . . . tell us the deepest and darkest, and whatever's going on, right? . . . I mean we see a variety of clients . . . severely sexually abused. . . . I also knew that there was some alleged accusation that the mother may have been poisoning the kids when they went for visits . . . you have to establish a rapport—a connection.

The driver's license examiner must exercise emotional labor to get through the day and deal with the queue of applicants who grow testy as they endure forms, exams, and long waits. The KSAs required of the Oregon Transportation Services Representative 1, for example, reflect this emotion work: "Skill in questioning people to get accurate and complete information. Skill in dealing with displeased, frustrated, confused, or hostile customers. Skill in doing detailed work under conditions of heavy workloads, time limitations, and noise."

The act of managing emotion at work is central to success in these jobs—both in terms of managing client emotions as well as the workers' managing their own. The New Jersey Agricultural Products Agent 2 who inspects and grades poultry products has far less variability on the job than social service counselors endure, and minimal amounts of relational work compared to the other two occupational listings, yet is compensated handsomely in comparison. While the driver's license examiner earns less than the other two positions, the examiner is required to meet and greet the public and interact with them as they apply and are examined for driver's licenses, receive them, or are denied. The social service counselor has an extraordinary amount of relational work yet earns only slightly more on average than the inspector checking truckloads of melons.

The ability required of the Illinois Meat and Poultry Inspector (with a starting monthly salary of $2,964) to "tolerate exposure to unpleasant odors in slaughter houses," and that required of the Oregon Social Service Specialist 1 (with a starting salary of $2,846, some $118 less than the Inspector) to "protect[ing] the lives of children" are compensated at comparable levels. Yet, even taking

Table 7.3

Breakdown of Job Occupants by Job Title

	Job Title	Salary Range	Women	Men	Percentage Women
Illinois	Public Service Representative	$2,160–$3,380	417	217	65.8
New Jersey	Examination Technician, Motor Vehicle Commission	$2,343–$3,178	38	27	58.5
Oregon	Transportation Services Representative 1	$2,067–$2,847	183	95	65.8
Illinois	Meat and Poultry Inspector	$2,964–$3,737	9	70	11.4
New Jersey	Agricultural Products Agent 2	$2,672–$3,639	6	15	28.6
Oregon	Shipping Point Inspector 2	$1,907–$2,595	3	5	37.5
Illinois	Child Welfare Specialist	$3,207–$4,738	562	174	76.4
New Jersey	Family Service Specialist 2	$3,533–$4,843	956	288	76.8
Oregon	Social Service Specialist 1	$2,846–$3,955	872	217	80.1

Sources: Illinois Department of Central Management Services, October 2005; New Jersey Department of Personnel, September 2005; Oregon Department of Administrative Services, Human Resource Services Division, June 2005.

into account any cost of living differentials between Illinois and Oregon, such "compensable equivalency" is difficult to reconcile.

The qualification for "heavy lifting" required of the New Jersey Agricultural Products Agent 2 and the ability "to perform heavy manual labor" and to have "good eyesight and sense of smell to detect irregularities in fruits, vegetables, or nuts" required of the Oregon Shipping Point Inspector 2 suggest that a greater market premium is placed on physical strength, vision, and olfactory senses than the more nuanced and higher-order skills required of emotion work. Compare the following skill sets: The Illinois Meat and Poultry Inspector (with a salary range of $2,964–$3,737) is required, in part, to "exercise sound judgment in the determination of wholesome meat and poultry products." The judgment required of the New Jersey Family Service Specialist 2 (with a salary range of $3,533–$4,843) in assessing "alleged abuse and neglect referrals" and in evaluating "applicants for foster and adoption care" is far more complicated and the stakes are much higher. Yet the salary differential is marginal ($142 per week at the entry level).

Physical labor is easy to capture but emotional labor is more nuanced. Listen to an employee of the Department of Corrections, expressing her frustration about her situation:

> My husband's job is a physical job and he can't understand, to think that you're sitting in an office, nice air-conditioned climate control—he's in a building that's 100 degrees some days, you know—and he can't understand how that can be frustrating. I said, yeah, it is. I said I would rather be out, cutting trees down or something, you know? . . . I'm responsible for an $18 million budget that we don't overspend . . . and we've got people that are responsible for heating and cooling and ventilation gauges [that] make three times what I make.

Jobs involving emotional labor require their own toolkit. In contrast to jobs that have few emotional labor demands, such as food inspector, the tools employed in relational work are not tangible. Compare the tools that are essential to the work of the Meat and Poultry Inspector as he "incises organs and glands of slaughtered meat producing animals" and "weighs additives and quantities of water at various times in the processing procedure," to those that are utilized in "people work." A correctional staff instructor provides an illustration:

> I mean you can't see it and it's hard to even write about but you feel it and you know and I probably—because I'm programmed to think that way that it comes out and it's like this little thing that says—it's like a meter. You're going over the edge. You know this is wrong. You can't do this. Like yesterday is an example. A young man [prisoner] who watered my plants comes in and they're good at manipulation, and he tells me, he's real nice . . . he said . . . I need to borrow something . . . I'd like to have one of the red pens like you

have. And he'd done a real nice job for me but that little meter inside telling me how am I going to say this in a way that I don't offend him, but he can't have that pen because I will get in trouble for that, you know. How am I going to say this appropriately without offending him . . . without hurting him. . . . That [is the] gauge that we're referring to.

Listen to a correctional counselor characterizing his work and the tools of his trade:

> [An inmate] can go from cooperative to uncooperative, fine to suicidal, you know . . . learning to read people . . . I just watch the body language. That's the biggest thing I do . . . I watch the eyes. The eyes tell a ton. Hand movements, you know, shoulders—you know it all plays into the game of reading the body language to tell if this person—is he gonna—is he docile or is he gonna be violent.

Multitasking is another key element of "people work," often in high-stress and chaotic environments, such as a records office:

> Multitasking . . . it's just the nature of the beast . . . you have to be able to juggle several things at one time . . . we do a lot of getting interrupted in the middle of calculating an inmate's sentence over here to answer the phone to go look up why they're B graded, or C graded, or Can you send me 6 inmates to work release? Even though you're in the middle of checking out a warrant of an inmate or something has to be right now—how I deal with it? My supervisor says I'm good at multitasking. I just can focus—set this down, close this off in my mind and then jump over here and do this. That's how I personally do it.

The concept of neutral competence provides a further window into the distinguishing skill characteristics of these three occupations. The food inspector can rely on this modus operandi; the driver's license examiner and the social service worker are not so similarly situated. The Oregon Shipping Point Inspector is required to "impartially render decisions regarding fresh fruit and vegetable grades and condition." The Illinois Child Welfare Specialist does not have this same bureaucratic imperative. Indeed, s/he is required to provide "direct service intervention" by reliance on a much broader range of organizational behaviors—including artifice—in order to do the job well. Read how an investigator describes his ability to become a chameleon and transform his behavior at will in order to elicit information:

> I've just got the ability to mold myself in whatever's required in that particular situation. I can turn it on and off at whatever I have to do . . . you have to be able to communicate with people out on the street . . . I can just be whoever I have to be; if I have to be nice guy and you know I'm fully comfortable talking to whoever, whatever, I can cozy up and talk to the neighborhood drug addict and get him to give me information.

Such emotion work is characteristic of relational work in all its human complexity. Inspecting a carton of marionberries for signs of rot is hardly commensurate with inspecting a child's home for signs of abuse and neglect. Or to put it even more bluntly, dealing with emotional scars is not in the same bailiwick as dealing with bruised tomatoes. Being a "mother hen" to her "chicks," as an employee of an adult transition center put it, and inspecting poultry require very different skill sets. Yet the compensation that attaches to each of these occupations fails to capture much difference between them. By naturalizing and essentializing[5] the work required of the social service counselor—work that affects the lives of families and children for years—the job is compensated at about the same level as that of the food inspector. Though this may reflect "market value," it leads us to ponder the wisdom of the market. As citizens' expectations for public services become more demanding, governmental agencies need to staff operations with the best workers. And the best workers expect to be compensated for the skills they bring to their work.

Conclusion

The skills that ensure the construction and maintenance of interpersonal relations are complex. Their expression is at the heart of interactive service work and public service. That emotional labor is legitimate work is surely undeniable. It can no longer be explained away as "invisible work" that women somehow naturally (and benevolently) perform; men perform it also. In this chapter, we have sketched its contours. The stories of those at the front line of public service delivery provide the color. A 911 call taker tells us, "Well, my first night here I had a murder. The guy killed both his parents, poisoned them to death, and had a handgun, and the officer is walking in the kitchen, and I'm like, I think the guy's got a gun—you know, that's what we deal with."

This 911 dispatcher knows that how he handles this one call, and the several other calls that he is simultaneously working, will be a determining factor in the life of this officer. It is his sole responsibility to elicit information from the son who has just committed a double murder in order to protect his police colleague. By any measure, the skills inherent in this work, and the work itself, are complex, legitimate, and necessary.

Salary inequities cannot be corrected in reality when they are understood only in concept. For human resource specialists, we encourage scrutiny of job descriptions, performance evaluations, and pay scales—scrutiny that will identify the disconnect between skills that are required, recognized, and remunerated. If a decade of reinventing government and performance management has taught us anything, surely we have learned that industrial-era systems fail to accommodate the service exchange.

Emotional labor is a missing link in the chain that produces lower wages for jobs that are held primarily by women. The requirements of emotional labor, predominantly emotional labor that involves *caritas*, result in work skills and abilities that are taken for granted, not listed as bona fide requirements of the job, and not compensated. Emotion management is a bona fide occupational skill, essential to effective job performance. It is the essence of "people work" in all its manifestations.

Once one sees emotional labor as compensable, one also sees the shortcomings of traditional job descriptions and pay scales. As we move farther and farther away from organizations designed to operate assembly lines, we must devise new structures that capture today's work and skill requirements. There is no better time than now to look again at that which worked in the past but has outlived its usefulness. "Seeing" the largely invisible emotional components of job classification and compensation systems enables us to more fully comprehend the tenacity of pay inequity in the workplace and to fashion remedies.

Notes

1. This finding differs from that of Guy and Newman (2004, p. 291), who report that wages of government workers fare better than all sectors of the economy, citing 2002 Government Accounting Office data. The reported widening of the pay gap for government workers between 2002 and 2005 is of significant interest and merits further exploration. We note it here as a point of departure from Guy and Newman (2004).

2. Illinois presents an interesting comparison with New Jersey, Oregon, and Florida. It has greater salary inequity between men and women in Exempt and Senior Administrator categories (See Appendix E). Working for the State of Illinois is not for the political neophyte. The state has a history (even tradition) of patronage politics. According to Robert Dees, compensation analyst in the Compensation Unit, Division of Technical Services, Central Management Services Agency, 1 percent of all state jobs are "double exempt"—exempt from *Rutan (Rutan v. Republican Party of Illinois (88–1872), 497 U.S. 62 (1990))* and exempt from the salary limit for new hires of up to 10 percent over previous private sector earnings (coded as Civil Service 43). People in these positions are responsible for administration of public policy and/or oversight of policy implementation for agencies/departments that do not receive any federal funding; 1.1 percent of all men and 0.9 percent of all women in Illinois occupy these positions. (Note: This does not include Secretary of State employees.) All jobs classified as "double exempt" fall into the Exempt category; the Career and Senior Administrators do not have this classification. Of the total Exempt employees, 21.2 percent are double exempt, and 14.3 percent of all female and 33.3 percent of all male employees in the state hold positions in this classification (Robert Dees, personal communication, December 6, 2005). According to Kent Redfield, University of Illinois at Springfield professor of political science and a noted expert on Illinois state politics, "The linkage of patronage and party systems to employment in Illinois is probably negative because of the promotion of party people who tend to be white male and, insofar as their 'diversity,' tends to involve traditional gender stereotypes which reinforces gender roles." Double exempt positions tend to be filled based on a "politics that is power and job oriented rather than policy oriented, resulting in the promotion/hiring of the politically connected and the politically faithful" (personal

communication, December 14, 2005). Roy Williams, Jr., executive director of the Illinois Association of Minorities in Government, puts it more bluntly: "In Illinois in particular, we play politics all the way down to the person who's raking leaves, picking up garbage. . . . [They] owe their job to a politician" (Wetterich 2005, p. 2). This strong political culture may serve to reinforce traditional gender dynamics.

3. Florida is not included in this comparison because the state switched to broadbanded job classifications in 2002 with salary ranges extending as wide as $100,000 per classification. This precludes meaningful comparison to similar jobs in other states with traditional paybands.

4. Of note, Spencer and Spencer (1993) and Hofrichter and Spencer (1996) refer to competencies with "below-the-waterline" characteristics. They present an "iceberg model," which shows "competencies as below the water line—and thus hard to see and measure." Mohrman, Cohen, and Mohrman (1995) make a similar argument about knowledge workers, asserting that no one can directly observe much of their labor. Their work is varied, abstract, and nonroutine. Emotional labor fits within this model—it requires spontaneous adaptation to the situation. It is not programmable, and the skills required to perform it are unobservable.

5. Naturalizing the work means that, consistent with the stereotype that women are nurturers, it is deemed "natural" for female social service counselors to care for others. This line of thought assumes that there is no inherent "skill" attached to the performance because it comes "naturally" to women. Essentializing the work means that, because the work of female social service counselors is characteristic of the work of all women in the helping professions, it follows that there is nothing unique, meaning skilled, about the work of female social service counselors.

— 8 —

Emotion Work Present and Future: Trends in Relational Occupations

I don't think you can ever be prepared for the first person that calls you up. My first suicide was—I had a gentleman who called up and said I just wanted someone to hear—he shot himself in the mouth and the whole time while the officer was getting there, all I hear are sounds—you know while he's dying and so I don't think you can ever be prepared for that. And I was also on the radio when an officer was shot and killed. I was the last person he talked to. . . .

Occupations with great emotional labor demands are among the fastest growing, while jobs susceptible to automation are on the decline. This fact points to the importance of relational work to the economy in general and to government, specifically. In this chapter, we look at how public service jobs have increased in number and to what extent they are projected to grow over the next decade. Discussion begins with the trade-off between cost efficiencies and emotion work.

Reliance on automated phone lines, contracted workers, and minimal staffing levels have distinct cost advantages, but each lowers service quality. As the trade-off is made between emotion work and reduced costs, program outcomes are affected. We do not quarrel with the need to keep costs down, but we urge sensitivity to the trade-off that is made when live voices are exchanged for impersonal recorded messages.

164

Intangible Benefits Versus Tangible Costs

Service work is labor intensive and labor is expensive. Automated phone lines are an attempt to replace relational work with information technology. To respond to simple informational needs, this is cost efficient. When recorded voicemail misses the mark, however, cost savings become expensive. Clearly, tension exists between the incentives to reduce costs using automation and the need to enhance personal service.

Agencies reduce costs not only by using automation; they also attempt savings by contracting with workers who have little if any commitment to the mission of the agency (Mastracci and Thompson 2005). Minimal staffing levels are another means of reducing labor costs. When operations are routine, this works okay, but when crises arise and hundreds or thousands of citizens are affected, there are too few workers to handle the demand. During hurricane or wildfire season, personnel budgets may be too lean to fully staff first responders in preparation for a worst-case scenario. Agencies would be overstaffed 90 percent of the time and over budget 100 percent of the time. Even in minor emergencies, workers can be deluged. For example, 911 call takers point out the problem when there is an accident at a heavily traveled intersection. Every driver who passes the accident picks up a cell phone and calls 911, and the lines become clogged.

> I don't think the public realizes how poorly staffed we are and how really unable we are to even tread water in a bad storm or other major event. You know, when you call Comcast (cable TV) you get that recording—we're aware of outages in such and such an area. We can't put [a recording] on 911 that "we're aware of the car accident at Ocala and Pensacola."

Human service agencies are usually understaffed, while the demand for services continues to increase. For example, when caseworkers see their caseloads grow beyond their capacity to keep up with the troubled families they are assigned, service suffers as they lose touch with families in their care. Describing the pressures on attorneys who work at the Office of the Public Guardian, we heard this:

> [T]here's a lot of pressure on the attorneys; they've got a huge caseload; it's a lot of pressure; they're in court every other day; they have to go out and see their clients; you know, it's not for everybody. You can see people that are overwhelmed and just can't get a grasp on their caseload. You've got five cases that are just going to hell, basically, all at the same time; they're not on top of their cases the way it's needed.

Both automation and understaffing improve productivity in terms of dollars and cents in the short run. In the long run, however, quality of service suffers. Why? Because the service demands of the work are ignored. Workers cannot do their full job—perform the emotion work required to be in touch with troubled families while keeping up to date with their other job demands. Demoralized workers leave or, worse, stay, but tend to their paperwork and meetings while ignoring the relational work that makes the difference between pushing paper and making a difference in a client's life. Turnover is expensive because experienced workers who walk out the door take organizational memory with them. Their departure also weakens the trust between clients and the agency. Newcomers must be trained, and the revolving door of recruiting, training, and new assignments starts over with each departure.

Our point is that a focus on tangible costs with little appreciation for the hidden investment that comes with emotion work results in service delivery problems that, at a superficial level, look like incompetence. Upon investigation, one sees a vacuum that is left when workers do not have the time to perform the "whole" job. Thus, increased "productivity" reaches a point of diminishing returns in relational work. The reason for this is obvious in the following account of a call received shortly after the attack on the World Trade Center, when Americans were hypersensitive to unexpected events. Had the call taker not been attentive to each and every call, she would have missed this report of a homicide:

> [A] young woman killed her mother and called and reported it right smack in the middle of a plane going over and causing a sonic boom. This was right after 9/11. Everyone called to report a boom somewhere since they didn't know what it was. Right in the middle of all those calls this girl called to report that she had stabbed her mom. Fortunately the call taker didn't answer the call by asking if this is about the sonic boom because there would have been a language barrier problem: the young woman was Chinese and English was her second language. [The call taker] listened to her long enough to realize, o-o-h, this is something very bad and it's not at all related to the boom.

There is a curvilinear relationship between costs and benefits. The problem with trying to align employee cost with service outcome is that the curve fails to reflect important inputs in the form of emotion work. When it is not performed, it is not immediately noticeable in terms of diminished returns. Unlike the withdrawal of funds, which has a direct and obvious effect—the utilities are turned off at the office—the withdrawal of emotion work manifests itself over time in lack of trust on the part of clients, client failure to keep appointments, and client failure to disclose information that would change how the worker interacts with the client. This is the corrosive effect of decreasing quality over time. Service failure is the ultimate result, but much damage has been done by the time the effect manifests itself through usual productivity measures. In other words, the parabola that is normally used to depict the cost/benefit curve is too blunt to be of value because it ignores invisible costs and benefits, and costs that only manifest as they accumulate over time.

With these constraints in mind, the following projections for employment growth show that service jobs will far outpace other types of work. These issues—trade-offs between authentic service quality and automated or superficial encounters—will continue to plague human capital planners and budget officers.

Government Employment

Every two years, the U.S. Bureau of Labor Statistics (BLS) publishes ten-year projections of changes in employment. The forecast shown in Figure 8.1 provides estimates to 2014.[1] As shown, employment in local government has experienced more growth since 1984 than either the state or federal level combined. This pattern is expected to continue through 2014. State-level employment has increased modestly, and federal government employment has declined. Both are expected to continue these trends in the future if state and federal agencies continue their current habit of contracting out much of their work. Doing so takes workers "off the books" so that they are not counted.

The greatest amount of emotion work is performed at the local level. It is at the level of cities and counties that the responsibility lies for day-to-day emergency preparedness, firefighters, law enforcement, public education, public health, and family and children's services. Some of these services are also provided at the state level. But both state and federal government focus more on policy guidance and rely on local governments to be their hands and feet to implement services.

All projected growth in the U.S. economy for the next decade occurs in the service-providing sector. State and local government employment comprises the largest portion of employment in the service sector and is projected to remain the largest industry within this sector in 2014 (Berman 2005, Table 1). Specifically, "educational services, health care and social assistance, and professional and business services represent the [service] industry sectors with the fastest projected employment growth" (Berman 2005, p. 47). Jobs in educational services will be both newly created ones and openings due to retirements and attrition, while most of the increases in health services in

Figure 8.1 **Employment in Federal, State, and Local Government, 1984 to 2004, and Projected to 2014** (in thousands)

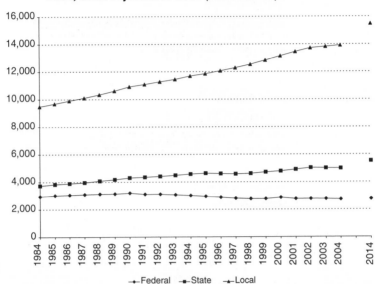

Sources: U.S. Bureau of Labor Statistics Current Employment Survey (1984–2004) and Berman 2005.

government will come from replacing workers who leave or retire.

In health services, state-level employment has declined and is predicted to continue on this trend while local-level employment increases. In all other service delivery areas, the number of jobs in "state and local government is anticipated to grow as the demand for community, health, and protective services expand with population growth and with the need to assume more of the responsibilities formerly borne by the federal government" (Berman 2005, p. 54). The devolution of service provision from the federal level to state and local government, along with the increase in contracted services, is reflected in historical decreases in the number of federal jobs. This is a trend expected to continue through the next decade.

Twenty percent of employment growth in health care and social assistance will be in government, and almost all of the growth in educational services takes place in the public sector. Education comprises more than half of all state and local government employment growth, and increases are due to initiatives such as universal preschool, all-day kindergarten, and reduced class size. All of these "should buoy the employment demand for educational services provided by local governments" through the next decade (Berman 2005, p. 54).

Figure 8.2 displays the breakdown of our respondents by their occupa-

Figure 8.2 **Occupational Categories of Survey Respondents**

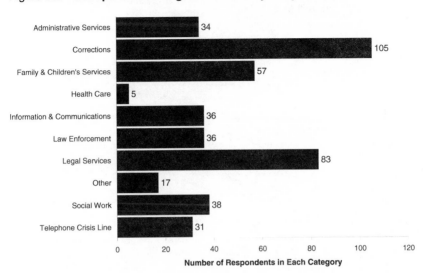

Number of Respondents in Each Category

tions.[2] Employment in our five occupations—attorneys, paralegals, social workers, dispatchers, and corrections officers—has grown over time and most are projected to grow at a faster-than-average rate in the next decade.

Occupations in legal services—lawyers and paralegals—are forecast to increase from new job growth as well as replacement needs, and about 25 percent of that growth takes place in government (Hecker 2005, p. 73). The number of social worker jobs is expected to increase by 22 percent, and the increase in the number of police, fire, and ambulance dispatcher jobs is close behind at 15.9 percent. Employment as bailiffs, corrections officers, and jailers is expected to grow more moderately, 7 percent into the next decade. Figure 8.3 depicts the changes in the numbers of these jobs over time and their projected changes to 2014[3] across all levels of government employment.

In most occupations, job openings from replacement needs outnumber job openings from employment growth (Hecker 2005, p. 78). Replacement needs and new job creation will create opportunities in all levels of government, but the state and local levels are expected to gain the most (Toossi 2005).

As Figure 8.3 shows, most of the jobs included in this study have shown some growth over the past two decades, and all of them are forecast to grow through the next decade. Although police, fire, and ambulance dispatchers are projected to grow by 15.9 percent, their numbers are relatively small compared to the other occupations in this chart. Corrections have expanded over time, and with "three strikes" laws in many states, overcrowding

169

Figure 8.3   **Occupations Examined in This Study, 1984 to 2004, and Projected to 2014**

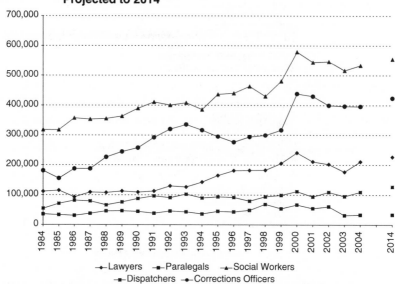

Lawyers   Paralegals   Social Workers
Dispatchers   Corrections Officers

Sources: U.S. Bureau of Labor Statistics Current Population Survey Outgoing Rotation Groups 1984–2004, and BLS projections 2014.

and new facilities have generated job growth, but our interviewees note that this job growth has not kept pace with demand. An administrator in corrections notes:

> I would say the larger stress has come from high up and it certainly isn't personalized. They wouldn't know me and that's just fine, but the demands of trying to reach the budgets that they've given us, trying to do more with less—that's just been the standard cry—do more with less. And understanding that at this point we pretty much have come to the end of our rope. That there's not much more we can do with less.

Several interviewees attributed their work-related stress to administrative and budget cuts rather than the nature of their work. Another corrections administrator concurs: "The first housing unit I worked on . . . had an officer at the door; today, they have one officer in that building." Resource allocations by agency generate jealousies and stress. In corrections, for instance, resources are allocated based on the number of beds at the facility. One significant threshold is 200: an institution that is officially classified as a 200-bed facility receives more resources than a smaller institution would, but overcrowding can result in both a 200-bed facility housing 300 inmates and a 100-bed facility housing 175 inmates. But due to budget cuts, the resources cannot be reallocated to address the increased demand.

Taxpayer wariness of rate hikes constrains growth in government employment, but the need for these emotional-labor-intensive services has not diminished. Jobs in social work and law have increased, and again, agencies like the Office of the Public Guardian are limited in their ability to hire more people, but that does not prevent the caseloads from growing. One attorney underscores the stress of working within austere fiscal conditions, and tells how budget cuts can threaten one's ability to accomplish an agency's mission:

> I started in a court room with about 700 children that I was representing. . . .
> [T]here were all these policies about how you're supposed to read every piece
> of paper in the pile . . . with 700 piles it's not possible that I'm doing what
> they're asking me to do and what I was doing was putting out fires and not
> really doing a lot of advocacy.

Evidence of increasing demands in the face of budget cuts and hiring freezes provides an interesting context within which to examine employment trends over time. Occupations in government that require significant degrees of emotional labor have grown. If the evidence in the vignette above characterizes other agencies and understaffing is a widespread problem, then increases in these highly relational jobs can be presumed to represent a fraction of the demand for emotional labor skills.

Employment Trends in Other Jobs with Emotional Labor Demands

Chapter 4 described the capacity of the O*NET Online database to identify occupations that involve high degrees of emotional labor. The database is searchable using 35 separate job skill keywords, alone or in combination. Nine of these 35 job skills were determined to comprise the emotional labor construct, based on empirical analyses and the theoretical foundation for emotional labor. Moreover, these 9 skills map nicely to the survey items we use to capture emotional labor in our data. To identify a larger group of occupations that involve high levels of emotion management demands, we conducted a search of all occupations in O*NET, using 9 emotional labor skills. Of the 60 occupations that matched at least 7 of those 9 emotional labor skills, about two-thirds are in government. These 38 jobs fall roughly into three categories: administration, education, and health services. Managers and administrators are projected to hold steady or increase slightly. Secretaries and administrative assistants, jobs whose numbers plummeted from the mid-1990s until about 2002, have leveled off and are projected to hold steady or increase slightly.

In contrast to the trends in these administrative occupations, employment in education and health services demonstrates more dramatic change. Elementary school teacher occupations have experienced growth and will continue to increase through the next decade. Teacher's aide jobs have increased at a lesser, but still significant, rate of about 50 percent since 1984. Secondary school teacher jobs fell moderately between 1984 and 1998, rose through 2001, and then declined again, but the forecast to 2014 projects somewhat stronger growth. In government, opportunities in nursing and "other educational services" have hovered between 300,000 and 400,000 jobs since 1984, with a slight increase projected for each through 2014.

Conclusion

Throughout these chapters, we argue that emotional labor is a critical component of fully one-third of all occupations, and that it is fundamental to public service and public management practice. In the best of circumstances, emotional labor is recognized so that job applicants can be screened for it, new employees can receive training in it, all employees can be evaluated for their adeptness at it, and especially skilled employees can be compensated for excelling in its performance. A call taker who trains new hires to answer 911 calls explains the skills that are sought:

> For the most part, we're looking for people that can think outside the box. We've got five basic questions that we ask, but you have to be able to take the response that you get and think, "Okay, this person just doesn't sound right—something else is going on here or the story doesn't sound right; the pieces aren't fitting together." You have to use your spider sense a little bit.
>
> *Interviewer:* What do you mean by "spider sense"?
> *Answer:* You know, that little feeling when your hairs turn up on your arms or on the back of your neck. Things that you pick up on that are gonna make or break what happens to the officer when they get on the scene and if you miss someone in the background hollering that they have a gun or you miss the popping noise in the background or you miss something critical you've now put the caller's life or the officer's life in jeopardy.

The need to recognize emotional labor is on the rise. Evidence from our interviews indicates that the demand for emotion-intensive work only increases, despite, and sometimes because of, hiring freezes or attrition. Government workers face greater and greater emotion management demands and fewer resources to address those demands. Many occupations with great emotional labor demands are among the fastest growing in Department of Labor forecasts through the next decade. Moreover, some of those highly relational occupations have been eliminated due to automation and outsourcing. Combining the data on employment growth in demanding emotional labor occupations with evidence that hiring has not kept pace with agency needs may suggest that the increases in emotional labor jobs in government represent no more than a shadow of the real demand for emotional labor in government.

The fact that there is a large service component to public service jobs should not surprise us. The need to select workers who are skilled in relational work should not surprise us. The lack of awareness of these facts is what should surprise us.

Notes

1. Historical data from the Current Population Survey (CPS) and Current Employment Statistics (CES) survey are used to track changes in employment by occupation for two decades leading up to the BLS projections. Together, these data illustrate the growth and decline of the occupations that we have examined most closely in this study, as well as changes in government employment overall, for more than thirty years.

2. This survey question permitted multiple answers. For example, a social worker for the Office of the Public Guardian may have reported that she worked in corrections and family and children services and social work. A total of 100 respondents chose more than one answer. Of these, 66 chose 2 occupational areas, 31 chose 3 areas, two chose 4 areas, and 1 person chose 5 areas.

3. Two precautions must be considered when examining Current Population Survey (CPS) data. First, the survey structure underwent a change in 1994, a change that has caused some researchers to avoid comparing some data from before and after that year. Second, the occupational classification system was altered significantly in 2000. Some occupations remained intact while others were created anew or split into separate occupations or reconstructed in another way. The BLS cautions against comparing across this classification transformation. This may help explain why trends appear to change in 2000: many occupations are measured differently using the new classification system. The effects of these data changes are found in all charts using CPS data before and after 2000.

— 9 —

Implications for Theory, Research, and Practice

Most scholarship on public service jobs begins with an unexamined assumption of the industrial notion of "work." Job analyses, recruitment, classification, compensation, and performance appraisals are all based on this paradigm. Even forward-thinking models of strategic human resource management are rooted in these assumptions. The leap of faith which assumes that all types of public service work are alike in all essential ways has allowed us to ignore a simple verity: person-to-person interactions require skills that are not called upon in person-to-object interactions.

Failure to acknowledge this difference has caused managers and scholars alike to ignore the essential components of the person-to-person service transaction. Job descriptions remain silent about the job demands that characterize most public service work. First, a quick review of how we arrived at this narrow conceptualization of work.

The History of "Paid" Work

Any history of work traces the transition of Western civilization from hunting-gathering societies to farming to city-states to urbanized communities (see, for example, Tausky 1984). As city-states emerged, kings needed scribes to record taxes, bookkeepers to keep records, and laborers to maintain public works. As the division of labor became more specialized, craft guilds developed, and their members were masons, woodworkers, weavers, smiths, carpenters, and bakers. As city-states gave way to metropolitan communities, crafts became more specialized and demand grew. Manufacturing developed.

To make a long story very short, by the 1800s the Industrial Revolution was under way. Far more potent than any political upheaval, the Industrial Revolution changed Western civilization because it determined where people lived (in cities) and their socioeconomic status (based on the type of work they performed). And it framed our attention on an arbitrary and compelling definition of work, an essential component of which is to explain the relative position of the subordinate to the superior, as well as the activities that the subordinate is to perform (Anthony 1977; Simon 1962).

"Work" became the term used to denote effort that is performed at the employer's behest and is directly linked to behavior that has a tangible outcome. Work in this sense requires deference, and the worker, as functionary, is the instrument of the employer. To differentiate voluntary work from servitude, an "objective" focus on skills grew popular. Jobs were specialized, designed, and circumscribed to focus only on the physical and cognitive skills necessary to perform requisite tasks. Such a targeted focus on empirically verifiable work behaviors created a system that seemed scientific, objective, and efficient. It suited assembly-line production processes and protected against patronage. That merit systems attempt to depersonalize work is emblematic of this paradigm. Thus, a theory of work in public service looks just like a theory of work in manufacturing. There has been scant attention directed at challenging this narrow conceptualization and its surrounding beliefs and fundamental values.

From Industrial Paradigm to Service Paradigm

By acknowledging emotional labor, we add "noise" to the long silence in our understanding of work. That which is not mentioned in this history is the requirement that in order for one person to enter into exchanges with another, there must exist the emotional intelligence and skill necessary to consummate the transaction. When person-to-person interaction is required, attributes that determine the success or failure of the interaction are subtle. As if our notion of work were constructed by watching employees from the comfort of a distant observation platform, subtleties are not seen. Because they are not seen, they are neither counted nor valued. Like the comparison between a weed and a flower, the difference rests in utility. If it is deemed to serve no purpose, it is a weed; if it is of use, it is a flower and is assigned a market value.

Economic theory holds that people work for instrumental reasons: they work to provide goods and services in return for money, which they spend on goods and services, and they work harder to get more. This does not explain the more interesting components of work performance. For example, the satisfying quality in work is itself complex and individualistic. Performance requires a mixture of skills, senses, demands, and exigencies. Workers react differently, influenced by their own temperaments, expectations, and perceptions. Even on the high tide of economic theory, workers imbue their work with moral duty and transcendental purpose.

The setting of work is as important as its content. The aim of public service work is responsibility toward the community—the "other." The insight, anticipation, and tenor of the communication between persons prior to, during, and after the exchange requires energy, focus, and sensing—in other words, emotional labor.

Emotion Work

The neglect of emotion stands in the way of a comprehensive understanding of work behavior. The word "emotion" is derived from the Latin verb *emovere*, which means "to move out, stir up, agitate." In terms of work behavior, emotion includes not only an appraisal of how something will affect the worker, but also an attraction or repulsion. "Emotional appraisal" means an evaluative judgment—usually instantaneous—of good or bad, pleasurable or dangerous. The sequence happens this way: There is a target to which the emotion relates; this target is causal in nature; the emotion experienced is purposive and the motivating target is rationally related to the emotion caused (Kiesling 2000).

Emotional competence varies with the individual. At high skill levels, it prepares the worker to dig through considerable complexity and make a reasoned, often nonverbal, instantaneous response. Less-skilled workers make inappropriate responses or responses that fail to facilitate the interaction. Emotion work is learned, just as is cognitive work. The human development literature tells us that a person's emotional education begins with earliest childhood and is acquired from parents, teachers, and other role models and authority figures. Another source of learning is on our own through a natural process of "figuring things out" (Kiesling 2000). Learning continues throughout the lifetime, although the older we get the more difficult it becomes to modify our fundamental emotional patterns or to increase our emotional repertoire.[1]

How does this play out in a work setting? Let's say that a 911 call taker answers an incoming call. The caller is screaming, "He's got a gun and he is banging on my door!" The call taker hears—and senses—the fear in the caller's voice and feels her own fear rise in regard to what she can expect to hear next. Sensing the situation, she immediately suppresses her own emotion and in a matter-of-fact voice, asks the most important question: What is your address? Securing that information, she must keep the caller on the line while simultaneously issuing a dispatch to a law enforcement officer. In this case, the job involves suppression of her own reaction so that she can manage the emotion of the caller.

Consider the opposite scenario. A hysterical caller is on the line, screaming. The 911 call taker cannot understand what the caller is saying. To quiet the caller, the call taker screams back. The caller is quieted by the unexpected response long enough to listen to the call taker as she then asks for the caller's location so that she can send help. Both of these reactions are stimulated in response to the caller, but the call taker had to make an instantaneous decision as to whether she should use a calming voice or a screaming voice in order to secure the information she needs to serve the citizen—to dispatch a law enforcement officer to the scene. The perceived need is noted immediately, and the information is processed and translated into an emotional response back to the caller. The emotional domain is as legitimate as the cognitive domain, and is more immediate and forceful.

The Ghost in the Room

A treasure trove of fascinating insights—and questions—arises from this exploration of emotion work. Chapter 1 began on the premise that emotional labor is ghostlike: some see it, some do not. When job candidates are interviewed, when the ability to work well in teams is required, when working amid conflict is important, and when jobs have high burnout rates, no one mentions the ghost, for it has no name. These chapters have attempted to illuminate the irony, to give the ghost a name, to provide empirical evidence to legitimize its presence.

The pursuit of a vocabulary that captures emotion work continues: Is it verbal judo? Putting on a game face? Rapport building? *Caritas*? Deep acting? Good cop, bad cop? Spider sense? Stage left? Emotional teflon? Mask, engagement, anesthesia, armor, mirror? Each of these terms highlights a particular dimension of artful affect. For example, we know that it requires management of one's own demeanor as well as the emotions of the other. In the words of one 911 call taker, "[A]ll you are is a voice. You're gonna be a good voice to help 'em or you're gonna be a voice that irritates them; you're gonna be a voice that is gonna give them complete confidence that someone's gonna get there quickly to help 'em and everything's gonna be okay." And, it requires instantaneous adjustments in response to changing circumstances. The ability to develop rapport is key, as evidenced in this description of the work of one call taker:

She only works part-time but she has developed the skills on the telephone to be able to get information out of people that other people couldn't. We had a guy call 911 over and over and over and over and over and over and over again and would say things like, the house is on fire. He did it every day for weeks, 20 times a day. It was a false address and we finally found the kid because she took the time to establish rapport with him. I don't think he gave her an address but he gave her the name of his father, and she found the address. He was just in last week to apologize to everybody.

Emotional labor is inherent to effective public service. It adds the "live" dimension to knowledge work in person-to-person transactions and requires the employee to "work feelingly."

To repeat the definition that captures artful affect as developed in Chapter 4:

Emotional labor is work that requires the engagement, suppression, and/or evocation of the worker's emotions in order to get the job done. The goal of this work is to influence the actions of the other. The performance encompasses a range of personal and interpersonal skills, including the ability to evoke and display emotions one does not actually feel, to sense the affect of the other and alter one's own affect accordingly, and to elicit the desired emotional response from the other. The ability to sense the affect of the other is accomplished through intuition and communication. Simply put, emotional labor requires affective sensitivity and flexibility with one's own emotions as well as those of the other.

The interviews and survey data reported in these chapters reveal corners, curves, and twists to emotional labor and contribute to a rapidly building cache of knowledge about the non-cognitive aspects of public service work. This is best summarized in an illustration. Figure 9.1 shows how it factors into job performance. It is an emotional performance that is bought and sold as a commodity; it is regulated by job demands; is organizationally mandated; and at the same time results from the autonomous discretion of the employee.

Explanation of Model

The model depicted in Figure 9.1 was constructed from data gathered in the survey of workers at the Office of the Public Guardian, the Department of Corrections, and the Tallahassee Police Department. To capture complex job attitudes and experiences, we created four index variables: *Waste of Time, Job Satisfaction, Burnout,* and *Efficacious EL.*

Valuing One's Work

To get a sense of how workers value their performance, we generated two additional index variables to capture whether work is viewed as a waste of time or whether it is worthwhile. A positive sense of value is defined by respondents'

Figure 9.1   Relationship Between Emotional Labor and Affective Outcomes

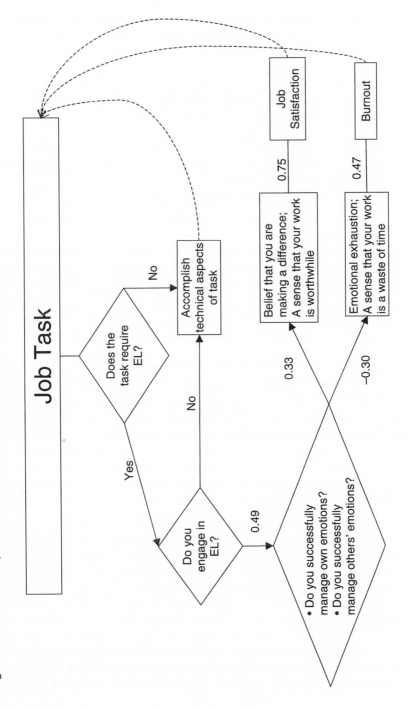

179

level of agreement with one survey item: "I am making a difference in my job." We call this variable *Job Makes a Difference*. A dimmer view of one's work is defined by the following four items, which we label *Waste of Time:*

- I feel like my work is a waste of time and energy.
- I leave work feeling optimistic (reversed).
- I feel like my work makes a difference (reversed).
- I leave work feeling energized (reversed).

These variables were correlated with burnout, job satisfaction, and efficacious emotional labor, as described in Chapter 5.

The illustration in Figure 9.1 simplifies public service by dividing tasks into two categories: those that demand emotional labor and those that do not. As workers encounter a task, they determine whether its successful execution requires emotion work. If not, then the technical aspects of the job are completed and the employee can move on to another job task. If the task requires emotional labor, then there remains a choice to exert emotional labor or not. If the worker fails to meet those emotional labor demands, or if, as discussed in the last chapter, the demands require the worker to pretend to feel emotions they do not actually feel, we hypothesize that this leads to emotional exhaustion, which decreases job satisfaction and increases burnout. Either outcome—burnout or job satisfaction—is then followed immediately by the demands of yet another task. The entire cycle starts again. This circular process can exacerbate dissatisfaction when *false face* emotion work is required, or can heighten one's sense of accomplishment and level of experience. Figure 9.1 illustrates the cumulative nature of emotional labor: prior success can bolster confidence and improve future "performances," and bad experiences color future encounters as well. Correlation coefficients are attached to several paths, and these are listed in Table 9.1.

The coefficients in Table 9.1 support several hypothesized relationships: a sense that one's work makes a difference is positively linked with job satisfaction ($r = 0.75$) and inversely related to burnout ($r = -0.18$). A sense that one's work is a waste of time is directly related to burnout ($r = 0.47$) and inversely related to job satisfaction ($r = -0.78$). And, when all types of emotional labor are combined, it is positively related to burnout ($r = 0.28$), job satisfaction ($r = 0.32$), and a sense that one is making a difference ($r = 0.40$). This underscores the importance of recognizing the emotional labor demands that workers face. Emotional labor brings about both satisfaction and burnout, and conversely, a sense of making a difference provides the confidence to engage in emotional labor. This is supported by the positive relationship between performing emotional labor and feeling that one is successful at it ($r = 0.49$). A sense of making a difference is strongly and directly related to satisfaction ($r = 0.75$) and equally strong but inversely

Table 9.1

Pearson's Correlation Coefficients on Emotional Labor and Affective Outcomes

	Emotional Labor	Burnout	Job Satisfaction	Work Makes a Difference	Efficacious Emotional Labor	Work is a Waste of Time
Emotional Labor	1.000					
Burnout	0.282	1.000				
Job Satisfaction	0.318	-0.287	1.000			
Work Makes a Difference	0.395	-0.186	0.749	1.000		
Efficacious Emotional Labor	0.491	-0.012	0.344	0.334	1.000	
Work is a Waste of Time	-0.254	0.470	-0.782	-0.779	-0.305	1.000

181

related to the sense of wasting one's time ($r = -0.78$). Emotional labor's link to respondents' assessments of the value of their work is illustrative as well. The inverse correlation between emotional labor and the sense that work is a waste of time ($r = -0.25$) points toward the salutary effect of emotion work. Workers who think their jobs are a waste of time are also those who tend not to engage in emotional labor or who feel that they are not good at it.

A closer examination of the types of work performed in the three research sites allows us to pinpoint those elements of the job that involve emotional labor (see Figure 9.2). These scenarios take us off the "distant observation platform" and show the importance of emotion work in person-to-person transactions. For example, emergency dispatch operators must answer each call and make an immediate decision about whether the caller's issues are emotionally charged. If so, the operator must differentiate between the need to gather factual information and the need to manage the caller's emotions, and perhaps her own, in order to elicit it. From there, the operator must proceed with the call such that, ideally, there is a positive outcome and satisfaction with a job well done. Errors at any point in the exchange with the caller are likely to result in a negative outcome.

In the case of prison units, corrections workers must approach each task with sensitivity to whether or not emotion work is required and, if so, what type. When it is, the worker must perform it in such a way as to achieve the goal of the interaction. When the exchange is effective, a positive outcome ensues. Failure to sense and manage the right type of interaction results in crowd control problems or disciplinary failures (see Figure 9.3).

With interviews conducted by OPG officials, investigators must develop rapport and intuit the correct approach for eliciting honest information that will be helpful in pursuing the child's best interest. Success results in assisting the child and feeling that one's work is worthwhile, while failure results in misinformation and burnout (see Figure 9.4).

While these models clarify decision points for the respective jobs, they also reveal how little we know about individual differences in performing such work. This raises a number of questions about how to incorporate emotion work skills into traditional human resources (HR) processes:

- Can individual skill in emotion work be assessed during the recruitment process?
- How can employees be trained to maximize their emotion management skills?
- How can workers be selected so that those with the best emotion work skills are in jobs where they are most needed?
- How can job descriptions be written to include emotional labor requirements?

Figure 9.2   Emotion Work Decision Tree for 911 Call Takers

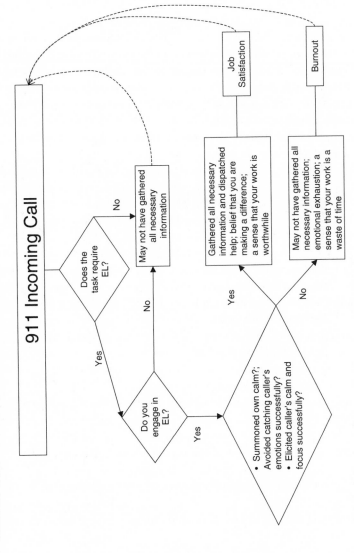

Figure 9.3 **Emotion Work Decision Tree for Corrections Officials**

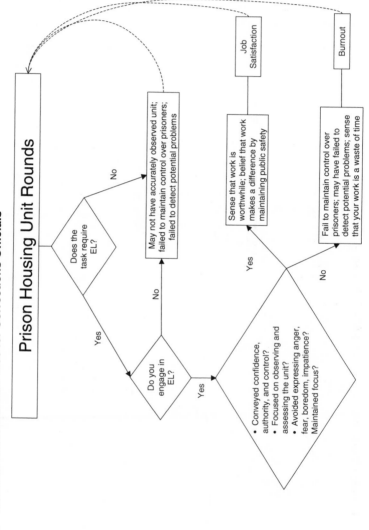

Figure 9.4 Emotion Work Decision Tree for Public Guardians

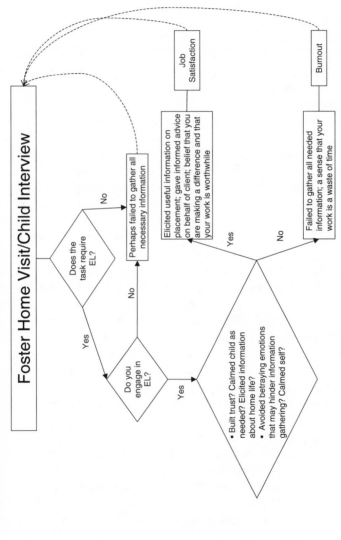

Foster Home Visit/Child Interview

Does the task require EL?

No → Perhaps failed to gather all necessary information

Yes

Do you engage in EL?

No

Yes

• Built trust? Calmed child as needed? Elicited information about home life?
• Avoided betraying emotions that may hinder information gathering? Calmed self?

Yes → Elicited useful information on placement; gave informed advice on behalf of client; belief that you are making a difference and that your work is worthwhile → Job Satisfaction

No → Failed to gather all needed information; a sense that your work is a waste of time → Burnout

Summary

There is no commonly understood term for emotion work. Thus, investigating it requires multiple forms of inquiry. This study used two modalities, face-to-face interviews and a survey questionnaire. Interviews revealed that each agency has its own terminology. Call takers for 911 talk about "hot calls"—riveting calls where the caller is emotional and the call taker must manage the caller's emotions. Investigators at the Office of the Public Guardian report that they put on their "game face" when they must be professional and in control, even in the most trying circumstances. Department of Corrections staff refer to putting on their "emotional armor" before confronting offenders.

What do the results of the survey reveal about emotion work? First, findings demonstrate that workers can express the degree to which they perform emotion work. Similar to how they report other work-related activities, they report on emotion work. Second, individual differences emerge in terms of their efficacy with emotion work. Workers report varying levels of ability and effectiveness in the performance of emotion work. Third, there are differences across agencies in the amount of emotion work performed by workers, but the differences in workers' ability to perform such work is not agency specific. This indicates that skill required to perform emotion work, just like cognitive labor, resides in the individual, not in the work environment, and is subject to individual differences. Fourth, the performance of emotional labor can contribute to pride in work and job satisfaction. Fifth, emotion work does not, ipso facto, contribute to burnout. In fact, in some instances it is motivating and makes the job meaningful. Rather, it is specifically the kind of emotion work that requires workers to express an emotion they do not feel that contributes to burnout.

We have much more to learn about this subject, but this research reveals at least shards of information that beg for deeper exploration. We know, for instance, that there are multiple dimensions to the performance of emotion work and that there are individual differences in terms of how accomplished people are at performing it. We know that the performance of emotion work is positively correlated with job satisfaction and pride in work. We know that the downside of emotion work is in those jobs that require workers to put on a false face—to suppress their own emotions and pretend to feel a different emotion. Even its negative effects, though, are mitigated when workers believe they are doing meaningful work.

Toward a New Theory of Public Service Work

This chapter began with a discussion about contemporary notions of work. We contend that emotional labor is ignored in the theory of work and in the paradigm that focuses our attention on work behaviors. Arguing that this conceptualization fails to take into account emotion work, the discussion turned to the centrality of person-to-person transactions that occur in public service. Because it is only in such transactions that emotion work matters, it is in precisely such venues that the theory of work needs to embrace an expanded notion of the labors that are exercised. Broadening a theory of work to embrace emotional labor will require a paradigm shift from industrial production to service transactions. Task-in-job currently functions as a means for separating the wholeness of the worker from the tasks performed. Requiring more than a crosswalk from standard job descriptions, a new paradigm of person-in-job will allow us to see all work that is performed, rather than the keyhole view we currently use.

The performance of emotion work requires active engagement with the wholeness of the job and the agency mission. It is this active engagement that provides the energy, commitment, and a sense of priorities that are essential. Judging from the findings described here, it also sets the stage for pride in the work performed and job satisfaction. The replacement of task-in-job thinking with person-in-job thinking will be the means for appreciating the wholeness of the worker in relation to the tasks performed.

To successfully complete a transaction, the worker must intuit the other's state of mind and make split-second adjustments in words, tone, or body language. A more accurate theory of work should encompass not only the performance of tasks as directed by one's superior, but also the fullness that workers bring to the job: dignity, courage, maturity, respect for citizens. It should embrace the inextricable relationship between the worker's subjective self, sense of the "other," and the objective content of the work.

To embrace this theory, one is required to grant more autonomy to workers, for emotion work is the ultimate knowledge work—the employer cannot "own" the worker's perceptions, reactions, and use of self-as-instrument to effect a successful transaction. This poses a conundrum as it constrains the degree to which employers can restrict the discretion of the worker. In a nation that extols the virtue of autonomy and self-reliance, this comprehension of the public service worker is not unreasonable.

Simplistic transference of marketplace efficiencies to public service transactions is exactly that—simplistic. If we are ready for a more comprehensive—and, yes, complex—understanding of work, then emotion work must be embraced. The first move is to acknowledge the capacity for nurturance, empathy, and care as well as the capacity for anger, fear, sadness and anxiety.

187

The second move is to delete the convention that emotional concerns are not as important as cognitive concerns. The belief that emotions are not quite rational—that they are too *feminine*—stands in the way of understanding service work. The third move is to embrace the totality of the worker, rather than parsing skills from the person. Does this open a Pandora's box for the HR office? Probably. Is this overdue? Yes.

As we move further and further away from organizations designed to operate assembly lines, we must devise new structures that capture today's work and skill requirements. Traditional HR structures impede a richer appreciation for emotional labor. From an institutional standpoint, job descriptions that ignore the emotional labor component of a position fail to reflect a comprehensive job analysis. Job analysis that identifies and labels, rather than ignores, emotional labor will contribute to a better understanding of the phenomenon and to an overhaul of the job description/compensation connection. There is no better time than now to look again at job descriptions that describe only part of the job. "Seeing" the largely invisible emotional components of job classification and compensation systems enables us to more fully comprehend the wholeness of job requirements. Making emotional labor visible is the first step; making it compensable is the next.

The most important point we have tried to make in this book is that emotional labor as we now understand it is far more nuanced and complex than that which was originally described when the construct first appeared in social science research. It is skilled work that takes a number of forms of artful affect. These range from nicer-than-nice exchanges with strangers to suppressing one's own emotions while exhibiting an opposite emotion in order to manage the behavior of the other. There are individual differences in workers' abilities to engage in these performances and there are different types and outcomes. While emotional engagement motivates workers and produces job satisfaction, the requirement to express emotions they do not actually feel produces burnout.

If we are to emphasize and honor the *service* in public service, we must pay attention to how public servants work "feelingly" in the citizen-state encounter. Such knowledge will influence how a job description is written, the skill mix sought as job applicants are screened, training and development protocols, "time-out" and retention strategies for employees, behaviors to evaluate in performance appraisals, compensation schemes, and supervisory methods. In sum, emotion work is at the heart of human capital concerns.

Note

1. For a comprehensive treatment of the subject of emotions, see Lewis and Haviland-Jones (2000), *Handbook of Emotions*.

Appendix A

GNM Emotional Labor Questionnaire

The purpose of this survey is to learn about the demands and characteristics of jobs that require employees to work in intense situations. There are no right or wrong answers; that which is important is your own personal experience on the job. Please be candid with your responses; they will be kept fully confidential.

For each of the following statements, indicate how often each occurs *by circling the number* based on the following scale:

1	2	3	4	5	6	7
Never	Rarely	Once in a while	Sometimes	Often	Usually	Always

	Never					Always	
1. I perform my job independently of supervision.	1	2	3	4	5	6	7
2. My job is interesting.	1	2	3	4	5	6	7
3. I am proud of the work I do.	1	2	3	4	5	6	7
4. I make my own decisions about how to do my work.	1	2	3	4	5	6	7
5. My performance appraisal accurately reflects how effective I am in my job.	1	2	3	4	5	6	7
6. My supervisor asks for my opinion on matters of concern.	1	2	3	4	5	6	7
7. I am doing something worthwhile in my job.	1	2	3	4	5	6	7
8. My work is challenging.	1	2	3	4	5	6	7
9. My work is satisfying.	1	2	3	4	5	6	7
10. My job provides career development opportunities.	1	2	3	4	5	6	7

	Never					Always	
11. There is a lot of variety in the kinds of things I do.	1	2	3	4	5	6	7
12. To be effective, I must be creative in my work.	1	2	3	4	5	6	7
13. I keep learning new things in my position.	1	2	3	4	5	6	7
14. My training prepared me to do my job well.	1	2	3	4	5	6	7
15. I am good at getting people to calm down.	1	2	3	4	5	6	7
16. I prefer working with people.	1	2	3	4	5	6	7
17. My job requires that I display many different emotions when interacting with others.	1	2	3	4	5	6	7
18. My job requires me to be "artificially" or "professionally" friendly to clients, callers, citizens, etc.	1	2	3	4	5	6	7
19. Working directly with people puts a lot of stress on me.	1	2	3	4	5	6	7
20. I help co-workers feel better about themselves.	1	2	3	4	5	6	7
21. I cover or manage my own feelings so as to appear pleasant at work.	1	2	3	4	5	6	7
22. My work requires me to guide people through sensitive and/or emotional issues.	1	2	3	4	5	6	7
23. My work involves dealing with emotionally charged issues as a critical dimension of the job.	1	2	3	4	5	6	7
24. I try to actually feel the emotions that I must display.	1	2	3	4	5	6	7
25. My job requires that I pretend to have emotions that I do not really feel.	1	2	3	4	5	6	7
26. My job requires that I manage the emotions of others.	1	2	3	4	5	6	7
27. My job requires that I hide my true feelings about a situation.	1	2	3	4	5	6	7
28. My work requires me to deal with unfriendly people.	1	2	3	4	5	6	7
29. In my work, I am good at dealing with emotional issues.	1	2	3	4	5	6	7
30. My work requires me to provide comfort to people who are in crisis.	1	2	3	4	5	6	7
31. I worry that this job is hardening me emotionally.	1	2	3	4	5	6	7
32. I leave work feeling tired and run down.	1	2	3	4	5	6	7
33. I leave work feeling emotionally exhausted.	1	2	3	4	5	6	7
34. I feel "used up" at the end of the workday.	1	2	3	4	5	6	7
35. I leave work feeling optimistic.	1	2	3	4	5	6	7
36. I leave work feeling energized.	1	2	3	4	5	6	7
37. I think about getting a different job.	1	2	3	4	5	6	7
38. I feel like my work is a waste of time and energy.	1	2	3	4	5	6	7
To unwind after a tough day, I confide in my							
39. Co-workers	1	2	3	4	5	6	7
40. Friends	1	2	3	4	5	6	7
41. Family	1	2	3	4	5	6	7
42. Other (please specify): _____	1	2	3	4	5	6	7

	Never					Always	
43. To cope with work stress, I engage in sports and/or hobbies.	1	2	3	4	5	6	7
44. I feel like my work makes a difference.	1	2	3	4	5	6	7
45. My work gives me a sense of personal accomplishment.	1	2	3	4	5	6	7
46. My job requires that I am nice to people no matter how they treat me.	1	2	3	4	5	6	7
47. I attempt to keep the peace by calming clashes between co-workers.	1	2	3	4	5	6	7
48. I help co-workers deal with stresses and difficulties at work.	1	2	3	4	5	6	7

General Information

The following information will be used only to develop categories for analysis purposes. It will NOT be shared with anyone else, nor will it be used to reveal your identity.

49. Are you:
    _____ Male
    _____ Female

50. Are you:
    _____ American Indian
    _____ Asian or Pacific Islander
    _____ Black, not of Hispanic origin
    _____ Hispanic
    _____ White, not of Hispanic origin
    _____ Other (please specify): _____

51. How old are you?
    _____ Under 20   _____ 45 thru 49
    _____ 20 thru 24   _____ 50 thru 54
    _____ 25 thru 29   _____ 55 thru 59
    _____ 30 thru 34   _____ 60 thru 64
    _____ 35 thru 39   _____ 65 thru 69
    _____ 40 thru 44   _____ 70 or over

52. What is your educational level? Indicate the highest level completed.
    _____ Less than high school
    _____ High school graduate or G.E.D.
    _____ Technical training or apprenticeship after high school

191

_____ Some college
_____ 2-year associate degree
_____ Graduated from college
_____ Some graduate school
_____ Master's degree
_____ Law degree (J.D., LL.B.)
_____ Doctorate degree (Ph.D., M.D., Ed.D., etc.)
_____ Other (please specify): _____

53. How long have you been working in your current job?
_____ Less than 1 year
_____ 1 year or more, but less than 2 years
_____ 2 years or more, but less than 3 years
_____ 3 years or more, but less than 4 years
_____ 4 years or more, but less than 5 years
_____ 5 years or more, but less than 6 years
_____ 6 years or more, but less than 7 years
_____ 7 years or more, but less than 8 years
_____ 8 years or more, but less than 9 years
_____ 9 years or more, but less than 10 years
_____ 10 years or more

54. a. Have you worked in a similar type job prior to this one?
_____ Yes
_____ No

b. If "Yes," for how long? _____

55. In which service area(s) do you work?
_____ Administrative services
_____ Corrections
_____ Family & children services
_____ Health care
_____ Information & communication
_____ Law enforcement
_____ Legal services
_____ Social work
_____ Telephone crisis line
_____ Other (please specify): _____

56. What is your marital status?

_____ Married
_____ Divorced
_____ Single
_____ Not married, but with a significant other
_____ Widow/er

57. Do you have childcare or dependent care responsibilities after work?
    _____ Yes
    _____ No

58. My salary is:

_____ Under $20,000	_____ $50,000–$59,999
_____ $20,000–$29,999	_____ $60,000–$69,999
_____ $30,000–$39,999	_____ $70,000–$79,999
_____ $40,000–$49,999	_____ $80,000 or above

Thank you very much for your participation.

If there is anything else you would like to tell me, please do so in the space provided below:

Appendix B

Research Design

We employed a research design similar to what Evan Lieberman (2005) refers to as nested analysis. He uses the term to denote a unified approach that joins intensive case-study analysis with statistical analysis. Such a protocol provides a synergy that enables hypothesis testing as well as theoretical insights gleaned from outliers and exceptions. This is an integrated strategy that draws on the distinct strengths of two different approaches. Coupling quantitative analyses of large-scale surveys with intensive interview protocols improves the probability of making valid causal inferences. This methodology relies on neither a "small n" analysis nor a "large n" analysis, but rather nests the interpretation of one within the other.

In this case, employees in three agencies were interviewed either singly or in focus groups and then paper-and-pencil questionnaires were distributed that probed individual experience and perceptions in more detail. This design allows identification of issues and dynamics from interviews that then provide insight to illuminate empirical data. The information gained from interviews reduces the likelihood of misinterpreting survey data while the quantitative data reduce the possibility of exaggerating or misinterpreting perspectives offered in personal interviews.

There was deliberate rather than random selection of interviewees so as to enable hypothesis generation about the subject matter. Lieberman explains that this "approach allows the scholar to identify the particular information that he or she wants to glean from the in-depth analysis of almost any case, and then to assess the potential added value of such analysis relative to a larger body of theory and data" (2005, p. 448). Moreover, this approach lightens the inferential burden that is otherwise carried by small n designs or large n designs when performed on their own.

This design allowed both qualitative and quantitative modes of analysis to inform the execution and interpretation of the other, and the analytic method allowed us to explore general relationships as well as specific experiences. Through it, we addressed the questions What is emotional labor? How does it affect job satisfaction? Burnout? Turnover? What are its correlates in terms of commitment, agency performance, co-worker relations?

Combining interviews with a paper-and-pencil survey allowed us to improve our analytic capacity while increasing our confidence in the central findings of the study. And, it enabled us to more clearly draw the distinction between emotional labor and traditional work skills. The information gleaned from each phase is complementary and the sum provides a more comprehensive understanding of emotional labor.

Sample Selection and Data Gathering

Three public agencies were chosen for this research, as described in Chapter 1. Data gathering occurred in two phases. The first phase involved interviews with professional staff at the Cook County Office of the Public Guardian in fall 2004. That was followed by interviews in spring 2005 at the Illinois Department of Corrections and with 911 call takers who work for the Tallahassee, Florida, Police Department. Interviews at the Office of the Public Guardian and Illinois Department of Corrections were individual, and interviews with 911 call takers were in small focus groups of about four workers each. These face-to-face sessions were designed to probe and query the degree to which workers performed emotion work, to learn how they experienced emotion work, and to hear in workers' own words how the performance of this work affected them. No common terminology emerged from the interviews, and it became obvious that each worker interpreted and expressed such work in his/her own terms. At the opening of the interviews, it was not unusual for participants to deny engaging in "emotion" work. As the discussion ensued, most would make an aha! declaration and clarify that, of course, they engaged in emotion work. They would follow that with examples. This experience made it obvious that surveying workers who are not accustomed to labeling emotional labor as such would require careful wording of questionnaire items.

Development of the Questionnaire

The questionnaire was constructed in a manner similar to that recommended by prior studies that have employed surveys on emotional labor, job satisfaction, burnout, and motivation.[1] In spring 2005, a 66-item pilot questionnaire was tested by 29 graduate students who were enrolled in public administration classes at Florida State University. After completing the survey, students were asked to report questions that were unclear or ambiguous or otherwise difficult to answer. Based on their comments, some items were deleted, some were reordered, and several questions plus the seven response categories were reworded for clarity. Factor analysis of the pilot results produced four factors: burnout (Cronbach's alpha = .771), emotional labor (Cronbach's alpha = .846), job satisfaction (Cronbach's alpha = .820), and pride in job (Cronbach's alpha = .839).

Survey Distribution

The questionnaire was distributed through departmental mail at the Office of the Public Guardian and the Department of Corrections. Interviews had revealed that there is not a commonly understood vernacular expression for emotional labor. To "prime the pump" and focus respondents' attention on the subject of emotion work, a cover letter was attached to each survey in an attempt to sensitize them to the purpose of the survey. In addition to explaining who the researchers were and asking respondents to complete the survey and return it by the deadline, the content of the letter included the "priming" questions shown below:

Cover Letter Used for Priming Respondents

This questionnaire is about *Emotional Labor*, which is related to job stress, burnout, and motivation. Before starting the questionnaire, think about how you might answer the following questions to get a better idea of the nature of Emotional Labor.

- Do you need to engage in *relationship building* in your job?
- Do you need to engage in *emotion management*—which means managing your own emotions as well as "taming" the emotions of others?
- How do you *unwind* from a tough day?
- What is the most *rewarding* thing about your job?
- Every occupation has its own *humor*—in the form of "sick jokes"—and this serves as a release for tensions. Does this relate to your job?

Office of the Public Guardian

OPG was contacted initially about this research project in July 2004, at which time Patrick Murphy, director of the agency, informed us of his impending election to the Circuit Court of Cook County, which would bring about the end of his tenure with OPG by December 1, 2004.[2] This project received a letter of support from OPG dated July 21, 2004, followed closely thereafter by approval from the Institutional Review Board (IRB) of the University of Illinois–Chicago. Interviews commenced thereafter and continued through November 2004. The team then waited for a new agency director to be named, and that occurred in early summer 2005. A new letter of support and memorandum of understanding were sought from Robert Harris, former Deputy Public Guardian and now Cook County Public Guardian. This was received and survey instruments were distributed to both the downtown and Roosevelt Road offices in late June 2005 and retrieved two weeks later. Of 270 employees, 139 surveys were returned for a response rate of 51.5 percent.

Department of Corrections

On December 7, 2004, Newman met with Director Roger Walker, Jr., and Mr. Sergio Molina (Chief, Office of Communications and Public Service) at the DOC headquarters office in Springfield, Illinois (formally, the Springfield General Office). The research project was introduced and formal permission was requested. A follow-up meeting was held on December 16, 2004, to discuss implementation of the project. This meeting was attended by Mastracci, Newman, Mr. Molina, and Mr. Steven Karr (Planning and Research Unit). In addition to the Springfield General Office as a research site, selection of the sample of correctional facilities was agreed upon. Consideration extended to having a sufficient number of facilities across levels of security (Levels 1–8, with Level 1 being the highest of 8 security level designations) and both male and female institutions. Convenience/location was also a factor; namely, close proximity to Chicago and Springfield. Based upon these criteria, six adult sites were identified by the researchers and approved by DOC, specifically:

- Stateville Correctional Center, Joliet IL (Level 1, maximum-security, male, capacity: $n = 1,506$)
- Stateville Northern Reception and Classification Center, Joliet IL (Level 7, low minimum-security, male, capacity: $n = 2,200$)
- Logan Correctional Center, Lincoln IL (Level 4, medium-security, male, capacity: $n = 1,050$)
- Lincoln Correctional Center, Lincoln IL (Level 4, medium-security, female, capacity: $n = 500$)
- Decatur Correctional Center, Decatur IL (Level 4, medium-security, female, capacity: $n = 500$)

• Decatur Adult Transition Center, Decatur IL (Level 8, transitional-security, male, capacity: n = 80)

The research protocol was approved by DOC and the University of Illinois at Springfield (UIS) Human Subjects Review Office. Formal approval to proceed with the research project was received from Director Walker on March 11, 2005. The DOC Research Agreement was signed (by Newman) and returned on March 15, 2005. The UIS Human Subjects Protocol was approved on March 16, 2005. As required by law, the DOC's consent form (DC 148) was utilized. In addition, UIS required that a more comprehensive consent form be utilized.

Research at the DOC was conducted in two stages. The first stage consisted of structured interviews with selected staff at four of the above six correctional facilities. (Due to heightened security issues and a change in management at Stateville, the researchers did not gain access to these two institutions.)

Selection of correctional staff was pre-arranged by the individual facility prior to the interview date. On March 11, 2005, Steve Karr sent an e-mail to each of the six facilities (addressed to the management staff), as follows:

> Director Walker has authorized a study regarding burnout and motivation in public service for which your facility was selected. The study will encompass staff interviews, focus group discussions, and questionnaires. Prior to site visits, either Meredith Newman, Sharon Mastracci, or Mary Ellen Guy will contact your facility to schedule activities with you or your designee to select study subjects. The Director's approval letter includes use of an audio tape recorder and for the Department to accommodate research staff through August of this year. More information will be forthcoming as details become available. However, research staff will be contacting your office shortly to begin subject selection. Please ensure that each staff participant completes DC148 Research Consent Form to be placed within their personnel file.

Mastracci and Newman interviewed a total of twenty-three correctional staff during the time period March 21, 2005, to March 31, 2005. Each facility made a conference room available, and individual staff members were interviewed in turn. Interviews followed a script, and were tape-recorded and subsequently transcribed. Details are as follows:

• March 21, 2005: Lincoln Correctional Center; 6 staff interviewed (5 women, 1 man);
• March 22, 2005: Logan Correctional Center; 6 staff interviewed (3 women, 3 men);
• March 30, 2005[3]: Decatur Adult Transition Center; 6 staff interviewed (1 woman, 5 men);

• March 31, 2005: Decatur Correctional Center; 5 staff interviewed (3 women, 2 men).

Stage 2 involved surveying the universe of DOC employees at the Springfield General Office. On April 27, 2005, Director Walker sent the following e-mail to these employees:

> You will receive a survey with your paycheck on Friday, April 29, 2005. The "Emotional Labor" Survey is being conducted by Dr. Meredith A. Newman, University of Illinois Springfield. The questionnaire is from researchers at the University of Illinois Springfield, the University of Illinois Chicago, and Florida State University. The questionnaire is about Emotional Labor, which is related to job stress, motivation, and employee burnout. Please take a few moments to complete the survey and return your completed survey to Brigitte Smith in the Executive Office Building, no later than Thursday, May 12, 2005. Please contact Brigitte Smith at extension 2002 with questions.

A total of 324 surveys were distributed on April 30, 2005 as follows:

Industries:	29
General Office:	242
Field:	41
School District:	12

Newman collected the returned questionnaires on May 16, 2005. A total of 136 usable questionnaires were returned for a response rate of 42 percent.

911 Call Takers

There was no cover letter used for the 911 call takers because each was handed the survey at the close of the focus group in which they participated. Thus, they had been "primed" through face-to-face communication with the researcher. The 40 call takers on duty on the 24-hour shift starting June 3, 2005, were included in these focus groups. This date was selected because it was the 24-hour time period when staffing was the heaviest, thus more of the call takers were on duty then than any other day of the week. Twelve focus groups of 3 to 4 call takers each were conducted. Each focus group was about an hour long and focused on 18 questions (shown in Chapter 1, Table 1.1). At the conclusion of each focus group, participants were handed the paper survey and asked to complete it within a week and drop it in a box left for collection. At the end of the week, the researcher returned to the dispatch center and collected the questionnaires. The research protocol was approved by the Tallahassee Police Department and the Florida State University Human Subjects Review Office.

Notes

1. See Churchill, Ford, and Walker (1974); Jones (1981); Maslach and Leiter (1997); Pines and Aronson (1988); Pugliese and Shook (1997); Steinberg (1999); and Steinberg and Figart (1999a and 1999b).

2. Mr. Murphy ran for the circuit court unopposed, so he anticipated winning the election—"even in Chicago!"—and therefore leaving OPG once the terms of newly elected judges began on December 1, 2004.

3. Mastracci only.

Appendix C

Variables for
Regression Analysis

Dependent Variable

The emotional labor index serves as the dependent variable. It is based on correlations among six survey items: 17, 22, 23, 26, 29, 30. It is generated as a standardized scale variable with a mean of 0 and a variance of 1.

Independent Variables

Independent variables are measured on a seven-point Likert scale with highest-valued responses indicating the strongest degree of agreement; years of experience is measured as the number of years (truncated at "ten or more"), and occupations are gauged as dummy variables. These are shown in Table C.1.

Work attitude variables range from 1 to 7 ("never" to "always"), so average values greater than 3.5 indicate that the survey item is a part of respondents' jobs at least some of the time. Values above that center point indicate increasing frequency. Respondents reveal that their work involves acting "artificially" or professionally friendly, calming others down, helping co-workers, and dealing with unfriendly people quite regularly. More infrequent aspects of work include worrying about becoming callous and experiencing stress by working with demanding publics. Each of the work attitude items varies by approximately the same variance, which suggests that they do not vary widely by agency.

The occupation variables and the variable "female" are dummies, so

Table C.1

Variable/Means

Variable	Mean	Std. Dev.	Min	Max
Dependent Var: Emotional Labor	0.00	0.80	−1.98	1.42
Must act artificially or professionally friendly to clients	5.38	1.57	1	7
Working with people produces a lot of stress	3.36	1.59	1	7
Good at calming people down	5.22	1.14	1	7
Help co-workers feel better about themselves	4.87	1.22	1	7
Pretend to have emotions that are not there	2.86	1.52	1	7
Must hide inappropriate feelings	3.90	1.62	1	7
Must deal with unfriendly people	4.65	1.37	1	7
Worry that work is hardening me emotionally	3.30	1.79	1	7
Years of experience	5.23	3.61	0	10
Occupation: Administration	0.11	0.31	0	1
Occupation: Corrections and Law Enforcement	0.34	0.47	0	1
Occupation: Family Services and Social Work	0.27	0.44	0	1
Occupation: Telecommunications	0.19	0.39	0	1
Occupation: Legal Services	0.27	0.44	0	1
Female	0.67	0.47	0	1

their means are interpreted as percentages. The total of all occupations, however, exceeds 100 percent because respondents could choose more than one category if they were, for instance, in prison administration. The largest category is corrections and law enforcement (34 percent), followed by family services and social work (27 percent), legal services (27 percent), telecommunications (19 percent), and administration (11 percent). Two-thirds of the respondents are female.

Appendix D

Emotional Labor Scales

Tables D.1 and D.2 are derived from Ronnie J. Steinberg's (1999) work on redesigning job evaluations. Four factors capture the content of emotion work: human relations, communications skills, emotional effort, and responsibility for client well-being. These factors are defined along two separate continua that measure lowest- to highest-levels of human relations and communications skills, as shown in Table D.1 and emotional effort and emotional demands, as shown in Table D.2.

Table D.1

Degrees of Emotion Work: Human Relations and Communications Skills

Level A	Level B	Level C	Level D	Level E
• Discussion of factual information • Ordinary personal courtesy • Contacts with clients or the public are incidental, not integral	• Exhibit polished courtesy • Promote and maintain credibility • Relate to the public to maintain organizational image	• Motivate, mentor, coach, or train employees and the public • May require hand-holding, reassurance, empathy, and rapport in nonsensitive situations • May require resolution of minor conflicts	• Considerable tact, patience, ability to reassure, empathy and rapport in providing direct services or comfort in sensitive situations • Use of persuasion and networking • Understanding of group dynamics. May involve dealing with emotionally charged issues in public forums • Conducting extensive consultations with external groups over emotionally charged issues • Subduing others in moderately difficult circumstances	• Creating a climate for commitment to the welfare of clients or the public • Coaching and guiding clients through difficult emotional, attitudinal, and developmental change • Providing comfort where people are in pain, dying, angry, distraught, or otherwise unpredictably physically violent, or emotional • Crowd control when crowd gets out of hand

Table D.2

Degrees of Emotion Work: Emotional Effort/Emotional Demands

Level A	Level B	Level C	Level D	Level E
• Occasionally deal with unfriendly people	• May deal occasionally with people who are in difficult or controversial circumstances	• Deal regularly with people who are difficult or with people who are emotionally impaired	• Deal with physically dangerous or violent people; or • Work directly with people who are in constant pain or facing emergencies; or • Work in highly sensitive or controversial circumstances	• Deal regularly with physically dangerous and unpredictably violent people • May also work directly with people (including family members) who are facing death or other sensitive situations

Appendix E

Description of Job Occupants

The tables that follow provide state-by-state comparisons and source data used for compiling the information that appears in Table 7.1.

Table E.1

Description of State Workers—Illinois, 2005

	Career[1]		Exempt[2]		Senior Administrator[3]		Total	
	Men	Women	Men	Women	Men	Women	Men	Women
Number	25,723	23,948	920	1,612	896	615	27,539	26,175
Percentage of service	51.8	48.2	35.9	63.7	57.5	40.7	51.2	48.7
Average salary	$49,596	$46,320	$78,328	$63,490	$79,452	$68,184	$51,527	$47,836
Women's salary per $1.00 earned by men		93¢		81¢		86¢		93¢

Source: Illinois Department of Central Management Services (October 2005).

[1] Career Service employees represent the largest category of state workers and represent the lowest skill levels.

[2] Exempt employees include staff attorneys, legal or technical advisors, engineers, physician medical, administrators, registered nurses, resident administrative heads of state charitable, penal, and correctional institutions, and confidential assistants.

[3] Policy-making positions and others in upper management as Senior Public Administrators.

Table E.2

Description of State Workers—New Jersey, 2004

	Career[1]		Unclassified[2]		Senior Executive[3]		Total	
	Men	Women	Men	Women	Men	Women	Men	Women
Number	27,063	34,254	6,362	3,492	182	126	33,607	37,872
Percentage of service	44.1	55.9	64.6	35.4	59.1	40.9	47.0	53.0
Average salary	$54,709	$46,248	$76,129	$70,531	$96,217	$92,636	$58,990	$48,642
Women's salary per $1.00 earned by men		85¢		93¢		96¢		82¢

Source: New Jersey Department of Personnel (September 2005).

[1]Career Service means those positions and job titles subject to the tenure provisions of Title 11A, New Jersey Statutes.

[2]Unclassified Service means those positions and job titles outside of the senior executive service, not subject to the tenure provisions of Title 11A, New Jersey Statutes or the NJ Administrative Code rules unless otherwise specified.

[3]Senior Executive Service (SES) means positions in state service designated by the Merit System Board as having substantial managerial, policy-influencing, or policy-executing responsibilities not included in the career or unclassified services. The SES does not include cabinet or subcabinet positions.

Table E.3

Description of State Workers—Oregon, 2005

	Career[1]		Exempt[2]		Senior Management[3]		Total	
	Men	Women	Men	Women	Men	Women	Men	Women
Number	13,097	15,664	2,524	2,572	324	223	15,945	18,459
Percentage of service	45.5	54.5	49.5	50.5	59.2	40.8	46.3	53.7
Average salary*	$40,409	$35,407	$59,770	$51,292	$88,291	$80,057	$44,447	$38,160
Women's salary per $1.00 earned by men		88¢		86¢		91¢		86¢

Source: Oregon Department of Administrative Services, Human Resource Services Division (June 30, 2005).

*Includes fixed differentials (not shift or other hourly differentials).

[1]Career Service means those positions and job titles in the Classified Service as defined in Oregon Revised Statutes 240.210.

[2]Select Exempt means selected positions and job titles in the Unclassified Service as defined in Oregon Revised Statutes 240.205 and includes those defined in state policy as Management Service. Select Exempt also includes legislative employees defined as Exempt Service in Oregon Revised Statutes 240.200.

[3]Senior Management means positions and job titles in State Unclassified Service as defined in Oregon Revised Statutes 240.205 and designated as Executive Service under state policy. Senior Executive excludes appointed or elected department directors, appointed or elected officials, as well as lawyers, licensed physicians, and dentists employed in their professional capacities.

Table E.4

Description of State Workers—Florida, 2005

	Career[1]		Selected Exempt[2]		Senior Management[3]		Total	
	Men	Women	Men	Women	Men	Women	Men	Women
Number	37,322	47,679	8,485	10,249	346	215	46,153	58,143
Percentage of service	43.9	56.1	45.9	54.1	61.7	38.3	44.0	56.0
Average salary	$35,825	$31,825	$56,503	$46,256	$106,284	$104,377	$39,829	$34,632
Women's salary per $1.00 earned by men		89¢		82¢		98¢		87¢

Source: Florida Department of Management Services, 2005.

[1] Career Service employees represent the largest category of state workers and the lowest skill levels.
[2] Selected Exempt employees are all managers, supervisors, confidential employees, and certain professionals, such as physicians and lawyers.
[3] Policy-making positions and other positions in upper management are in the Senior Management Service. This category contains appointed department heads.

Table E.5

Description of Job Occupants and Salary Ranges—Illinois

Job Title	Salary Range	Women	Men	Percentage Women
Public Service Representative	$2,160–$3,380	417	217	65.8
Meat and Poultry Inspector	$2,964–$3,737	9	70	11.4
Child Welfare Specialist	$3,207–$4,738	562	174	76.4

Sources: Illinois Office of the Secretary of State, Department of Personnel, December 2005 (Public Service Representative); and Illinois Department of Central Management Services, October 2005.

Table E.6

Description of Job Occupants and Salary Ranges—New Jersey

Job Title	Salary Range	Women	Men	Percentage Women
Examination Technician, Motor Vehicle Commission	$2,343–$3,178	36	27	57.1
Agricultural Products Agent 2	$2,672–$3,639	6	15	28.6
Family Service Specialist 2	$3,533–$4,843	956	288	76.8

Source: New Jersey Department of Personnel, September 2005.

Table E.7

Description of Job Occupants and Salary Ranges—Oregon

Job Title	Salary Range	Women	Men	Percentage Women
Transportation Services Representative 1	$2,067–$2,847	183	95	65.8
Shipping Point Inspector 2	$1,907–$2,597	3	5	37.5
Social Service Specialist 1	$2,846–$3,955	872	217	80.1

Source: Oregon Department of Administrative Services, Human Resource Services Division, June 2005.

216

Appendix F

Factors Used in Analysis

Table F.1

Factors That Emerge from the Data

Factor	Survey Items	Cronbach's alpha
Burnout	19, 31, 32, 33, 34	$\alpha = .872$
Emotion Work (per se)	17, 22, 23, 26, 29, 30	$\alpha = .893$
Emotional Labor (personal efficacy)	15, 20, 24, 47, 48	$\alpha = .883$
Emotional Labor (false face)	18, 21, 25, 27, 28, 46	$\alpha = .716$
Job Satisfaction	5, 9, 10, 11, 13	$\alpha = .786$
Pride in Job	2, 3, 7, 8, 14, 44, 45	$\alpha = .860$
Waste of Time	35, 36, 38, 44	$\alpha = .769$

Note: Each of these factors has sufficiently high internal reliability, as measured by Cronbach's alpha. The coefficients are above the desirable threshold for paper-and-pencil inventories of psychological constructs.

Bibliography

Abel, Emily K., and Margaret K. Nelson, eds. 1990. *Circles of Care. Work and Identity in Women's Lives*. Albany, NY: State University of New York Press.

Abraham, R. 1998. "Emotional Dissonance in Organizations: Antecedents, Consequences and Moderators." *Genetic, Social, and General Psychology Monographs* 124: 229–46.

Addams, Jane. 2002 [1902]. *Democracy and Social Ethics*. Chicago: University of Illinois Press.

Adelmann, Pamela K. 1995. "Emotional Labor as a Potential Source of Job Stress." In *Organizational Risk Factors for Job Stress*, ed. Steven L. Sauter and Lawrence R. Murphy, 371–81. Washington, DC: American Psychological Association.

Albrecht, K., and R. Zemke. 1985. *Service America! Doing Business in the New Economy*. Homewood, IL: Dow-Jones-Irwin.

American Federation of State, County and Municipal Employees (AFSCME) Council 31. 2005. "Informational Pickets Raise Safety, Staffing Issues at DOC Sites," April 8, 2005. www.afscme31.0rg/printable.asp?objectID=851. Accessed April 7, 2007.

American Psychiatric Association. 1994. *Diagnostic and Statistical Manual of Mental Disorders*. 4th ed. (DSM-IV). Washington, DC: American Psychiatric Publishing.

Anker, R. 1998. *Gender and Jobs: Sex Segregation of Occupations in the World*. Geneva, Switzerland: International Labour Office.

Anthony, P.D. 1977. *The Ideology of Work*. London: Tavistock.

Argyris, Chris. 1964. *Integrating the Individual and the Organization*. New York: John Wiley & Sons.

Ashforth, B., and R. Humphrey. 1993. "Emotional Labor in Service Roles: The Influence of Identity." *Academy of Management Executive* 18 (1): 88–115.

Baines, Carol, Patricia Evans, and Sheila Neysmith, eds. 1998. *Women's Caring. Feminist Perspectives on Social Welfare*, 2nd ed. Ontario, Canada: Oxford University Press.

Batuji, Jacqueline. 1974. "Aspects of Semantic Neology." *Languages* 8 (36): 6–19.

Bellas, Marcia L. 1999. "Emotional Labor in Academia: The Case of Professors." *Annals of the American Academy of Political and Social Science* 561: 96–110.

Berman, Jay M. 2005. "Industry Output and Employment Projections to 2014." *Monthly Labor Review* 128 (11): 45–69.

Bolton, Sharon C. 2000. "Who Cares? Offering Emotion Work as a 'Gift' in the Nursing Labour Process." *Journal of Advanced Nursing* 32 (3): 580–86.

219

Boone, Louis E., and Donald D. Bowen, eds. 1987. *The Great Writings in Management and Organizational Behavior.* New York: Random House.

Bowen, D.E., and B. Schneider 1988. "Service Marketing and Management: Implications for Organizational Behavior." In *Research in Organizational Behavior,* ed. L.L. Cummings and B.M. Staw, 10: 43–80. Greenwich, CT: JAI Press.

Bowen, D.E., R.B. Chase, T.G. Cummins, and Associates. 1990. *Service Management Effectiveness: Balancing Strategy, Organization and Human Resources, Operations and Marketing.* San Francisco: Jossey-Bass.

Box, Richard C., and Deborah A. Sagen. 1998. "Working with Citizens: Breaking Down Barriers to Citizen Self-Governance." In *Government Is Us: Public Administration in an Anti-Government Era,* ed. Cheryl Simrell King and Camilla Stivers, 158–74. Thousand Oaks, CA: Sage.

Brabeck, Mary M., ed. 1989. *Who Cares? Theory, Research, and Educational Implications of the Ethic of Care.* New York, NY: Praeger.

Breusch, T.S., and A.R. Pagan. 1979. "A Simple Test for Heteroscedasticity and Random Coefficient Variation." *Econometrica* 47: 1287–94.

Brotheridge, Celeste M., and Alicia A. Grandey. 2002. "Emotional Labor and Burnout: Comparing Two Perspectives of 'People Work.'" *Journal of Vocational Behavior* 61: 17–39.

Brotheridge, Celeste M., and Raymond T. Lee. 2003. "Development and Validation of the Emotional Labour Scale." *Journal of Occupational and Organizational Psychology* 76: 365–79.

———. 1998. "On the Dimensionality of Emotional Labour: Development and Validation of the Emotional Labour Scale." Paper presented at the First Conference on Emotions in Organizational Life, San Diego, CA, August.

Brown, S.W., E. Gummesson, E. Edvardsson, and B.Gustavsson. 1991. *Service Quality: Multidisciplinary and Multinational Perspectives.* Lexington, MA: Lexington Books.

Brownlow, Louis, Charles Merriam, and Luther Gulick. 1937. *Administrative Management in the Government of the United States.* Washington, DC: President's Committee on Administrative Management.

Buber, Martin. 1958. *I and Thou.* 2nd ed. New York: Charles Scribner's Sons.

Bulan, Heather Ferguson, Rebecca J. Erickson, and Amy S. Wharton. 1997. "Doing for Others on the Job: The Affective Requirements of Service Work, Gender, and Emotional Well-Being." *Social Problems* 44: 235–56.

Burnier, DeLysa. 2004. "Lost and Found: Gender, Narrative, Miss Burchfield and the Construction of Knowledge in Public Administration." Paper presented at the annual meeting of the Midwest Political Science Association Meeting, Chicago, IL, April.

———. 2003. "Other Voices/Other Rooms: Towards a Care-Centered Public Administration." *Administrative Theory & Praxis* 25 (4): 529–44.

———. 1995. "Reinventing Government from a Feminist Perspective: Feminist Theory and Administrative Reality." *Forum Magazine* (Fall). Available at www-as.phy.ohiou.edu/FORUM/burnier.html. Accessed January 14, 2005.

Buunk, B.P., and Wilmar B. Schaufeli. 1999. "Reciprocity in Interpersonal Relationships: An Evolutionary Perspective on Its Importance for Health and Well-Being." In *European Review of Social Psychology,* ed. W. Stroebe and M. Hewstone, 10 (1): 259–340.

Champoux, Joseph E. 1991. "A Multivariate Test of the Job Characteristics Theory of Work Motivation." *Journal of Organizational Behavior* 12 (5): 431–46.

Cherniss, Cary. 1993. "The Role of Professional Self-Efficacy in the Etiology and Amelioration of Burnout." In *Professional Burnout: Recent Developments in Theory and*

Research, ed. Wilmar B. Schaufeli, Christina Maslach, and Tadeusz Marek, 135–49. Washington DC: Taylor & Francis.

_____. 1980. *Staff Burnout: Job Stress in Human Services*. Beverly Hills, CA: Sage.

Churchill, Gilbert, Neil M. Ford, and Orville C. Walker, Jr. 1974. "Measuring the Job Satisfaction of Industrial Salesmen." *Journal of Marketing Research* 11 (August): 254–60.

City of Tallahassee. 2003. *FY2003 Performance Management Process Document: Supervisor/Manager.* Tallahassee, FL: City of Tallahassee.

Clayton, Betsy. 2000. "Day Care Costs Slam Parents." *News Press.* www.cityguide.news-press.com/fe/childcare/pocketbook.shtml. Accessed June 23, 2001.

Cleveland, Frederick A. 1909. *Chapters on Municipal Administration and Accounting.* New York: Longmans, Green.

Colindres, Adriana. 2005. "Prison Workers Approve Contract." *State Journal-Register*, August 22.

Connellan, T., and R. Zemke. 1993. *Sustaining Knock Your Socks Off Service.* New York: AMACOM.

Conrad, C., and K. Witte. 1994. "Is Emotional Expression Repression Oppression? Myths of Organizational Affective Regulation." In *Communication Yearbook*, ed. Stanley A. Deetz, 17: 417–28. Newbury Park, CA: Sage.

Cook County Public Guardian. 2002. "Client Interview Form, Revised." February.

Cordes, C.L., and T.W. Dougherty. 1993. "A Review and an Integration of Research on Job Burnout." *Academy of Management Review* 18: 621–56.

Cunningham, Maddy. 2003. "Impact of Trauma Work on Social Work Clinicians: Empirical Findings." *Social Work* 48: 451–59.

Daley, M.R. 1979. "Preventing Worker Burnout in Child Welfare." *Child Welfare* 48: 443–50.

Daniels, Arlene Kaplan. 1987. "Invisible Work." *Social Problems* 34 (5): 403–15.

Davis, J.B. 2005. "Finding Calm After the Call" *ABA Journal* 91 (March): 75.

Davis, Robert C., Pedro Mateu-Gelabert, and Joel Miller. 2005. "Can Effective Policing Also Be Respectful? Two Examples in the South Bronx." *Police Quarterly* 8: 229–47.

Dawis, René V., Lloyd H. Lofquist, and David J. Weiss. 1968. "A Theory of Work Adjustment (A Revision)." University of Minnesota: Minnesota Studies in Vocational Rehabilitation, xxiii.

Diefendorff, James M., and Erin M. Richard. 2003. "Antecedents and Consequences of Emotional Display Rule Perceptions." *Journal of Applied Psychology* 88: 284–94.

Domagalski, Theresa A. 1999. "Emotion in Organizations: Main Currents." *Human Relations* 52 (6): 833–52.

Drucker, P.F. (1980). *Managing in Turbulent Times*. New York: Harper & Row Publishers.

Edelwich, Jerry, and Archie Brodsky. 1980. *Burn-Out. Stages of Disillusionment in the Helping Professions.* New York: Human Sciences Press.

Einsiedel, Albert, and Heather Tully. 1981. "Methodological Considerations in Studying the Burnout Phenomenon." In *The Burnout Syndrome. Current Research, Theory, Interventions*, ed. John W. Jones, 89–106. Park Ridge, IL: London House Press.

England, Paula, and Nancy Folbre. 1999. "The Cost of Caring." *Annals of the American Academy of Political and Social Science* 561 (1): 39–51.

Erickson, Rebecca J. 1997. "Putting Emotions to Work." In *Social Perspectives on Emotion,* ed. David D. Franks, Rebecca J. Erickson, and Beverly Cuthbertson-Johnson, 4: 3–18. Greenwich, CT: JAI Press.

_____. 1991. "When Emotion Is the Product: Self, Society, and Inauthenticity in a

Postmodern World." Unpublished doctoral dissertation, Washington State University.

Erickson, Rebecca J., and Christian Ritter. 2001. "Emotional Labor, Burnout, and Inauthenticity: Does Gender Matter?" *Social Psychology Quarterly* 64 (2): 146–63.

Erickson, Rebecca J., and Amy S. Wharton. 1997. "Inauthenticity and Depression: Assessing the Consequences of Interactive Service Work," *Work and Occupations* 24 (2): 188–214.

Feldhusen, J. 1984. "The Teacher of Gifted Students." *Gifted Child Quarterly* 3 (1): 88–91.

Ferguson, Kathy. 1984. *The Feminist Case Against Bureaucracy.* Philadelphia: Temple University Press.

Figart, Deborah M. 2000. "Equal Pay for Equal Work: The Role of Job Evaluation in an Evolving Social Norm." *Journal of Economic Issues* 34 (1): 1–19.

Figley, Charles R. 2002. "Compassion Fatigue: Psychotherapists' Chronic Lack of Self Care." *Journal of Clinical Psychology* 58: 1433–41.

_____., ed. 1995. *Compassion Fatigue: Coping with Secondary Traumatic Stress Disorder in Those Who Treat the Traumatized.* New York: Brunner/Mazel.

Filby, M.P. 1992. "The Figures, the Personality, and the Bums: Service Work and Sexuality." *Work, Employment, and Society* 6 (March): 23–42.

Fineman, Stephen, ed. 1993. *Emotion in Organizations.* Newbury Park, CA: Sage.

Fisher, B. and Joan Tronto. 1990. "Toward a Feminist Theory of Caring." In *Circles of Care: Work and Identity in Women's Lives*, ed. Emily K. Abel and Margaret K. Nelson, 35–62. Albany: State University of New York Press.

Flanagan, Maureen A. 1990. "Gender and Urban Political Reform: The City Club and the Woman's City Club of Chicago in the Progressive Era." *American Historical Review* 95 (4): 1032–50.

Fletcher, Joyce K. 1999. *Disappearing Acts: Gender, Power, and Relational Practice at Work.* Cambridge, MA: MIT Press.

Florida Department of Management Services. 2002. *State of Florida Annual Workforce Report: January Through December, 2001.* Tallahassee, FL. Available at www.state.fl.us/dms/hrm/reports/workforce_01.pdf. Accessed September 6, 2002.

Folbre, Nancy. 2001. *The Invisible Heart. Economics and Family Values.* New York: The New Press.

Follett, Mary Parker. 1942 [1925]. "Power." In *Dynamic Administration: The Collected Papers of Mary Parker Follett*, ed. Henry C. Metcalf and L. Urwick, p. 99. New York: Harper.

Freudenberger, H.J. 1980. *Burn-Out: The High Cost of High Achievement.* Garden City, NY: Anchor Press.

Gaines, Jeannie, and John M. Jermier. 1983. "Emotional Exhaustion in a High Stress Organization." *Academy of Management Journal* 26 (4): 567–86.

Gerstein, Lawrence H., Charles G. Topp, and Gregory Correll. 1987. "The Role of the Environment and Person When Predicting Burnout Among Correctional Personnel." *Criminal Justice and Behavior* 14 (3): 352–69.

Gilligan, Carol. 1982. *In a Different Voice.* Cambridge, MA: Harvard University Press.

Glomb, Theresa M., John D. Kammeyer-Mueller, and Maria Rotundo. 2004. "Emotional Labor Demands and Compensating Wage Differentials." *Journal of Applied Psychology* 89: 700–714.

Golembiewski, Robert T. 1981. "Organizational Development Interventions: Limiting Burn-Out Through Changes in Policy, Procedures and Structure." *Proceedings of the First National Conference on Burnout.* Philadelphia, PA.

Golembiewski, Robert T., and Robert F. Munzenrider. 1988. *Phases of Burnout. Developments in Concepts and Applications.* New York: Praeger.

Golembiewski, Robert T., Robert F. Munzenrider, and Jerry G. Stevenson. 1986. *Stress in Organizations. Toward a Phase Model of Burnout*. New York: Praeger.

Grandey, Alicia A. 2000. "Emotion Regulation in the Workplace: A New Way to Conceptualize Emotional Labor." *Journal of Occupational Health Psychology* 5: 95–110.

_____. 1998. "Emotional Labor: A Concept and Its Correlates." Paper presented at the First Conference on Emotions in Organizational Life, San Diego, CA, August.

Green, Richard T. 2002. "Alexander Hamilton: Founder of the American Public Administration," *Administration & Society* 34 (5): 541–62.

Gulick, Luther. 1976. "Democracy and Administration Face the Future." Lecture delivered at Indiana University in the New Horizons of Knowledge Series, The School of Public and Environmental Affairs, April 1.

Guy, Mary E. 2003. "Ties That Bind: The Link Between Public Administration and Political Science." *Journal of Politics* 65 (3): 641–55.

Guy, Mary E., and Jennifer A. Killingsworth. 2007. "Framing Gender, Framing Work: The Disparate Impact of Traditional HRM Practices." In *Strategic Public Personnel Administration: Building and Managing Human Capital for the 21st Century*, ed. A. Farazmand, 2: 399–418. Westport, CT: Greenwood.

Guy, Mary E., and Meredith A. Newman. 2004. "Women's Jobs, Men's Jobs: Sex Segregation and Emotional Labor." *Public Administration Review* 64 (3): 289–98.

Guy, Mary E., and Jason B. Thatcher. 2004. "Diversity, Administration, and Governance." In *Sound Governance: Policy and Administrative Innovations*, ed. Ali Farazmand, 187–208. Westport, CT: Praeger.

Hecker, Daniel E. 2005. "Occupational Employment Projections to 2014." *Monthly Labor Review* 128 (11): 70–101.

Heckscher C., and A. Donnellon. eds. 1994. *The Post-Bureaucratic Organization: New Perspectives on Organizational Change*. Thousand Oaks, CA: Sage.

Henderson, Angela. 2001. "Emotional Labor and Nursing: An Under-Appreciated Aspect of Caring Work." *Nursing Inquiry* 8 (2): 130–38.

Himmelweit, Susan. 1999. "Caring Labor." *Annals, AAPSS* 561 (January): 27–38.

Hirschmann, Nancy J., and Ulrike Liebert, eds. 2001. *Women and Welfare. Theory and Practice in the United States and Europe*. Piscataway, NJ: Rutgers University Press.

Hochschild, Arlie. 1983. *The Managed Heart: Commercialization of Human Feeling*. Berkeley: University of California Press.

_____. 1979. "Emotion Work, Feeling Rules, and Social Structure." *American Journal of Sociology* 85 (3): 551–75.

Hofrichter, David A., and Lyle M. Spencer, Jr. 1996. "Competencies: The Right Foundation for Effective Human Resources Management." *Compensation & Benefits Review* November/December: 21–26.

Hummel, Ralph P. 1994. *The Bureaucratic Experience. A Critique of Life in the Modern Organization*. 4th ed. New York: St. Martin's Press.

_____. 1987. *The Bureaucratic Phenomenon*. New York: St. Martin's Press.

Hummel, Ralph P., and Camilla Stivers. 1998. "Government Isn't Us: The Possibility of Democratic Knowledge in Representative Government." In *Government Is Us: Public Administration in an Anti-Government Era*, ed. Cheryl Simrell King and Camilla Stivers, 28–48. Thousand Oaks, CA: Sage.

Jackson, S.E., R.L. Schwab, and R.S. Schuler. 1986. "Toward an Understanding of the Burnout Phenomenon." *Journal of Applied Psychology* 71 (4): 630–40.

Jacobs, J. 1989. *Revolving Doors: Sex Segregation and Women's Careers*. Stanford, CA: Stanford University Press.

Johnson, R.R. 2004. "Citizen Expectations of Police Traffic Stop Behavior." *Policing: An International Journal of Police Strategies and Management* 27: 487–97.

Jones, John W., ed. 1981. *The Burnout Syndrome: Current Research, Theory, Interventions*. Park Ridge, IL: London House Press.

Jun, Jong. 1999. "The Need for Autonomy and Virtues: Civic-Minded Administrators in Civil Society." *Administrative Theory & Praxis* 21: 218–26.

Kanter, Rosabeth M. 1977. *Men and Women of the Corporation*. New York: Basic Books.

Karlsson, Jan C. 1990. "The Purpose, Value and Meaning of Work." *Economic and Industrial Democracy*, 11 (2): 129–39.

Kerr, Brinck, Will Miller, and Margaret Reid. 2002. "Sex-based Occupational Segregation in U.S. State Bureaucracies, 1987–97." *Public Administration Review* 62 (4): 412–23.

Kiesling, Herbert J. 2000. *Collective Goods, Neglected Goods: Dealing with Methodological Failure in the Social Sciences*. Singapore: World Scientific.

King, Cheryl Simrell, and Camilla Stivers. 1998. *Government Is Us: Public Administration in an Anti-Government Era*. Thousand Oaks, CA: Sage.

Kittay, Eva Feder, and Ellen K. Feder. 2002. *The Subject of Care. Feminist Perspectives on Dependency*, Lanham, MD: Rowman & Littlefield.

Kramer, Robert. 2003. "Beyond Max Weber: Emotional Intelligence and Public Leadership." In *Proceedings of 10th Annual Conference of Network of Institutes and Schools of Public Administration in Central and Eastern Europe*, Hanulova, Slovakia, ed. Jane Finlay and Marek Debicki, 126–46.

Lawler, Edward E. III. 1995. "The New Pay: A Strategic Approach." *Compensation & Benefits Review* July–August: 14–22.

————. 1986. *High Involvement Management*. San Francisco: Jossey-Bass.

Lawson, Loralie. 1993. "Theory of Work Adjustment Personality Constructs." *Journal of Vocational Behavior* 43: 46–57.

Ledford, Gerald E., Jr. 1995. "Paying for the Skills, Knowledge, and Competencies of Knowledge Workers." *Compensation & Benefits Review* July–August: 55–62.

Lee, Cynthia, Kenneth Law, and Philip Bobko. 1999. "The Importance of Justice Perceptions on Pay Effectiveness: A Two-Year Study of a Skill-based Pay Plan." *Journal of Management* 25 (6): 851–73.

Leidner, Robin. 1993. *Fast Food, Fast Talk: Service Work and the Routinization of Everyday Life*. Berkeley: University of California Press.

Leininger, Madeleine M., ed. 1988. *Caring: An Essential Human Need. Proceedings of the Three National Caring Conferences*. Detroit, MI: Wayne State University Press.

Leiter, Michael P., and Christina Maslach. 2000. *Preventing Burnout and Building Engagement. A Complete Program for Organizational Renewal*. San Francisco: Jossey-Bass.

————. 1988. "The Impact of Interpersonal Environment on Burnout and Organizational Commitment." *Journal of Organizational Behavior* 9: 297–308.

Lewis, Michael, and Jeannette M. Haviland-Jones. 2000. *Handboook of Emotions*. 2nd ed. New York: The Guilford Press.

Lieberman, Evan S. 2005. "Nested Analysis as a Mixed-Method Strategy for Comparative Research." *American Political Science Review* 99 (3): 435–52.

Lief, H.I., and R.C. Fox. 1963. "Training for 'Detached Concern' in Medical Students." In *The Psychological Basis of Medical Practice*, ed. H.I. Lief, V.F. Lief, and N.R. Lief, 12–35. New York: Harper and Row.

Lipsky, Michael. 1980. *Street-Level Bureaucracy: Dilemmas of the Individual in Public Services*. New York: Russell Sage Foundation.

Lowi, Theodore. 1964. "American Business, Public Policy, Case Studies, and Political Theory." *World Politics* 16 (4): 677–715.

224

Martin, Susan Ehrlich. 1999. "Police Force or Police Service? Gender and Emotional Labor." *Annals of the American Academy of Political and Social Science* 561 (1): 111–26.

Maslach, Christina. 1982. *Burnout: The Cost of Caring*. Englewood Cliffs, NJ: Prentice Hall.

———. 1981. "Burnout: A Social Psychological Analysis." In *The Burnout Syndrome*, ed. John W. Jones, 30–53. Park Ridge, IL: London House Press.

———. 1976. "Burned-Out." *Human Relations* 5: 16–22.

Maslach, Christina, and Susan E. Jackson. 1986. *Maslach Burnout Inventory: Manual*. 2nd ed. Palo Alto, CA: Consulting Psychologists Press.

———. 1984. "Burnout in Organizational Settings." In *Applied Social Psychology Annual*, ed. S. Oskamp, 5: 133–53. Beverly Hills, CA: Sage.

———. 1981. "The Measurement of Experienced Burnout." *Journal of Occupational Behavior* 2: 99–113.

———. 1979. "Burned-Out Cops and Their Families." *Psychology Today* 12: 59–62.

———. 1978. "Lawyer Burnout." *Barrister* 8: 52–54.

Maslach, Christina, and Michael P. Leiter. 1997. *The Truth About Burnout. How Organizations Cause Personal Stress and What to Do About It*. San Francisco: Jossey-Bass.

Maslach, Christina, Wilmar B. Schaufeli, and Michael P. Leiter. 2001. "Job Burnout." *Annual Review of Psychology* 52 (1): 397–422.

Mastracci, Sharon H., Meredith A. Newman, and Mary E. Guy. 2006. "Appraising Emotion Work: Determining Whether Emotional Labor Is Valued in Government Jobs." *American Review of Public Administration* 36 (2): 123–38.

Mastracci, Sharon H., and James R. Thompson. 2005. "Nonstandard Work Arrangements in the Public Sector: Trends and Issues." *Review of Public Personnel Administration* 25 (4): 299–324.

Maynard-Moody, Steven, and Michael Musheno. 2003. *Cops, Teachers, Counselors: Stories from the Front Lines of Public Service*. Ann Arbor: University of Michigan Press.

McEwen, Melanie, and Evelyn M. Wills. 2002. *Theoretical Basis for Nursing*. Philadelphia: Lippincott Williams & Wilkins.

McSwite, O.C. 2004. "Creating Reality Through Administrative Practice: A Psychoanalytic Reading of Camilla Stivers' *Bureau Men, Settlement Women*." *Administration & Society* 36: 406–26.

———. 1997. *Legitimacy in Public Administration: A Discourse Analysis*. Thousand Oaks, CA: Sage.

Mohrman, Susan A., Susan G. Cohen, and Allan M. Mohrman, Jr. 1995. *Designing Team-based Organizations: New Forms for Knowledge Work*. San Francisco: Jossey-Bass.

Morris, J. Andrew, and Daniel C. Feldman. 1997. "Managing Emotions in the Workplace." *Journal of Managerial Issues* 9 (3): 257–74.

———. 1996. "The Dimensions, Antecedents, and Consequences of Emotional Labor." *Academy of Management Review* 21 (4): 986–1010.

Naff, Katherine C. 2001. *To Look Like America: Dismantling Barriers to Women and Minorities in Government*. Boulder, CO: Westview Press.

National Bureau of Economic Research (NBER). 2005. Current Population Survey (CPS) merged outgoing rotation group data, 1979–2004. www.nber.org/data/morg.html. Accessed December 24, 2006.

Newman, Meredith A. 1994. "Lowi's Thesis and Gender: Implications for Career Advancement." *Public Administration Review* 54 (3): 277–84.

Newman, Meredith A., and Mary E. Guy. 1998. "Taylor's Triangles, Follett's Web." *Administrative Theory & Praxis* 20 (3): 287–97.

Newman, Meredith A., Sharon H. Mastracci, and Mary E. Guy. 2005. "Burnout Versus Making a Difference: The Hidden Costs and Benefits of Emotion Work." Paper presented at the annual meeting of the American Political Science Association, Washington DC, September.

Nicholson, N. 1977. "Absence Behavior and Attendance Motivation: A Conceptual Synthesis." *Journal of Management Studies* 41: 231–52.

Noddings, Nel. 1984. *Caring: A Feminine Approach to Ethics and Moral Education.* Berkeley: University of California Press.

Oxford English Dictionary (OED) Online. 2006. The *Oxford English Dictionary* website. Accessed on January 22, 23, and 30, 2006.

O*NET Online Knowledge Site. www.onetknowledgesite.com/pages/Onet_Insert.cfm. Accessed December 20, 28, and 30, 2005; January 18, 20, and 26, 2006.

O*NET Online. http://online.onetcenter.org/skills/. Skills search conducted on February 18 and 20, 2006.

Ollilainen, Marjukka. 2000. "Gendering Emotions, Gendering Teams: Construction of Emotions in Self-Managing Teamwork." In *Emotions in the Workplace: Research, Theory, and Practice*, ed. Neal M. Ashkanasy, Charmine E.J. Hartel, and Wilfred J. Zerbe, 82–96. Westport, CT: Quorum Books.

Paine, Whiton Stewart. 1981. "The Burnout Syndrome in Context." In *The Burnout Syndrome*, ed. John W. Jones, 1–29. Park Ridge, IL: London House Press.

Parkinson, B. 1991. "Emotional Stylists: Strategies of Expressive Management Among Trainee Hairdressers." *Cognition and Emotion* 5: 419–34.

Paules, Greta Foff. 1991. *Dishing It Out: Power and Resistance Among Waitresses in a New Jersey Restaurant.* Philadelphia: Temple University Press.

Pearlman, Laurie Anne, and Paula S. MacIan. 1995. "Vicarious Traumatization: An Empirical Study of the Effects of Trauma Work on Trauma Therapists." *Professional Psychology Research and Practice* 26: 558–656.

Pierce, Jennifer L. 1999. "Emotional Labor Among Paralegals." *Annals of the American Academy of Political and Social Science* 561: 127–42.

————. 1995. *Gender Trials: Emotional Lives in Contemporary Law Firms.* Berkeley: University of California Press.

Pines, Ayala, and Elliot Aronson. 1988. *Career Burnout: Causes and Cures.* New York: The Free Press.

Pines, Ayala, and Ditsa Kafry. 1981. "Coping with Burnout." In *The Burnout Syndrome*, ed. John W. Jones, 139–50. Park Ridge, IL: London House Press.

Pines, Ayala, and Christina Maslach. 1980. "Combatting Staff Burnout in a Day Care Center: A Case Study." *Child Care Quarterly* 9: 5–16.

Pugliesi, Karen. 1999. "The Consequences of Emotional Labor: Effects on Work Stress, Job Satisfaction, and Well-Being." *Motivation and Emotion* 23 (2): 125–54.

Pugliesi, Karen, and Scott L. Shook. 1997. "Gender, Jobs, and Emotional Labor in a Complex Organization." In *Social Perspectives on Emotion*, ed., David D. Franks, Rebecca J. Erickson and Beverly Cuthbertson-Johnson, 4: 283–316. Greenwich, CT: JAI.

Putnam, Linda L., and Dennis K. Mumby, 1993. "Organizations, Emotion and the Myth of Rationality." In *Emotion in Organizations*, ed. Stephen Fineman, 36–57. Newbury Park, CA: Sage.

Quinn, John F. 2003. *Corrections, A Concise Introduction.* 2nd ed. Prospect Park, IL: Waveland Press.

Rafaeli, Anat, and Robert I. Sutton. 1987. "Expression of Emotion as Part of the Work Role." *Academy of Management Review* 12 (1): 23–37.

Regan, Helen B., and Gwen H. Brooks. 1995. *Out of Women's Experience.* Thousand Oaks, CA: Corwin Press.

Richards, Jane M. 2004. "The Cognitive Consequences of Concealing Feelings." *Current Directions in Psychological Science* 13 (4): 131–34.

Rivlin, Alice. 2003. Elliott Richardson Lecture on Ethics and Integrity in the Public Service. Delivered at the Annual Meeting of the American Society for Public Administration, March 15–18, Washington, DC.

Rogers, Martha E. 1994 [1990]. "Nursing: Science of Unitary, Irreducible, Human Beings: Updated 1990." In *Martha E. Rogers: Her Life and Her Work,* ed. Violet M. Malinski, Elizabeth Ann Manhart Barrett, and John R. Phillips, 244–49. Philadelphia: F.A. Davis.

————. 1994 [1985]. "High Touch in a High-Tech Future." In *Martha E. Rogers: Her Life and Her Work,* ed. Violet M. Malinski, Elizabeth Ann Manhart Barrett, and John R. Phillips, 288–91. Philadelphia: F.A. Davis.

Ryerson, Diane, and Nancy Marks. 1981. "Career Burnout in the Human Services: Strategies for Intervention." In *The Burnout Syndrome,* ed. John W. Jones, 151–64. Park Ridge, IL: London House Press.

Schachter, Hindy Lauer. 2004. "Josephine Goldmark. Champion of Scientific Management and Social Reform." In *Outstanding Women in Public Administration. Leaders, Mentors, and Pioneers,* ed. Claire L. Felbinger and Wendy A. Haynes, 31–48. Armonk, NY: M.E. Sharpe.

————. 2002. "Women, Progressive-Era Reform, and Scientific Management," *Administration & Society* 34 (5): 563–77.

Schaubroeck, J., and J.R. Jones. 2000. "Antecedents of Workplace Emotional Labor Dimensions and Moderators of Their Effects on Physical Symptoms." *Journal of Organizational Behavior* 21: 163–83.

Schaufeli, Wilmar B., and D. Enzmann. 1998. *The Burnout Companion to Study and Practice: A Critical Analysis.* London: Taylor and Francis.

Schaufeli, Wilmar B., Christina Maslach, and Tadeusz Marek. 1993. "The Future of Burnout." In *Professional Burnout: Recent Developments in Theory and Research,* ed. Wilmar B. Schaufeli, Christina Maslach, and Tadeusz Marek, 253–59. Washington DC: Taylor and Francis.

Schultz, Vicki. 2000. "Life's Work." *Columbia Law Review* 100 (7): 1881–1964.

Seeman, M. 1991. "Alienation and Anomie." In *Measures of Personality and Social Psychological Attitudes,* ed. J. Robinson, P. Shaver, and L.Wrightsman, 291–95. San Diego, CA: Academic Press.

Shareef, Reginald. 1994. "Skill-based Pay in the Public." *Review of Public Personnel Administration* 14 (3): 60–74.

Sharrad, H. 1992. "Feeling the Strain: Job Stress and Satisfaction of Direct-Care Staff in the Mental Handicap Service." *British Journal of Mental Subnormality* 38 (1): 32–38.

Shaw, Jason, Nina Gupta, Atul Mitra, and Gerald Ledford. 2005. "Success and Survival of Skill-based Pay Plans." *Journal of Management* 31(February): 1–22.

Shuler, Sherianne, and Beverly Davenport Sypher. 2000. "Seeing Emotional Labor: When Managing the Heart Enhances the Work Experience." *Management Communication Quarterly* 14 (1): 50–89.

Simon, H. 1976. *Administrative Behavior.* 3rd ed. New York: The Free Press.

Simon, R., and L.E. Nath. 2004. "Gender and Emotion in the United States: Do Men and Women Differ in Self-Reports of Feelings and Expressive Behavior?" *American Journal of Sociology* 109 (5): 1137–76.

Simon, Yves R. 1962. *A General Theory of Authority.* Westport, CT: Greenwood Press.

Sloan, M.M. 2004. "The Effects of Occupational Characteristics on the Experience and Expression of Anger in the Workplace." *Work and Occupations* 31(1): 38–72.

Spencer, L.M., and S.M. Spencer. 1993. *Competence at Work: Models for Superior Performance.* New York: John Wiley & Sons.

Staden, Helene. 1998. "Alertness to the Needs of Others: A Study of the Emotional Labour of Caring." *Journal of Advanced Nursing* 27: 147–56.

Stamm, B. Hudnall. 2005. "Professional Quality of Life: Compassion Satisfaction and Fatigue Subscales, R-IV (ProQOL)." www.isu.edu/~bhstamm. Website accessed December 15, 2005, and January 30, 2006.

State of Florida. Department of Management Services. 2005. *2005 Annual Workforce Report.* http://dms.myflorida.com/content/download/27985/129868. Accessed November 28, 2006.

State of Illinois. Department of Central Management Services. 2005a. Information provided through a public records request (October).

_____. 2005b. Job Specification 07218. www.state.il.us/cms/downloads/pdfs_specs/07218.pdf. Accessed September 26, 2005.

_____. 2005c. Job Specification 26070. www.state.il.us/cms/downloads/pdfs_specs/26070.pdf. Accessed September 26, 2005.

State of Illinois. Office of the Secretary of State. Department of Personnel. 2005. Information provided through a public records request (December 13).

State of New Jersey. Department of Personnel. 2004a. Job Specification 62152. http://webapps.dop.state.nj.us/jobspec/62152.htm. Accessed December 13, 2005.

_____. 2004b Information provided through a public records request (September).

_____. 2004c. Job Specification 33892. http://webapps.dop.state.nj.us/jobspec/33892.htm. Accessed December 12, 2005.

_____. 2004d. Job Specification 56440. http://webapps.dop.state.nj.us/jobspec/56440.htm. Accessed December 13, 2005.

State of Oregon. Department of Administrative Services. Human Resource Services Division. 2005a. Information provided through a public records request (June).

_____. 2005b. Classifications Specifications. Available at www.hr.das.state.or.us/hrsd/class/6612.htm. Accessed December 19, 2005.

_____. 2005c. Classifications Specifications. Available at www.hr.das.state.or.us/hrsd/class/5451.htm. Accessed December 19, 2005.

_____. 2005d. Classifications Specifications. Available at www.hr.das.state.or.us/hrsd/class/0331.htm. Accessed December 19, 2005.

Steinberg, Ronnie J. 1999. "Emotional Labor in Job Evaluation: Redesigning Compensation Practices." *Annals of the American Academy of Political and Social Science* 561 (1): 143–57.

Steinberg, Ronnie J., and Deborah M. Figart. 1999a. "Emotional Labor Since *The Managed Heart.*" *Annals of the American Academy of Political and Social Science* 561 (1): 8–26.

_____. 1999b. Emotional Demands at Work: A Job Content Analysis." *Annals of the American Academy of Political and Social Science* 561 (1): 177–91.

Stenross, Barbara, and Sherryl Kleinman. 1989. "The Highs and Lows of Emotional Labor: Detectives' Encounters with Criminals and Victims." *Journal of Contemporary Ethnography* 17 (4): 435–52.

Stivers, Camilla. 2008. "A Civic Machinery for Democratic Expression: Jane Addams on Public Administration." In *Jane Addams and the Practice of Democracy: Multidisciplinary Essays on Theory and Practice,* ed. Wendy Chmielski, Marilyn Fischer, and Carol Nackenoff. Champaign, IL: University of Illinois Press.

_____. 2005. "A Place Like Home: Care and Action in Public Administration." *American Review of Public Administration* 35 (1): 26–41.

_____. 2002. *Gender Images in Public Administration. Legitimacy and the Administrative State.* 2nd ed. Thousand Oaks, CA: Sage.

_____. 2000. *Bureau Men, Settlement Women: Constructing Public Administration in the Progressive Era.* Lawrence: University of Kansas Press.

Strickland, W. 1992. "Institutional Emotional Norms and Role Satisfaction: Examination of a Career Wife Population." *Sex Roles* 26: 423–39.

Sutton, Robert I. 1991. "Maintaining Norms About Expressed Emotions: The Case of Bill Collectors." *Administrative Science Quarterly* 36 (2): 245–68.

Sutton, Robert I., and Anat Rafaeli. 1988. "Untangling the Relationship Between Displayed Emotions and Organizational Sales: The Case of Convenience Stores." *Academy of Management Journal* 31 (3): 461–87.

Tausky, Curt. 1984. *Work and Society.* Itaska, IL: F.E. Peacock.

Taylor, F.W. 1911. *The Principles of Scientific Management.* New York: W.W. Norton.

Thompson, George J. 2006. *Verbal Judo: The Gentle Art of Persuasion.* New York: Harper Collins Reprints.

_____. 1983. *Verbal Judo: Words as a Force Option.* Springfield, IL: Charles C. Thomas.

Thompson, Victor A. 1975. *Without Sympathy or Enthusiasm: The Problem of Administrative Compassion.* Tuscaloosa, AL: University of Alabama Press.

Tolich, M. 1993. "Alienating and Liberating Emotions at Work: Supermarket Clerks' Performance of Customer Service." *Journal of Contemporary Ethnography* 22 (3): 361–81.

Toossi, Mitra. 2005. "Labor Force Projections to 2014: Retiring Boomers." *Monthly Labor Review* 128 (11): 25–44.

Tracy, Sarah J., and Karen Tracy. 1998. "Emotion Labor at 911: A Case Study and Theoretical Critique." *Journal of Applied Communication Research* 26 (4): 390–411.

Traut, Carol Ann, Steve Feimer, Craig F. Emmert, and Kevin Thom. 2000. "Law Enforcement Recruit Training at the State Level: An Evaluation." *Police Quarterly* 3: 294–314.

Tschan, Franziska, Sylvie Rochat, and Dieter Zapf. 2005. "It's Not Only Clients: Studying Emotion Work with Clients and Co-Workers with an Event-Sampling Approach." *Journal of Occupational and Organizational Psychology* 78: 195–220.

United Nations High Commissioner for Refugees (UNHCR). 2003. *Partnership: An Operations Management Handbook for UNHCR's Partners.* Rev. ed. www.unhcr.ch.

U.S. Department of Commerce, Bureau of Labor Statistics. 2007. "All employees, thousands; government; seasonally adjusted and not seasonally adjusted" data extracted on February 21, 2007: http://data.bls.gov/PDQ/outside.jsp?survey=ce

U.S. Department of Commerce. Census Bureau. 2005 (May). "School Enrollment—Social and Economic Characteristics of Students: October 2003." Available at www.census.gov/prod/2005pubs/p20–554.pdf. Accessed November 3, 2005.

U.S. Department of Labor. Bureau of Labor Statistics. 2005a. "Women in the Labor Force: A Databook, Report 985, May 2005." Available at www.bls.gov.cps/wlf-table19–2005.pdf. Accessed November 16, 2005.

_____. 2005b. "Employment and Earnings, January 2005. Household Data Annual Averages, Table 39." Available at www.bls.gov/cps/cpsa2004.pdf. Accessed November 8, 2005.

_____. 2004. Current Employment Survey. Available at www.bls.gov/ces/home.htm#data. Accessed Jan 5, 2008.

U.S. Equal Employment Opportunity Commission. 2003. "Job Patterns for Minorities and Women in Private Industry-National Aggregate. Table 1. Occupational Employment in Private Industry by Race/Ethnic Group/Sex and by Industry, United States, 2003." Available at www.eeoc.gov/stats/jobpat/2003/national.html. Accessed November 14, 2005.

Van Riper, Paul P. 1983. "The American Administrative State: Wilson and the Founders: An Unorthodox View." *Public Administration Review* 43 (6): 477–90.

_____. 1976. *History of the U.S. Civil Service.* Westport, CT: Greenwood Press.

Verbal Judo Institute. Questions and Answers about Verbal Judo. www.verbaljudo.com/ kata. Accessed on December 17, 2006, and January 20, 2006.

Waldo, Dwight. 1948. *The Administrative State: A Study of the Political Theory of American Public Administration.* New York: The Ronald Press Company.

Waldron, Vincent. 1994. "Once More with Feeling: Reconsidering the Role of Emotion in Work." In *Communication Yearbook,* ed. Stanley A. Deetz, 17: 388–416. Newbury Park, CA: Sage.

Webber, A. 1991. "Crime and Management: An Interview with NYC Police Commissioner Lee O. Brown." *Harvard Business Review* 70 (May–June): 110–30.

Weber, Max. 1968. *Economy and Society: An Outline of Interpretive Sociology.* Volume 3. New York: Bedminster Press.

_____. 1987 [1922]. "Legitimate Authority and Bureaucracy." In *The Great Writings in Management and Organizational Behavior,* ed. Louis E. Boone and Donald D. Bowen, 5–19. New York: Random House, Inc. (Reprinted from Max Weber, *The Theory of Social and Economic Organization,* trans. A.M. Henderson and Talcott Parsons, ed. Talcott Parsons, 1947. London: Wm. Hodge & Co., Ltd.)

Wetterich, Chris. 2005. "Frustration over City Hiring Grows." *The State Journal Register,* (December 12), p. 2.

Wharton, Amy S. 1999. "The Psychosocial Consequences of Emotional Labor." *Annals of the American Academy, AAPSS* 561: 158–76.

_____. 1996. "Service with a Smile: Understanding the Consequences of Emotional Labor." In *Working in the Service Society,* ed. C.L. MacDonald and C. Sirianni, 91–112. Philadelphia: Temple University Press.

_____. 1993. "The Affective Consequences of Service Work: Managing Emotions on the Job." *Work and Occupations* 20 (2): 205–32.

Wharton, Amy S., and Rebecca J. Erickson. 1995. "The Consequences of Caring: Exploring the Links Between Women's Jobs and Family Emotion Work." *Sociological Quarterly* 36: 273–96.

White, Leonard D. 1926. *Introduction to the Study of Public Administration.* New York: Macmillan.

Willoughby, William F. 1927. *Principles of Administration: With Special Reference to National and State Government of the United States.* Washington, DC: Brookings Institution.

Williams v. Saxbe (1976), 413 F. Supp. 665, 11EPD 10,840 (D.D.C. 1976).

Wouters, Cas. 1989. "The Sociology of Emotions and Flight Attendants: Hochschild's Managed Heart." *Theory, Culture, and Society* 6 (1): 95–123.

Zapf, Dieter. 2002. "Emotion Work and Psychological Well-Being. A Review of the Literature and Some Conceptual Considerations." *Human Resource Management Review* 12: 237–68.

Zapf, Dieter, Claudia Seifert, Barbara Schmutte, Heidrun Mertini, and Melanie Holz. 2001. "Emotion Work and Job Stressors and Their Effects on Burnout." *Psychology and Health* 16: 527–45.

Zapf, Dieter, C. Vogt, Claudia Seifert, Heidrun Mertini, and Amela Isic. 1999. "Emotion Work as a Source of Stress: The Concept and Development of an Instrument." *European Journal of Work and Organizational Psychology* 8: 371–400.

Zellner, Arnold. 1962. "An Efficient Method of Estimating Seemingly Unrelated Regressions and Tests for Aggregation Bias." *Journal of the American Statistical Association* 57: 348–68.

Index

231

About the Authors

Mary E. Guy holds the Jerry Collins Eminent Scholar Chair in the Askew School of Public Administration and Policy. She is past president of the American Society for Public Administration and a fellow of the prestigious National Academy of Public Administration. Her research focuses on issues related to managing public agencies, especially in terms of human capital. Her writings are marked by a special emphasis on diversity and the changing workplace.

Meredith A. Newman is professor and director of the School of Public Administration at Florida International University. Prior to her current career in academia, Newman served with the Australian Foreign Service (in France and Vietnam), the U.S. Department of State (in Senegal, Malaysia, and Republic of Singapore), and the World Bank. Professor Newman is widely published in the areas of public management, administrative theory, gender and worklife issues, and human resources.

Sharon H. Mastracci is an assistant professor of public administration at the University of Illinois–Chicago. She studies employment policies targeting women and low-wage workers, gendered aspects of work, innovations in public personnel management, and the sociology of work. She is the author of *Breaking Out of the Pink Collar Ghetto: Policy Solutions for Non-College Women* (2004), and serves on the editorial board of the *Review of Public Personnel Administration*.